D0787729

Cognitive Science Series, 9

Cognitive Science Series

The Transfer of Cognitive Skill

Mark K. Singley
John R. Anderson

Harvard University Press
Cambridge, Massachusetts
London, England
1989

Library of Congress Cataloging-in-Publication Data
Singley, Mark K.
    The transfer of cognitive skill.
    (Cognitive science series: 9)
    Bibliography: p.
    Includes index.
    1. Transfer of training—Case studies.   I. Anderson,
    John R. (John Robert), 1947–   . II. Title.
    III. Series.
LB1059.S523 1989   370.15   88-28404
ISBN 0-674-90340-4 (alk. paper)

To our wives,
Arlene and Lynne,
and our parents,
Dorcas and Luther, and Adeline and John

Preface

When Singley first came to Carnegie-Mellon in 1982 to study with Anderson, the ACT* theory of skill acquisition was in its final stages of development and the time was ripe for application. What better domain than transfer to test a learning theory, we thought. By taking this approach, we were following a long tradition in which the question "What is learned?" is answered by tests of transfer. We looked first at transfer in text editing and then at transfer in calculus. This book presents the results of that research as well as numerous other theoretical and empirical analyses that are relevant to transfer.

As we began to reflect on our work, it became apparent that we were proposing something analogous to Thorndike's identical elements theory of the transfer process. In short, we assumed that transfer was based on those elements that are shared between tasks. In any identical elements theory, the critical question is how to define the elements. Using the ACT* theory as a starting point, we identified production rules as the elements of skill and thus as the basis for transfer. We found production rules well cast in this role by virtue of certain useful properties, notably their independence and abstractness. The theory we present here can be viewed as a resurrection of Thorndike's theory of identical elements, with production rules and their declarative precursors taking on the role of the elements.

With regard to Thorndike, it is possible to ask whether his theoretical glass is half full or half empty. In writing this book, we chose to stress the former (perhaps to get the reader's blood pumping), casting our theory as a modernization of his. We could just as easily have stressed the many differences between his theory and our own. In fact, our work represents something of a resolution to a conflict that has raged since Thorndike's day concerning the specificity of transfer. Thorndike proposed an identical elements theory, but because of his lack of a mental representation language, his elements were superficial and tied to overt behavior. In short, Thorndike's elements made no provision for transfer at an abstract level. With production rules, however, transfer can be localized to specific components (in keeping with Thorndike's theory) and yet still be quite abstract and mentalistic.

We thank the many people who have shared in both the conceptual and the physical preparation of this book. Many of the ideas presented here had their first expression in meetings of the ACT* research group, which has included Frank Boyle, Gary Bradshaw, Fred Conrad, Al Corbett, Rob Farrell, Wayne Gray, Robin Jeffries, Bonnie John, Irv Katz, Claudius Kessler, Ken Koedinger, Matthew Lewis, Jean McKendree, Bob Milson, Peter Pirolli, Lynne Reder, Brian Reiser, Jeff Shrager, and Ross Thompson. Special thanks go to Claudius Kessler and Matthew Lewis, who participated significantly in the research effort and whose work is reported here in some detail. Peter Pirolli and Peter Polson read the entire manuscript and made many insightful suggestions regarding content and organization. Kelley George ably managed the physical preparation of the manuscript, including figures and tables. Mari-Jo Dagostino and Judy Rosa provided timely proofreading assistance. At Harvard University Press, Michael Aronson encouraged our efforts and helped us define the direction and scope of the work; Virginia LaPlante provided a skillful polishing. Finally, we are grateful for the generous support we received for this work from the Army Research Institute and the Air Force Human Resources Laboratory, Contract MDA903-85-K-0343.

Contents

The Transfer of Cognitive Skill

1 / The Study of Transfer

The aim of this book is to apply some of the modern formalisms of cognitive psychology to an age-old practical problem: the transfer of learning. The study of transfer is the study of how knowledge acquired in one situation applies (or fails to apply) in other situations. There is a host of theoretical and practical reasons for reviving interest in transfer now. Transfer provides an important test-bed for learning and performance theories. Newell and Simon (1972) pointed out that a certain research agenda is imposed on cognitive psychologists by logical necessity. A performance theory is first worked out in detail. Only then can issues of learning be addressed. The underlying logic is that one must understand the end points of a transition before understanding the transition itself.

In a sense, the study of transfer is the next logical step in the research program outlined by Newell and Simon. To understand transfer, one must have detailed theories of both learning and performance. In addition, these theories must apply to not one skill but two. Although transfer is a complex, higher-order phenomenon, there is currently no reason to suspect that its understanding will lie outside the bounds of a well-specified theory of learning and performance. In short, the study of transfer is a stringent but necessary test for all comprehensive theories of cognition.

Aside from its relevance to theoretical issues, the problem of transfer is perhaps the fundamental educational question. It is rare that people learn things in school which apply directly to life and work. For education to be effective, curricula must be designed with an eye toward transfer. This concern becomes increasingly important in a world where rapid technological change often penalizes those who are narrowly skilled and inflexible. Interacting with educational questions are questions of technological design. It has been claimed that, in comparison with simpler machines like automobiles and copiers, transfer among different kinds of computer systems is relatively difficult (Nakatani, 1983). Perhaps transfer should be considered more explicitly in the design process.

A recurring observation in the study of transfer is that knowledge acquired in one situation fails to transfer to another, and a major theoretical issue concerns why this is so. Our perspective on this issue is that such failures are an inevitable consequence of the limited power and generality of human knowledge. Just having knowledge that logically implies a solution to a task is not enough. One must learn how to apply that knowledge to the task in specific situations. This leads to our interest in cognitive skill, which may be characterized as the application of knowledge to a task. Most of this book is devoted to assessing the adequacy of the ACT* (pronounced "act-star") theory (Anderson, 1983) in providing an analysis of the transfer of cognitive skill. However, it is first necessary to frame the issue of transfer historically.

Transfer in Historical Perspective

Issues of transfer have fallen in and out of the main focus of psychology at several times in the past. Each school has had its own interests and approaches. Throughout its history, however, the study of transfer has been dominated by certain recurring themes, both substantive and methodological.

General versus specific transfer

Perhaps the dominant substantive issue in transfer research has been whether transfer is specific and limited in scope or whether it is broad and ranges across diverse tasks and disciplines. The first psychologist to study transfer systematically was the associationist Thorndike (Thorndike and Woodworth, 1901), and he took primary interest in this issue. Thorndike disagreed with the prevailing opinion concerning education during his time, namely the doctrine of formal discipline. This doctrine, credited to Locke (Higginson, 1931) and upheld by a number of early educational psychologists (Angell, 1908; Pillsbury, 1908; Woodrow, 1927), claimed that studying such otherworldly subjects as Latin and geometry was of significant value because it served to discipline the mind. The doctrine of formal discipline subscribed to the faculty view of mind, which extends back to Aristotle and was first formalized by Reid in the late eighteenth century (Boring, 1950). The faculty position held that the mind was composed of a collection of general faculties, such as observation, attention, discrimination, and reasoning, which were exercised in much the same way as a set of muscles. The content of the exercise made little difference; most important was the level of exertion (hence the fondness for Latin and geometry). Transfer in such a view is broad and takes place at a general level, sometimes spanning domains that share no content. For example, training in chess should transfer to computer programming since both skills involve use of the general reasoning faculty.

Thorndike undertook a research program extending some thirty years to show that transfer was much narrower in scope than would be predicted by the doctrine of formal discipline. According to Thorndike, the mind was composed not of general faculties but rather of specific habits and associations, which provided a person with a variety of narrow responses to very specific stimuli. In fact, the mind was just a convenient name for countless special operations or functions (Stratton, 1922). Thorndike's theory of transfer, known as the theory of identical elements, stated that training in one kind of activity would transfer to another only if the activities shared common stimulus-response elements: "One mental function or activity improves others insofar as and because they are in part identical with it, because it contains elements common to them. Addition improves multiplication because multiplication is largely addition; knowledge of Latin gives increased ability to learn French because many of the facts learned in the one case are needed in the other" (Thorndike, 1906, p. 243). Thus, Thorndike was happy to accept transfer between diverse skills as long as it could be shown that the transfer was mediated by identical elements. Generally, however, Thorndike concluded that "the mind is so specialized into a multitude of independent capacities that we alter human nature only in small spots, and any special school training has a much narrower influence upon the mind as a whole than has commonly been supposed" (Thorndike, 1906, p. 246).

In his first series of experiments (Thorndike and Woodworth, 1901), Thorndike subjected the strong version of the doctrine of formal discipline to an empirical test. The strong version claims that transfer ranges across diverse tasks when those tasks involve the same general faculty. In one study, no correlation was found between memory for words and memory for numbers. In another, accuracy in spelling was not correlated with accuracy in arithmetic. Thorndike interpreted these results as evidence against the general faculties of memory and accuracy.

However, Thorndike was not content with attacking only the strong version of the theory. To further substantiate his own theory of identical elements, he devised a much more stringent test which involved presenting subjects with tasks more closely related, tasks he defined as falling within the same *function group*. A function group was defined as a particular operation generalized across a limited set of inputs. For example, the addition of the integers constituted a single function group. Thorndike's position was that transfer was quite limited even within function groups, and that any change in the inputs would have a detrimental effect on the function: "Any disturbance whatsoever in the concrete particulars reasoned about will interfere somewhat with the reasoning, making it less correct, or slower, or both" (Thorndike, 1922, p. 36).

To test this position, Thorndike gave a group of subjects skilled in algebra a series of algebraic exercises involving either customary or novel algebraic expressions (Thorndike, 1922). Table 1.1 presents the exercises as well as the results of the experiment. In most cases, changing the form of the data did have a detrimental effect on performance. However, in one of the six exercises, performance was not damaged, and overall, subjects supplied right answers to about 50 percent of the novel exercises. These results offer little support for the strong version of Thorndike's theory of identical elements. They in fact provide

Table 1.1.   Representative results from Thorndike's (1922) experiment on the effect of changed data on reasoning.

Problem	Customary	Percent incorrect	Novel	Percent incorrect
Square	$x + y$	6	$b_1 + b_2$	28
Square	a^2x^3	34	r^3r^2	47
Factor	$x^2 - y^3$	22	$1/x^3 - 1/y^2$	41
Multiply	x^a and x^b	55	4^a and 4^b	70
Simplify	$ac - [a(b + c)]$	25	$p_1p_3 - [p_1(p_2 - p_3)]$	53
Solve	$e^2 + ef = 8/x; x$	52	$e^2 + ef = 8/p; p$	53

evidence for substantial positive transfer within algebraic function groups.

In another experiment (Thorndike and Woodworth, 1901), Thorndike trained subjects to cross out the words in a prose passage containing both the letters e and s (e–s). Following this training, subjects did better on transfer tasks that involved crossing out words that contained either e–r or s–p than words that contained two new letters. Thorndike interpreted these results as consistent with his common elements view. However, those subjects who had e–s training did better on words with two new letters than did control subjects who had no training whatsoever. Once again, there was evidence for a kind of general skill transfer within a function group. Generally, Thorndike observed more transfer than could be explained by common stimulus-response elements alone.

Besides this lack of empirical support, Thorndike was criticized from a purely logical standpoint by educational psychologists more sympathetic to the doctrine of formal discipline (Meiklejohn, 1908; Wallin, 1910; Orata, 1928). One of the primary objections was that Thorndike's mechanistic stimulus-response conception of mind was incompatible with the traditional notion of transfer which stressed adaptation and flexibility. In many transfer situations, what one already knows is somehow insufficient; some kind of transformation or adaptation of existing knowledge is required. However, Thorndike's view precluded any kind of intelligent adaptation or reconstruction: "In the same organism the same neurone action will always produce the same result, in the same individual the really same situation will always produce the same response" (Thorndike, 1903, p. 7). Given concrete stimulus-response pairs as the elements of skill, Thorndike's theory of identical elements was in a sense denying the existence of transfer entirely, in that transfer was possible only in those situations where the same responses to the same stimuli were required. In effect one was simply doing more of the same, as opposed to something adaptive and new.

Another problem was that, in the absence of an explicit representation language for cognitive skill, Thorndike was somewhat vague about the exact nature of his elements. In fact, there has been considerable debate on this point, much of it focusing on the meaning of the troublesome term *identical* (Orata, 1928; Ellis, 1965). Given a literal interpretation, an identical elements theory makes the prospect of learning and transfer rather absurd and quixotic: "What can we say of a theory that the training of the mind is so specific that each particular act gives facility only for the performing again of that same act just as it was before? Think of learning to drive a nail with a yellow hammer, and then realize your helplessness if, in time of need, you should borrow your neighbor's hammer and find it painted red. Nay, further think of learning to use a hammer at all if at each other stroke the nail has gone further into the wood, and the sun has gone lower in the sky, and the temperature of the body has risen from the exercise, and in fact, everything on earth and under the earth has changed so far as to give each new stroke a new particularity all of its own, and thus has cut it off from all possibility of influence upon or influence from its fellows" (Meiklejohn, 1908, p. 126).

The problem, of course, is that no two situations are truly identical; they are merely perceived as such psychologically. Predating the cognitive revolution, Thorndike's theory was tied to the physical world and made no use of abstract mental representations. Quite simply, Thorndike did not have the formal and theoretical tools to develop his ideas properly. Thorndike was successful in toppling a mistaken theory, the doctrine of formal discipline. In its place he put one that was largely vacuous. Despite these criticisms, Thorndike defined most of the issues that dominate discussions of transfer to the present day.

Theories that smack more or less of formal discipline have been circulated with regularity over the years. Perhaps the most influential and long-standing has been Piaget's theory of cognitive development. It is difficult to overestimate the impact of Piaget's theory, not only in developmental psychology but also in such diverse fields as biology and philosophy. Although the theory is wide-ranging and complex, we may restrict ourselves to those claims of the theory concerning the abstract nature of knowledge and its relation to stages of development. According to Piaget, children pass through an invariant sequence of fairly stable stages on their way to cognitive maturity. These stages are defined by certain modes of thought, which have been given an abstract yet precise mathematical characterization in the theory. Critical to a stage theory like Piaget's are the claims that the onset of a particular stage is rapid, not continuous, and that, once a child is within a stage, all reasoning is mediated by the characteristic structures of that stage. If, for example, a child is in the concrete operations stage, that child should exhibit concrete operations on a wide range of tasks. Thus, Piaget's position was that knowledge is quite abstract and that particular knowledge structures apply broadly (speaking of Piaget's theory

in terms of knowledge applying to tasks is somewhat misleading in that the theory is a structural and not a process theory).
On these grounds, a loose parallel may be drawn between the
Piagetian view and the doctrine of formal discipline. Both identify a commonality between tasks at a very high level. One
major difference between the two, however, is that Piaget felt
strongly that abstract thinking cannot be taught or trained, and
that children cannot be pushed through the developmental sequence.

Piaget used a wide range of problem-solving tasks to study
the developmental sequence, many of which have subsequently
become staples for research in developmental psychology. Although Piaget himself used these tasks primarily for exploratory
purposes, subsequent researchers have used them more or less
as litmus tests to classify children into their respective stages.
For example, the concrete operations stage is identified through
successful performance on such tasks as conservation (number,
liquid, solid, and weight), class inclusion, and seriation. Years
of replication of Piaget's work, however, has shown that progress through the developmental stages is not as orderly and
well-defined as Piaget originally thought. Most important, recent research has shown that children do not necessarily perform equally well on all tasks that define a particular stage, and
this suggests that knowledge is not totally abstract but is somewhat specific to the task at hand.

The experimental evidence is perhaps clearest for those tasks
defining the concrete operations stage, which roughly spans the
ages 7 through 12. Consider three of Piaget's benchmark tasks:
conservation of number, conservation of solid, and conservation
of weight. According to the theory, performance on these tasks
should be completely coupled; children should show mastery of
either all or none simultaneously (Seigler, 1986). In fact, children
seem to acquire these concepts in sequential order, with conservation of number appearing first at age 6, conservation of solid
next at age 8, and conservation of weight last at age 10 (Katz and
Beilin, 1976; Miller, 1976); Piaget termed this decoupling *horizontal decalage* but had no explanation for it. Additionally,
it has been shown that, within a single task, children may do
well on some versions and not on others. For example, in the
conservation-of-number task, children may conserve sets of
three objects but not sets of five (Kinsbourne, 1978). Similarly, in
the class inclusion task, performance varies widely depending
upon superficial features, such as wording and problem context
(Winer, 1980). For example, questions involving the classifica-

tion of animals are much easier than those involving the classification of flowers (Inhelder and Piaget, 1964).

Thus, it appears that the role of domain-independent, abstract
knowledge has been somewhat overstated in the Piagetian theory. This realization has led certain developmental theorists
(e.g., Flavell, 1978) to call for the abandonment of sweeping
stage theories like Piaget's which attempt to characterize all of a
child's thinking at a certain age by a single deep structure.
Indeed, with the advent of the information-processing approach, the focus in developmental psychology has largely
shifted away from stage theories and toward the study of incre-
mental development within specific content domains.

Meaningful versus rote learning

The traditional doctrine of formal discipline and Thorndike's
theory of identical elements in essence define the two extreme
ends of the general-specific transfer continuum. Certainly many
intermediate positions are possible. Indeed, many early critics of
the theory of identical elements claimed that Thorndike had
shown not that transfer was necessarily limited in scope, but
merely that in the absence of *effective training* it was (Meredith,
1927; Woodrow, 1927; Orata, 1928). Several studies done in
direct opposition to Thorndike showed that the likelihood and
breadth of transfer was largely dependent on the type of instruction offered and the subsequent organization of the skill (Judd,
1908; Ruger, 1910; Coxe, 1925; Orata, 1928; Dorsey and Hopkins, 1930). The question of whether there is transfer between
tasks often has no dogmatic answer; transfer often depends on
whether a common representation of the tasks can be found and
communicated to subjects.

Perhaps the first demonstration of the importance of representation was the classic refraction study by Judd (1908). In this
experiment, young boys were asked to throw darts at an under-
water target. During training, the target was submerged twelve
inches, but in the transfer task, it was brought up to four. The
critical manipulation was that half of the subjects received instruction on the theory of refraction, and the other half did not.
Interestingly, the two groups were indistinguishable during
training, when both groups were occupied primarily with the
mechanics of dart throwing. However, the difference between
the two groups emerged strikingly on the transfer task. Those
subjects without theory were quite confused, and their errors
were large and persistent. However, those subjects with instruc-

tion adapted very rapidly. Apparently, an understanding of the basics of refraction helped them to generate the appropriate action in the new situation.

Results such as these supported the position that transfer was largely dependent on the kind of representation subjects had of the task. However, to associationists like Thorndike, representation was not an issue. Thorndike claimed that all learning could be reduced to a single type: the forming and strengthening of connections between stimuli and responses. In such a view, the difference between learning a simple association between two nonsense syllables and learning a complex mathematical postulate was entirely quantitative; the latter simply involved forming more associations.

In contrast, gestalt psychologists like Wertheimer, Koffka, and Katona made a qualitative distinction between what they called *senseless learning*, the kind studied by the associationists, and *meaningful learning*, the kind where "eyes are opened . . . real grasping, real understanding occurs" (Wertheimer, in Katona, 1940). Meaningful learning arises not from the formation of connections through rote memorization but rather from a deep understanding of the structural relations within a problem. To draw this distinction experimentally, the gestalters were naturally drawn to the study of transfer. Their claim was that, whereas senseless learning would show little or no transfer, meaningful learning would show quite a bit. To the gestalters, transfer occurred not through the piecemeal sharing of common elements but rather through the *transposition* of an entire structure. Where Thorndike erred was in his insistence that "the essential element in the structure of psychology is habit and no organization at a higher level exists" (Allport, 1937, p. 248).

A clear illustration of the difference between Thorndike's identical elements and the gestalt notion of transposition is the comparison of two different musical melodies. Thorndike's measure of similarity presumably would be based upon the number of shared notes in the two melodies. However, the gestalters recognized that melodies are perceived as organized wholes whose essential character resides in the *functional relations* between the notes, not in the notes themselves. Such an analysis captures the fact that, although two melodies may share no notes, they nevertheless may be perceived as virtually identical, as in the case when a melody is played in different keys (Wertheimer, 1945). The gestalters' principal insight was simply that the whole is often more than the sum of its parts.

Subjects, then, can approach a task in more than one way,

and the method of attack can have profound implications for transfer. Wertheimer (1945) found that, given the same task, subjects adopt different strategies, some more "meaningful" than others. Figure 1.1a shows the classic demonstration of this fact, namely Wertheimer's task of finding the area of a parallelogram. His young subjects were shown the procedure for dropping perpendiculars to convert a parallelogram to a rectangle, a shape for which a tried and true formula for computing area was already known. However, only some of his subjects grasped the

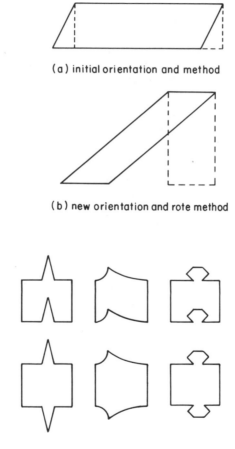

(a) initial orientation and method

(b) new orientation and rote method

(c) sensible (top) and insensible transfer tasks

Figure 1.1. *Wertheimer's finding the area of a parallelogram. M. Wertheimer,* Productive Thinking *(New York: Harper & Row, 1943, © 1959 by Valentin Wertheimer). Reprinted by permission.*

sense of this transformation; others adopted a rote strategy of dropping lines and measuring line segments. On the original task, the rote and meaningful strategies were more or less functionally equivalent, as in Judd's refraction study. However, the two strategies were easily discriminated by a series of transfer tasks. Figure 1.1b shows one task in which subjects were presented with a parallelogram in a different orientation. Some subjects continued to drop vertical lines, as was required by the original task, but was now inappropriate. Figure 1.1c shows another transfer task, in which subjects were presented with a series of irregular figures, some of which nonetheless could be transformed in much the same way as the parallelogram. Subjects with the proper understanding of the transformation solved the "sensible" figures readily and rejected the others as malformed. These demonstrations show that transfer results are often useful in determining what has been learned in those situations where more than one type of learning is possible.

Whereas Wertheimer relied on the natural variability in the methods of his subjects, Katona (1940) set out to induce different strategies and representations experimentally. Katona performed a series of experiments involving a variety of puzzle problems (card tricks, matchstick problems) where subjects were taught either a rote strategy that applied to a particular problem or a more general strategy that was based on the structural relations of an entire set of problems. Figure 1.2 shows the matchstick problem, where subjects either memorized the series of physical actions used to solve a particular problem or studied the following more meaningful principle: "Here are five squares

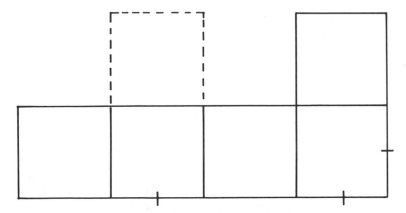

Figure 1.2. *Katona's matchstick problem.*

composed of sixteen equal lines. We want to change these five squares into four similar squares. Since we have sixteen lines and want four squares, each square must have four independent side lines, which should not be side lines of any other square at the same time. Therefore, all lines with a *double function,* that is, limiting two squares at the same time, must be changed into lines with a *single function* (limiting one square only)" (Katona, 1940, p. 60). The standard result in these experiments was that, whereas the rote subjects had slightly better performance on the problem they had memorized, the meaningful subjects showed much better transfer to similar problems. This finding was replicated by Hilgard, Irvine, and Whipple (1953) and, more recently, by Simon (1975), who showed that a general recursive strategy for solving the tower-of-Hanoi problem applied to problems with any number of disks, whereas a rote strategy did not.

Thus, when considering issues of transfer, we must consider the strategies and representations used by subjects. Some may be more conducive to transfer than others. It is interesting to note, however, that throughout their attack on Thorndike and the associationists, the gestalters did not deny the basic notion of identical elements and its relevance to transfer; they merely stressed the preeminence of structural identity over the kind of piecemeal identity that Thorndike advocated (Wertheimer, 1945).

Analytic versus nonanalytic approaches

Most of the early studies of transfer did little to determine the actual locus of the effect, that is, which pieces of knowledge were being carried over to the new situation. In many classroom studies it was sufficient simply to demonstrate that transfer had occurred at all (Ellis, 1965). Underwood (1957) called such experiments *nonanalytic,* for obvious reasons. Nonanalytic experiments abounded for at least two reasons. First of all, researchers had no knowledge representation language to specify the elements of skill. As a result, as Thorndike (1903) admitted, "it was often not possible to tell just what features of two mental abilities were thus identical" (Thorndike goes on to say, however, that "there is rarely much trouble in reaching an appropriate decision in those cases where training is of practical importance"). Second, even if the elements could have been specified explicitly, data collection techniques were often incapable of winnowing out the effects of a particular learned component on the execution of a complex skill.

Although the identification and independent measurement of elements was and continues to be a difficult problem, it can be made somewhat easier by the choice of an appropriate task, particularly one that is relatively simple, discrete, and therefore easily structured. The verbal learners adopted just such a task for extensive study: the learning of lists of paired associates. The verbal learners took the problem of transfer out of the classroom and placed it firmly in the laboratory, where it was subjected to a thorough analysis. Much was learned about the peculiarities of transfer as it manifests itself in this relatively narrow and circumscribed domain.

In the typical study, subjects were asked to learn in succession two lists of paired stimuli and responses, most often familiar words or nonsense syllables. The two lists often differed in terms of stimulus or response similarity. For example, the stimuli in the two lists might be synonyms, or the responses antonyms. In such a way, the relative contributions of stimulus and response similarity could be assessed independently. The structure of this task was clean and lent itself to a relatively straightforward analysis.

A wide range of transfer results from such studies were systematically integrated by Osgood (1949) with his transfer and retroaction surface. Figure 1.3 shows Osgood's three-dimensional surface, which conveys that transfer is a curvilinear

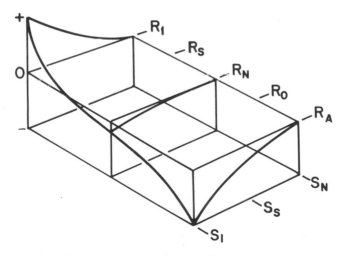

Figure 1.3. *Osgood's transfer surface (the stimulus dimension, in the foreground, ranges from S_I [identical stimuli] to S_N [neutral stimuli]; the response dimension, along the back edge, ranges from R_I [identical responses] to R_A [antagonistic responses]).*

function of both stimulus and response similarity. The side edge shows shifts in stimulus similarity, ranging from identical stimuli (S_I) in the two lists, through similar stimuli (S_S), to neutral stimuli (S_N). The back edge shows shifts in response similarity, ranging from identical responses (R_I), through similar responses (R_S), neutral responses (R_N), and partially opposite responses (R_O), to directly antagonistic responses (R_A). The vertical dimension expresses the amount of transfer, ranging from largely positive (+) to largely negative (−). The surface is perhaps best understood by considering its extreme anchors:

1. In the back left corner, maximal transfer occurs when both stimuli and responses are identical in the two lists (this is in some sense a degenerate transfer condition and is really a case of overlearning). Transfer diminishes but remains positive as both stimuli and responses depart from identity and approach similarity.

2. In the front left corner, maximal interference occurs when the stimuli are identical in the two lists but the responses are antagonistic. Once again, interference diminishes as both stimuli and responses approach similarity.

3. Along the back edge, where the stimuli in the two lists bear no resemblance whatsoever, the amount of transfer is zero and is unaffected by shifts in response similarity.

Although Osgood's surface represents a fairly accurate summary of verbal learning transfer results, various aspects have been called into question. The criticisms concern both the correct placement of certain regions of the surface and the comprehensiveness of the surface as a whole. For example, although several points along the stimulus similarity dimension have been sampled, the continuous gradients implied by the smooth curves have never truly been substantiated, especially in the intermediate regions of the curves (Postman, 1971). Concerning comprehensiveness, Bower and Hilgard (1981) pointed out that the surface does not accommodate a particular design in which the stimuli and responses in the second list are identical to those in the first but are simply repaired (the so-called A-B, A-Br design). Various studies (Gagné, Baker, and Foster, 1950; Porter and Duncan, 1953) have shown that this condition produces the most negative transfer, but it is not represented anywhere on the surface. To remedy some of these deficits, Martin (1965) proposed an even more elaborate decomposition involving separate surfaces for forward associations, backward associations, and response availability. The particulars of these various formulations are of no real concern here. What is most important is that the verbal learners pioneered a highly analytic approach to the study of transfer.

An interesting question is whether the recall of a list of paired associates constitutes cognitive skill. On the one hand, the task has a rather shallow, disjointed organization and seems to involve no cognition other than retrieval from long-term memory. On the other hand, there does seem to be a certain skill involved: with practice, subjects actually get better at learning new lists. More specifically, there is a well-documented general practice effect distinct from the specific effects summarized in Osgood's surface. This general practice phenomenon, called *learning to learn,* has been found in domains ranging from paired associates learning (Ward, 1937; Bunch and McCraven, 1938; Thune, 1950) to maze learning in rats (Marx, 1944) to concept learning in monkeys (Harlow, 1949). Ironically, this general practice effect was viewed largely as a contaminating factor and consequently was not studied as exhaustively as the specific effects.

Lateral versus vertical transfer

While the verbal learners were taking the study of transfer out of the classroom and into the laboratory, a group of educational psychologists, led by Gagné, were striving for a similar level of analysis with more complex classroom tasks. Their interest was in designing well-formed curricula that maximized learning and transfer and could be used in conjunction with the new "programmed instruction" technology. Programmed instruction, which arose out of the behaviorist tradition (Skinner, 1954), decomposed the teaching of a complex topic such as algebra into a set of discrete subtopics or *frames*. The approach stressed the role of feedback and cumulative learning; that is, each frame was mastered before moving on to the next. To be principled, programmed instruction required that the developer first identify the elements of skill or frames to be sequenced and then apply some sequencing strategy. All too often, however, this ideal was not realized (Gavurin and Donahue, 1961; Roe, Case, and Roe, 1962; Buckland, 1968). Many programs of instruction were largely ad hoc (VanPatten, Chao, and Reigeluth, 1986).

Gagné and his colleagues set out to put curriculum design on firmer footing. After observing that learning rates in programmed instruction varied by as much as a factor of two, Gagné argued that individual differences were due not to differences in intelligence but rather to differences in prerequisite knowledge (Gagné and Paradise, 1961). Cognitive skill was best represented as a hierarchy of super and subordinate capabilities called *learning sets* (Harlow, 1949). The successful acquisition of a particular learning set in the hierarchy was almost completely dependent on the mastery of sets subordinate to it. At the top of these skill hierarchies sat the highest-order skill, the goal of the instructional sequence. At the bottom sat basic abilities of the type that might be measured by standardized intelligence tests.

Gagné's skill hierarchies brought to light the distinction between what he called *lateral* and *vertical* transfer (Gagné, 1966). Lateral transfer was defined as the kind of transfer that spreads over a broad set of situations at roughly the same level of complexity. For example, transfer between different programming languages, between different puzzle problems like tower-of-Hanoi and missionaries-and-cannibals, or between speaking English and French all qualify as instances of lateral transfer. Vertical transfer, however, concerns transfer between lower-level and higher-level skills that exist in a part-whole, prerequisite relationship to one another. In a sense, Gagné's skill hierarchies defined the conditions for vertical transfer within a particular skill: vertical transfer was nearly guaranteed when subordinate learning sets in the hierarchy had been mastered.

Figure 1.4 presents Gagné's skill hierarchy for solving first-order algebraic equations. The hierarchy consists of seven distinct subordinate levels, arranged in order of complexity and terminating with the basic skills of integration, symbol recognition, and knowledge of number. Arcs between various nodes in the tree indicate specific prerequisite relations.

Hierarchies such as these were said to be constructed largely through a process of rational task analysis, the details of which were generally unspecified. As Gagné put it, to identify the prerequisites of a particular learning set, one simply asks the following question: "What would the student have to know how to do in order to achieve this new task, when given only instructions" (Gagné and Paradise, 1961, p. 4). One asks this question recursively at all levels until the entire hierarchy has been defined. The recursion stops at the level of so-called basic skills, which may be more or less basic, depending on the complexity of the root node of the hierarchy.

This was how the elements of skill were defined. As for how they were sequenced in the curriculum, Gagné reported that there were many equally good alternate routes through most

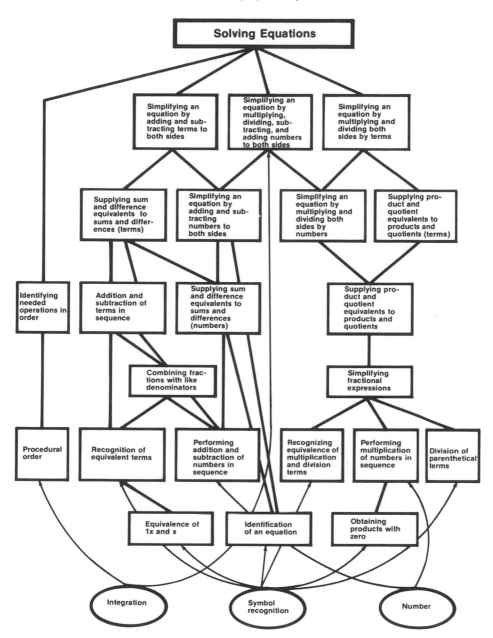

Figure 1.4. *Gagné's skill hierarchy for solving simple equations.*

hierarchies. The one inviolable rule was that, as one moved from lower to higher levels, one did not move to a superordinate node without mastering all the prerequisites. In Gagné's view, many educational problems arise from violations of this rule: "Of course, the individual learner may be set a problem which is beyond him in the sense that he must acquire all the subordinate principles himself before he achieves a solution. Solving a problem under such circumstances may happen on certain occasions and in particular individuals, but to advocate such an approach as a practical learning method makes no sense" (Gagné, 1966, p. 165). In fact, Resnick (1976) showed that when nodes are skipped in the hierarchy, that is, when students are given tasks beyond their skill level, the variability among students increases. The better students are able to span the gap; the worse students are not.

Gagné's skill hierarchies have been subjected to several empirical tests (Gagné and Paradise, 1961; Gagné and Bassler, 1963; Gagné and Staff, 1965). For example, Gagné and Paradise (1961) set out to validate the skill hierarchy shown in Figure 1.4. Their method was to present students with programmed instruction based on the hierarchy and to monitor the various transitions between levels. Transitions were classified into four types, based on the subjects' performance on adjacent levels in the hierarchy:

1. LOWER+ HIGHER+   This denotes the situation where a subject masters both the subordinate and the superordinate skills. This situation is consistent with Gagné's theory: if subjects master all lower-level skills, transfer should be total and positive to the higher-level skills.

2. LOWER− HIGHER−   This situation, also consistent with the theory, occurs when subjects fail on lower-level skills and subsequently fail on higher-level skills.

3. LOWER− HIGHER+   This situation is in direct contradiction to the theory. It is unclear whether a high occurrence of such transitions indicates a disconfirmation of the theory or simply a poor task analysis.

4. LOWER+ HIGHER−   Gagné hedged a bit here, claiming that this situation neither confirmed nor disconfirmed the theory. His position was that a higher-level set may be failed, even though all relevant lower-level sets are achieved, because a subject receives insufficient instruction or practice on the higher-level set. According to Gagné, a high occurrence of such transitions indicates a poorly administered rather than a poorly designed learning program.

To get a measure of support for his theory, Gagné simply divided the number of confirming types (types 1–2) by the total number of relevant types (types 1–3). Gagné compiled data for fifteen transitions, all of which were within the range of .91 to 1.00 on his measure. Generally, as subjects moved up the hierarchy, the proportion of + + transitions decreased in favor of − − transitions. Indeed, for the three transitions to the penultimate level in the hierarchy (the highest level measured), the failure rate was nearly 81 percent. This points to the general ineffectiveness of the learning program. As further support for this view, the mean percentage of so-called irrelevant types (LOWER +, HIGHER −) was 13 percent but ranged as high as 50 percent on some transitions.

Many researchers have failed to find any effect for principled curriculum design (VanPatten, Chao, and Reigeluth, 1986). Notable among these failed attempts were the *scramble* studies, where carefully designed programs of instruction were pitted against versions whose frames had been randomly ordered (Gavurin and Donahue, 1961; Roe, Case, and Roe, 1962; Levin and Baker, 1963; Payne, Krathwohl, and Gordon, 1967; Niedermeyer, 1968; Pyatte, 1969). One moderately successful study was done by Buckland (1968), who found that less capable students were hurt by the scrambled curriculum but more capable students were not. This is in agreement with Resnick's analysis.

In sum, Gagné's notion of skill hierarchies, while quite intuitive and almost certainly true at some level, has been lacking in empirical support. One problem with confirming the theory has been that the requisite task analysis is something of an art. Gagné himself pointed out that many analyses of the task in Figure 1.4 were possible, with some better than others: "In doing the analysis, we accepted in general the approach to solution of simple equations which had been designed into the program. This particular approach is by no means the only one. In other words, there are perhaps several *possible* learning set hierarchies which could be worked out to support this final task, and it is quite conceivable that some are "better" than others in the sense of being more efficient or more transferable to later learning" (Gagné and Paradise, 1961, p. 5).

In short, Gagné was running into the same representational buzz saw faced by Thorndike and the gestalters. Many decompositions of cognitive skill are possible; some promote transfer better than others. Indeed, many of the failures to confirm the theory have been criticized for having the wrong representation of the skill (VanPatten, Chao, and Reigeluth, 1986).

Gagné's hierarchical, bottom-up view has not been the sole position advanced on vertical transfer. Other instructional sequences have been advocated by a variety of educational psychologists. These include Bruner's spiral curriculum, where topics are introduced and reintroduced at increasing levels of detail (Bruner, 1966); Ausubel's progressive differentiation, where complex topics are preceded by more general statements called advance organizers (Ausubel, 1968); and Reigeluth's elaboration theory, where instruction starts at a very general level, zooms in to capture detail, and pulls back again to reinforce major points (Reigeluth and Stein, 1983; see also Norman, 1973). Unfortunately, these theories have received less empirical scrutiny than Gagné's (with the exception of Ausubel's), and this makes comparisons difficult. Progress has been limited somewhat in this area by the difficulty of performing the kinds of full-blown classroom studies that are required. Recent advances in intelligent tutoring may make the study of vertical transfer more tractable.

Contemporary Studies of Transfer

With the advent of the information-processing approach in psychology, many traditional learning and transfer issues were temporarily set aside. Researchers adopted the strategy of first working out the details of performance theories before turning their attention to the study of higher-order phenomena. As a result, the transfer of cognitive skill has been largely neglected by cognitive psychologists throughout the last quarter-century.

Analogical transfer

One topic that has received considerable recent attention, however, is analogical transfer in problem solving. To solve a problem by analogy, a subject is first reminded (or told) of a similar problem whose solution is known. The subject then maps the solution of that problem (the source) to the current problem (the target). Many studies use problem isomorphs, that is, problems that differ in terms of superficial features but have the same problem-solving operators and search space at some deeper level.

A wide range of studies have shown that, at least in the situations concocted by experimental psychologists, people are quite bad at noticing similarities between problems and drawing on analogous solutions (Reed, Ernst, and Banerji, 1974; Hayes

and Simon, 1977; Weisberg, DiCamillo, and Phillips, 1978; Holyoak, 1985). In one such study (Perfetto, Bransford, and Franks,
1983), subjects were first asked to rate for truthfulness sentences
such as "A minister marries several people each week." Then
the subjects were presented with a set of insight problems
adapted from Gardner (1978). It just so happened that many of
the rated sentences hinted rather blatantly at solutions to the
problems. For example, the preceding sentence can be applied
to the following problem: "A man who lived in a small town in
the U.S. married twenty different women of the same town. All
are still living and he has never divorced any of them. Yet, he
has broken no law. Can you explain?" (Perfetto et al., 1983, p.
25). Surprisingly, prior exposure to the sentences had no effect
on subjects' probability or type of solution. Subjects did, however, make use of the sentences if told explicitly of their relevance.

In another series of studies (Gick and Holyoak, 1980, 1983),
subjects were presented with Duncker's (1945) classic radiation
problem: "Suppose you are a doctor faced with a patient who
has an inoperable stomach tumor. You have at your disposal
rays that can destroy human tissue when directed with sufficient intensity. How can you use these rays to destroy the tumor
without destroying the surrounding healthy tissue?" (adapted
from Gick and Holyoak, 1983). Prior to their exposure to the
target problem, subjects read a story about an analogous military problem and its solution. In the story, a general wishes to
capture an enemy fortress. Radiating outward from the fortress
are many roads, each of which is mined in such a way that the
passing of any large force will cause an explosion. This precludes a full-scale direct attack. The general's plan is to divide
his army, send a small group down each road, and converge on
the fortress. The common strategy in both problems is to divide
the force, attack from different sides, and converge on the target. After reading this story, however, only about 30 percent of
the subjects could solve the radiation problem, which is little
improvement over the 10 percent baseline solution rate (Gick
and Holyoak, 1980). A series of follow-up experiments (Gick
and Holyoak, 1983) found that neither the addition of a concluding statement conveying the common underlying principle
nor a diagram depicting that principle made the military story
any more useful to subjects.

Why do subjects perform so poorly? According to our simple
two-stage model of analogical problem solving, difficulties arise
either in the initial noticing that problems are similar or in the

subsequent mapping from source to target. As far as the notic-ing component is concerned, many studies have shown that explicit hints about the relevance of the source problem improve subject performance dramatically (e.g. Gick and Holyoak, 1980, 1983; Perfetto et al., 1983; see also Reed, Ernst, and Banerji, 1974). This indicates that being reminded of the right problem is often more problematic than mapping the solution. Ross (1982) showed that the reminding process is quite sensitive to many of the same interfering and facilitating effects (such as context and fan) found in traditional studies of recognition memory. How-ever, despite the seeming unreliability of spontaneous analogi-cal transfer, some researchers have recently championed analogical reasoning as perhaps the most powerful knowledge acquisition tool in humans (Neves, 1981; VanLehn, 1983; Ander-son and Thompson, in press). In these proposals, analogical problem solving often goes by the name of learning by example, which can be thought of simply as analogical reasoning with a supplied source.

Although "noticing" is often tantamount to "solving," the mapping process is perhaps the greater obstacle in more diffi-cult problems. A series of studies involving puzzle problem isomorphs showed that, even when informed of the relevance of the source, subjects often have trouble drawing correspon-dences between the two domains and are unable to solve the target problem (Reed, Ernst, and Banerji, 1974; Simon and Reed, 1976; Hayes and Simon, 1977; Kotovsky, Hayes, and Simon, 1985). The difficulty in many cases seems to be that subjects adopt representations of the two problems that rely too heavily on superficial features, which are radically different, and not heavily enough on deep, functional relationships, which are often the same. Of course, shallow representations typify prob-lem solving in the novice. This fact was noticed first by the gestalters (e.g. Duncker, 1945) and more recently has been sub-stantiated extensively (Chi, Feltovich, and Glaser, 1981; Chi, Glaser, and Rees, 1982). In a series of sorting tasks, Chi discov-ered that, on the one hand, novice physics students sorted mechanics problems in terms of superficial features, like type of device involved (pulley, inclined plane) or physics words men-tioned in the problem text. On the other hand, experts sorted on the basis of abstract, solution-relevant features. For ex-ample, they might group together all problems solved by the conservation-of-momentum principle. Similar results were found in domains as diverse as algebra word problem solving (Silver, 1979) and text editing (Kay and Black, 1985). Given that novices almost by definition are unable to formulate "deep" representations, it is no wonder that in many situations they find drawing functional correspondences between two problems difficult.

Aside from problems in noticing and mapping, subjects may have shown little transfer in the isomorph experiments simply because the experimenter had not ensured that something was learned in the first place. Typically in these studies, subjects get only one trial on both source and target problems. Needless to say, one trial may not be enough to learn anything substantial about a difficult problem like the tower-of-Hanoi (Hayes and Simon, 1977) or missionaries-and-cannibals (Reed, Ernst, and Banerji, 1974; Thomas, 1974; Simon and Reed, 1976). For example, in one study control subjects were given an additional trial on the source problem, and little improvement was observed (Reed et al., 1974). If subjects cannot solve the source, how can they be expected to solve the target? Indeed, a series of studies by Smith (1986) overturned some of the prior results of Hayes and Simon (1977) by showing that substantial transfer was possible between tower-of-Hanoi isomorphs, given sufficient practice on source problems.

Specificity of transfer

Recently there has been a surge of interest in documenting the specificity of transfer in a wide range of school-related and work-related tasks. One area of research has involved the classic Wason card task (Wason, 1966). Subjects were shown four cards which had printed on them the symbols A, E, 4, and 7. The task was to judge the validity of the following rule, which referred only to these four cards: "If a card has a vowel on one side, then it has an even number on the other side."

The subjects were instructed to turn over only those cards that had to be turned over for the correctness of the rule to be judged. Forty-six percent of the subjects elected to turn over both E and 4, which is a wrong combination of choices. The E had to be turned over, but the 4 did not, since neither a vowel nor a consonant on the other side would have falsified the rule. Only 4 percent elected to turn over E and 7, which are the correct choices. An odd number behind the E or a vowel behind the 7 would have falsified the rule. Another 33 percent of the subjects elected to turn over the E only. The remaining 17 percent of the subjects made other incorrect choices.

One might dismiss this failure as subjects' simply not appreciating the logic of the conditional. However, Cheng et al. (1986) showed that subjects do no better if they have had formal training in logic. The problem is not that subjects do not know the logic of the conditional, but rather that they do not transfer this knowledge to the card task.

Subsequent research showed quite remarkably that subjects can achieve high levels of performance if the card selection task is presented in other logically equivalent forms. For instance, in one isomorphic version of the problem, subjects are told that "If a person is drinking alcohol, then he must be over 21" and are asked whom to check to validate the rule: someone drinking alcohol, someone drinking a soft drink, someone over 21, or someone under 21. In this case, subjects have no difficulty whatsoever choosing the proper options, namely, someone drinking alcohol and someone under 21. Cheng et al. (1986) argued that this is because subjects possess a "permission schema" which allows them to reason about such situations but does not provide a basis for transfer to the card selection task. Nonetheless, the permission schema can be used to judge a wide variety of situations. For instance, subjects in the same study were able to use it to reason about whether passengers entering a country had been checked for cholera. Thus, in this case Thorndike's extreme version of the identical elements model is again wrong. There is a real range of transfer for the permission schema. It is nevertheless remarkably narrow compared to the generality of the conditional logic that underlies it.

The Ghost of General Transfer

A fundamental transfer question is whether transfer is necessarily limited in scope or whether it is broad and ranges across diverse disciplines. The broad view, first advocated as the doctrine of formal discipline, was discredited by Thorndike, who claimed that transfer was quite specific and was based on the existence of identical elements. Thorndike, however, was challenged by the gestalters, who showed that a broad range of transfer outcomes was possible and that the generality and applicability of knowledge was largely dependent upon its representation. Modern cognitive psychology has been greatly concerned with the influence of knowledge representation on intellectual performance. The possibility of transfer cannot be denied outright; its occurrence depends heavily on the nature of instruction and the organization of knowledge. It seems, then, that what Thorndike called the "superstition of general training" is making something of a comeback. A variety of researchers have recently called for the identification and codification of "general" cognitive skills. Simon (1980) claimed that powerful general problem-solving methods do exist, and what's more, they can be taught. Brown, Bransford, Ferrara, and Campione (1983) decried the emphasis on the teaching of content in today's schools and called for more emphasis on the teaching of general methods for learning. Rubinstein (1980) reported that at the time over thirty colleges and universities offered interdisciplinary courses in general problem solving. A growing number of researchers in computer science and education are championing computer programming as a powerful new vehicle for teaching general problem solving (Winston, 1977; Papert, 1980; Linn and Fisher, 1983). What, then, is the current status of the notion of general transfer? Is it dead, or very much alive?

One reason why the notion of general transfer keeps rising from the grave is that it is such an attractive proposition for psychologists and educators alike. It is the one effect that, if discovered and engineered, could liberate students and teachers from the shackles of narrow, disciplinary education. Sustaining these longings is the fact that it is very difficult to prove something does not exist. There is always another manipulation in the psychologist's toolbox to try.

Unfortunately, despite these yearnings, the evidence for the existence of general transfer is not good (Simon, 1980). First of all, there were the classic disconfirming studies of formal discipline (Thorndike and Woodworth, 1901; Thorndike, Aikens, and Hubbell, 1902; Thorndike, 1922). A further series of studies, initiated by Thorndike (1924), demonstrated that the study of such abstract subjects as Latin and geometry in high school had no greater facilitating effect on tests of reasoning than did more mundane subjects like bookkeeping and shopwork (Carroll, 1940; Rapp, 1945; Wesman, 1945; Strom, 1960). More recent studies (e.g. Jeffries, 1978) have shown no transfer of general problem-solving skills across widely different types of problems. In a typical study, Post and Brennan (1976) trained subjects for several weeks on a general heuristic procedure for solving algebra word problems. Their instructions included such things as "determine what is given" and "check your result." On a problem-solving post-test, the performance of the trained subjects was no better than that of a control group. Besides this spate of negative evidence, there has been no positive evidence of general transfer besides a few highly questionable studies (Dorsey and Hopkins, 1930; Fawcett, 1935; Hartung, 1942). In one such study, Bartlett (reported in Hayes, 1980) gave subjects an IQ test before and after taking a university-sponsored problem-solving course. On average, subjects added seven points to their IQs (from 127 to 133). However, no control was run, and it is quite possible that test familiarity or some other confounding factor contributed to the gain. In sum, there has as yet been no strong demonstration of the existence of general transfer.

Why has general transfer in problem solving been so hard to detect? One possibility is that general heuristic methods are not really that useful. This view is consistent with the current emphasis in cognitive psychology on the role of domain-specific knowledge in skilled performance (Chase and Simon, 1973; Lesgold, 1984). The picture is evolving of an expert whose skill is composed of thousands of specific responses to specific situations. For example, Chase and Simon (1973) estimated that chess experts have between 10,000 and 100,000 board positions committed to memory. Not surprisingly, problem-solving methods based on specific knowledge geared toward particular situations, the so-called *strong* methods, outperform widely applicable methods based on general knowledge, the *weak* methods (Newell, 1973).

General methods are often useless in problem solving because their prescriptions are too vague to apply. Table 1.2, for example, presents a set of general problem-solving heuristics advocated by Rubinstein (1975). These heuristics all have the ring of truth and seem quite reasonable on the surface. However, their application to a particular problem is difficult, given the abundance of abstract nouns in search of referents. In the first heuristic, the problem solver is told to avoid detail in the initial formulation of the problem, but what is detail in the mind of a novice? Indeed, it may require substantial expertise to determine which details are relevant and which are not in a particular situation. In the second heuristic, the problem solver is told to prune alternative solution paths by watching for signs of progress. Again, how is a novice to recognize signs of progress? Generally speaking, as methods get more abstract and widely applicable, their useful role in problem solving gets more tenuous. For practical purposes, the search for referents puts a cap on the generality of methods.

Another reason why general transfer has been so hard to detect is that, at least in adults, many of the weak methods are highly practiced and therefore drop out of the transfer equation. The reason for this is not profound but simply a consequence of

Table 1.2.   Rubinstein's problem-solving heuristics.

1. *Total Picture*
   Before you attempt a solution to a problem, avoid getting lost in detail. Go over the elements of the problem rapidly several times until a pattern or a total picture emerges. Try to get the picture of the forest before you get lost in the trees.

2. *Withhold Your Judgment*
   Do not commit yourself too early to a course of action. You may find it hard to break away from the path, find it may be the wrong one. Search for a number of paths simultaneously, and use signs of progress to guide you to the path that appears most plausible.

3. *Models*
   Verbalize, use language to simplify the statement of the problem, write it down. Use mathematical or graphical pictorial models. Use abstract models such as symbols and equations, or use concrete models in the form of objects.
   A model is a simpler representation of the real world problem; it is supposed to help you.

4. *Change in Representation*
   Problem solving can also be viewed as a change in representation. The solutions of many problems in algebra and mathematics in general consist of transformations of the given information so as to make the solution, which is obscure, become transparent in a new form of representation. Most mathematical derivations follow this route.

5. *Asking the Right Questions*
   Language in all its forms is a most powerful tool in problem solving. Asking the right question, uttering the correct word, or hearing it, may direct your processing unit to the appropriate region in your long-term storage to retrieve complete blocks of information that will guide you to a successful solution.

6. *Will to Doubt*
   Have a will to doubt. Accept premises as tentative to varying degrees, but be flexible and ready to question their credibility, and, if necessary, pry yourself loose of fixed convictions and reject them. Rejection may take the form of innovation, because to innovate is, psychologically, at least, to overcome or discard the old if not always to reject it outright.

7. *Working Backward*
   Do not start at the beginning and follow systematically step by step to the end goal.
   The solution path is as important as the answer and, in problems where the goal is specified, the path is the solution.

8. *Stable Substructures*
   In complex problems it helps to proceed in a way that permits you to return to your partial solution after interruptions. Stable substructures that do not collapse or disappear when you do not tend to them will serve this purpose.

9. *Analogies and Metaphors*
   Use an analogy whenever you can think of one. An analogy provides a model which serves as a guide to identify the elements of a problem as parts of a more complete structure. It also helps recognize phases as elements of a complete process.

10. *Talk*
    When you are stuck after an intensive effort to solve a problem, it is wise to take a break and do something else. It is also helpful to talk about your problem at various stages in your search for a solution. Talking to someone may help you pry loose of the constraints we mentioned, because your colleague may have a different world view and he may direct you to new avenues of search when he utters a word or asks a question.

Source: Moshe F. Rubinstein, *Patterns of problem solving* (Englewood Cliffs, N.J.: Prentice-Hall, © 1975). Reprinted by permission.

how transfer is measured. Even if a component plays a large part in both training and transfer tasks, that component will have no measurable effect on transfer unless the performance of that component *improves* as a result of training. If the component is already well-practiced before training begins, learning will be negligible and no savings will be realized on the transfer task. This point highlights the fact that all cognitive skills are learned not in isolation but rather against a backdrop of well-practiced support skills which go virtually undetected in any measurement of learning and transfer. This may be one reason why Jeffries (1978) found no transfer between missionaries-and-cannibals problems and waterjug problems even though both involved extensive use of means-ends analysis (Atwood and Polson, 1976; Jeffries, Polson, Razran, and Atwood, 1977). Presumably, Jeffries's adult subjects had already acquired and automated means-ends analysis prior to her experiment. Nothing significant was gained through their repeated practice other than a slight speedup. In short, weak methods show no transfer because they show no improvement.

Given the available evidence, the prospect of general transfer is rather dim. The problem faced by the architect of general transfer is a difficult one. He or she must discover a general method that is indomitable by strong methods, concrete enough to be applied easily, and yet novel to most adult subjects.

It seems a fair generalization of the literature to assert that transfer, when it does occur, depends on shared or overlapping content. The shared content can be quite specific, as in a rule for simplifying equations or an arithmetic fact. Or it can be quite general, as in a problem-solving method or language comprehension facility. The reason there is little general transfer is that the general components tend to be well-learned upon entering most training situations.

There is another way in which general transfer might occur, having to do with the idea behind the doctrine of formal discipline. The formal discipline view is based on two premises: (1) the mind is a general-purpose computing system (like a computer's CPU) that can be deployed to execute very different tasks, and (2) it is something whose computation can improve. The appropriate analogy is muscle. Strengthening muscle in one task improves its performance in another task. It is now abundantly clear that the mind is not a muscle in this sense. Thus the conjunction of premises (1) and (2) cannot be true. Moreover, premise (2) is known to be true because the mind can improve its performance on specific tasks in very much the same way that muscle gains strength. Thus, premise (1) must be the problem. Hence, we can conclude that the units of knowledge in the mind are functionally separate with respect to their potential for improvement.

But what of two tasks which require the same underlying knowledge? Why is there sometimes failure of transfer here? Why should subjects trained in logic not succeed at the Wason card selection task? This might be seen as a perversity in the design of the mind, but we do not think so. We think there is an inevitable and necessary difference between having knowledge in the abstract and being able to use it in a particular situation.

Consider an extreme example. Suppose someone has been told the rules of chess. Then theoretically that person has the knowledge to play a perfect game of chess; he or she can use these rules to generate all possible moves and countermoves and thus select the best move in all cases. Of course, to expect this amount of transfer from instruction on the rules of chess is ridiculous. Brute force deployment of knowledge is computationally too expensive. What a person has to learn is how to deploy this knowledge in specific game situations. For instance, he or she might learn the value of a forking pattern by playing several games involving that pattern. While the value of the pattern is a logical deduction (or nearly so) from the rules of chess, how should the beginner know to focus attention (and deductive resources) on this pattern in preference to the millions of other patterns possible? The basic point is that any piece of knowledge can be deployed in many ways, and a person has to learn which pieces are useful. To make matters worse, the amount of knowledge a person has is much more than just the rules of chess, and in many situations, like the Wason task, a large fraction of it is potentially relevant. Why should someone realize that his or her training in logic should be brought to bear on the task? And why in this form? And even if that knowledge is brought to bear in the right form, it is a nontrivial task to get a problem-solving system to map it onto the task in the right way. As Cheng et al. documented, people bring this knowledge to bear only in special situations where it is obviously relevant. It seems that situated learning (Rogoff and Lave, 1984) is an inevitable consequence of the huge combinatorial space of ways to use knowledge.

From this perspective, the acquisition of knowledge per se is not the fundamental issue. Rather, the fundamental issue concerns the acquisition of a particular use of knowledge and the range of circumstances over which that use will extend (assuming the strong version of Thorndike's identical elements model cannot be right). We think that the ACT* theory of skill acquisition provides a suitable framework for understanding this issue.

The ACT* Theory of Skill Acquisition

Previous attempts at understanding the transfer of cognitive skill have had limited success, largely because of inadequate theoretical and formal tools. It is especially timely to revive interest in transfer now because detailed, comprehensive theories of skill acquisition now exist (e.g. VanLehn, 1983; Rosenbloom and Newell, 1986). Of these theories, we chose to apply the ACT* theory (Anderson, 1983) to the problem.

The ACT* theory of skill acquisition lies within a broader class of theories that use production systems to model human cognition (Newell and Simon, 1972; Thibadeau, Just, and Carpenter, 1982). In its basic formulation, a production system consists of a set of condition-action rules, called *productions,* and a working memory. For example, a simple production for inserting characters in the text editor EMACS would be:

> IF   the goal is to insert a character = char
>   and the editor is EMACS
>   and the desired character position is marked by
>   the cursor
> THEN type = char.

In this production, the symbol = *char* denotes a variable that matches any character. A production such as this fires when the conditions of the IF clause of the production match the contents of working memory. The IF clause can contain references not only to the current goal but also to other contextual elements. When more than one production matches on a particular cycle of the system, certain conflict resolution principles apply to select a single production for application. This enforces a strict seriality on the flow of control (for a more detailed description of production systems, see Waterman and Hayes-Roth, 1978; Brownston, Farrell, Kant, and Martin, 1985).

ACT* differs from many production system architectures in that, in addition to production memory, a second kind of long-term memory is involved: a declarative memory. Whereas productions represent procedures, declarative structures are used to encode facts, such as "John is married" or "the delete key deletes characters." Although the focus here is on the learning of procedures, the declarative component cannot be ignored in the study of procedural learning.

The ACT* theory breaks down the acquisition of cognitive skill into two major stages: a *declarative* stage, where a declarative representation of the skill is interpreted by general productions, and a *procedural* stage, where the skill is directly embodied in domain-specific productions. The transition from the declarative to the procedural stage is achieved by the process of knowledge compilation. Knowledge compilation consists of two separate mechanisms: the *composition* mechanism collapses sequences of general productions into highly specific productions, and the *proceduralization* mechanism deposits domain knowledge from long-term memory directly into productions. Taken separately, these compilation mechanisms can account for many of the phenomena associated with practice: elimination of piecemeal application of operators, dropout of verbal rehearsal, fewer working memory errors, and power-law speedup (Anderson, 1982).

An important recent modification to the theory has been the addition of structural analogy as a mechanism for translating initial declarative encodings into action. Extensive studies of novice LISP programmers (Anderson, Farrell, and Sauers, 1984; Pirolli and Anderson, 1985), as well as studies of arithmetic and algebra instructional materials (Neves, 1981; VanLehn, 1983), have exposed the importance of example problems to the initial performance of a skill. Anderson (1986) showed how an analogy mechanism coupled with the standard knowledge compilation mechanisms can not only achieve the transition from declarative to procedural knowledge but also generalize the resultant procedural representation. This is done by abstracting common features of the source and target of the analogy.

Modeling transfer in ACT*

When the ACT* theory is applied to the study of transfer, single productions are the units of cognitive skill, the elements that Thorndike was searching for. A first approximation to an understanding of transfer involves comparing two sets of productions for different tasks. To the extent that the production sets overlap, transfer would be positive from one task to the other. To get a slightly more quantitative prediction, weights might be assigned to the productions according to their frequency of use in the transfer task.

This simple formulation is in fact a modern version of

Thorndike's theory of identical elements. Where it differs from that formulation is primarily in the fact that, unlike Thorndike's superficial elements, productions are versatile and powerful computational formalisms. As shown by Chomsky (1957), behaviorist systems like Thorndike's lack the computational power to handle many of the difficult processing problems faced by humans. However, productions systems have the computational power of Turing machines (Anderson, 1976). Productions are abstract and can be used to represent many different yet functionally equivalent methods at various levels of generality. For example, production systems can be used quite naturally to model both the rote and the meaningful methods studied by the gestalters. Productions are often used to represent cognitive processes which have no impact on the external world yet nonetheless play an important role in skilled behavior, like planning and problem decomposition. Therefore, not only external but also internal actions are considered in calculations of transfer. Indeed, one can model general problem-solving methods like analogy and means-ends analysis by production rules. Thus, transfer of general problem-solving methods can be analyzed as just a special case of transfer defined on the identity of productions.

Production system models of transfer have already been applied with reasonable success (Moran, 1983; Polson and Kieras, 1985; Singley and Anderson, 1985; Kieras and Bovair, 1986). Although these initial attempts look promising, the purely procedural approach is at best a useful first approximation to understanding something as complex as transfer of cognitive skill. Notably lacking is any mention of the declarative component in calculations of transfer. The ACT* theory makes a strong claim about the importance of declarative knowledge during the early stages of skill acquisition. However, simple production system models of transfer make no allowance for declarative knowledge, so there can be no declarative component in the transfer equation. In some well-defined cases this omission can lead to erroneous predictions.

A declarative-procedural taxonomy

Given the fundamental distinction between declarative and procedural knowledge in ACT*, we may define a broad taxonomy of transfer types based upon the type of knowledge acquired in the training task and the type of knowledge applied in the transfer task. Figure 1.5 shows that either declarative or proce-

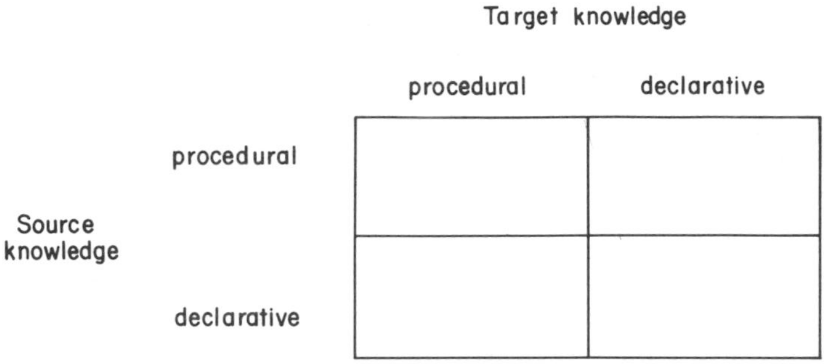

Target knowledge

procedural   declarative

	procedural	declarative
procedural		
declarative		

Source
knowledge

Figure 1.5. *Taxonomy of transfer types.*

dural knowledge may serve as the source or the target, thus generating a 2 × 2 taxonomy. The four different types of transfer can be characterized as: procedural to procedural, declarative to procedural, declarative to declarative, and procedural to declarative.

Procedural-to-procedural transfer is the kind of transfer captured by the simple production system formulations. Procedural-to-procedural transfer occurs when productions acquired in the training task apply directly to the transfer task. This type of transfer is automatic as long as the transfer task is represented in a way that allows the productions to apply (sometimes a reworking of the representation of the transfer task is required before this kind of procedural transfer takes place). A precondition is that a fair amount of practice on the training task is done so that the appropriate productions are formed.

Since the productions apply directly and without modification in the transfer task, this type of transfer might be criticized as not being transfer at all. Thorndike's theory received this criticism, namely that transfer had to be more than just doing the same thing over again, that true transfer required the "making over" of old knowledge to fit the new situation. However, because of their abstract and general character, the same production rules can underlie performance in rather different tasks and different contexts. The intelligence in the system does not reside in the transfer mechanisms but rather in the initial learning mechanisms which cast the productions at the proper level of abstraction.

Declarative-to-procedural transfer occurs when declarative structures acquired in the training task aid in the acquisition of productions in the transfer task. The transition from declarative to procedural knowledge occurs routinely in the acquisition of a single skill; in this sense, transfer of this type is quite common. Declarative structures can also contribute to the acquisition of a new skill if the structures happen to serve as precursors of productions in that skill. Interestingly, the same declarative structures can constitute the base of many skills which, once compiled, have little overlap at the production level. It is in these situations that inclusion of the underlying declarative component is most important in calculations of transfer.

In the ACT* theory, the transition from declarative to procedural knowledge is mediated largely by the process of structural analogy. Analogy takes the declarative representation of an old solution and modifies that solution for use in the present problem. As a by-product, a production rule is generated which captures the essence of the solution and generalizes across irrelevant features in the source and target. Here, then, is where flexibility and adaptation reside in the system: in the analogical mapping of declarative structures. Through this mapping, a production rule is created at an appropriate level of abstraction. Since analogy is a complex, error-prone process (Halasz and Moran, 1982), this type of transfer is much less certain than procedural-to-procedural transfer. The spate of analogical transfer studies showing little or no transfer attest to this fact.

Declarative-to-declarative transfer occurs whenever existing declarative structures either facilitate or interfere with the acquisition of new declarative structures. As we reviewed, this is a widely studied topic in psychology, occupying years of effort of the verbal learners. More recently, psychologists have studied such diverse topics as the fan effect in sentence memory (Anderson, 1983; Reder and Ross, 1983), the effect of domain-specific knowledge on memory (Chase and Simon, 1973; Voss, Vesonder, and Spilich, 1980), and the role of macrolevel knowledge structures in comprehension (Schank and Abelson, 1977; Bower, Black, and Turner, 1979). All of these topics are in a sense instances of declarative-to-declarative transfer. Needless to say, being concerned primarily with the transfer of cognitive skill, we have nothing new to say about this type of transfer in this book.

Procedural-to-declarative transfer involves cognitive skills that facilitate the acquisition of declarative knowledge. Are there skills of this type? Certainly yes. Most notable are the basic language skills of reading and speech comprehension without which no one could assimilate modern culture. After these basic skills are mastered, the acquisition of more sophisticated study skills, such as summarizing text, asking questions, and note taking, may improve performance further (Day, 1980; Brown, 1981; Brown, 1982). Since the acquisition of cognitive skill always involves the acquisition of some declarative base, these advanced study skills hold out considerable promise for general transfer. This type of transfer may be somewhat of a special case for our purposes, however. Once again, our interest is primarily in the acquisition and transfer of procedural, not declarative, knowledge.

Overview of the Study

The goal of our research is to identify the elements and mechanisms of transfer working within the ACT* framework. We restrict ourselves to transfer from either procedural or declarative knowledge to procedural knowledge. Our approach is characterized by four features: novice representations, emphasis on learning, multiple trials, and fine-grained analyses. We place heavy emphasis on novice rather than expert representations of skill because this allows a much larger role for declarative and control structure components in the transfer equation. These representations are determined through a combination of rational task analysis, protocol analysis, and quantitative modeling. At this stage in theory development, we feel that, given a subject's representation, we can fairly accurately predict the direction and magnitude of transfer. The task that remains most difficult, however, is determining the representation.

An emphasis on learning is important because, before we can possibly understand what is transferred, we must understand what is learned. In fact, common elements models of transfer are totally explained in terms of learning, in that the elements of transfer are merely subsets of the elements of learning. For this reason, we devote a large share of our attention to issues of learning.

Multiple trials are essential because many studies have probably underestimated transfer by failing to ensure that something was learned in the first place. It is not surprising that transfer is minimal when subjects have only a single trial in both the base and transfer tasks. To better understand both learning and transfer, we trace our subjects' performance over multiple trials. This methodology yields more sensitive measures of transfer than single trials, in much the same way that time to relearn is a more sensitive measure of retention than recall or recognition.

Finally, in any account of learning and transfer, the level of analysis is critical. Central to our effort is the goal of determining the loci of transfer at the finest grain of analysis possible. Most desirable would be a grain size that allowed for the separation and independent measurement of all learning and transfer components. This would allow the most rigorous test of any common elements theory of transfer. Given imperfect theories of skill representation and imperfect behavioral measures, however, this is presently and perhaps forever impossible. Unable to determine a priori the proper grain of analysis, we have conducted a series of analyses at several different grain sizes. We hope to understand learning and transfer by successive approximation, using the more aggregate measures to guide our analysis at more detailed levels.

This book first provides an in-depth analysis of the process by which cognitive skill is acquired in ACT*. Productions in ACT* have a number of features which make them suitable as the identical elements upon which to base a theory of transfer. They are discrete and independent entities, which have a range of application across diverse situations. They have a degree of abstractness that avoids many of the difficulties in the original Thorndike formulation. Data from the LISP tutor (Anderson, 1987) make the point that production rules do indeed have these properties. Learning in the LISP tutor is a paradigm case of vertical transfer, where knowledge from earlier lessons transfers to later lessons.

After examining vertical transfer, we turn our attention to the more critical issue of lateral transfer. We analyze the transfer among various text editors as a function of the number of productions they share. This position receives remarkable support through a series of microanalyses in which transfer sites are localized to very specific components of the skills.

Negative transfer among skills is obtained in a variety of ways within the identical productions model. The primary way is essentially an Einstellunglike phenomenon whereby productions optimal for one skill are transferred to another where they are nonoptimal. Another text-editing study, as well as other research from our laboratory, provides support for this position.

Production-based transfer implies that when a skill is well-tuned for one application, there may not be transfer to another skill that uses the knowledge in related ways. We describe a calculus experiment that provides support for this prediction. Specifically, we find no transfer among the skills of translating word problems into equations, selecting calculus operators to apply to these equations, and applying these operators. Other results from our laboratory show a similar encapsulation of knowledge.

We present a detailed simulation model of learning in the calculus experiment, which starts with a declarative representation of the instruction given in calculus, uses the weak methods of analogy and means-ends analysis to solve problems, and compiles productions specific to the particular skills. One outcome of this simulation is the realization that our prediction of total encapsulation of knowledge is too strong. The productions used in the various calculus activities do share a common declarative base. Learning one component should transfer to another component to the extent they reinforce the common base. However, this transfer should be observed only during the early stages of learning. Another calculus experiment isolates the declarative transfer of components to the beginning stages of skill acquisition.

The ACT* perspective on transfer illuminates much of the recent research done in other laboratories. It also casts light on what we feel is the most important remaining conceptual problem in research on transfer, the issue of representation. As it turns out, all transfer predictions depend critically on assumptions about the representation of the task. This raises the question of whether one can always fashion the task representation to avoid disconfirmation of a theory of transfer. Our answer is that important constraints from other sources can be applied to determine representations independently of transfer data.

Appendix: Transfer Designs and Formulas

To study transfer, one must first decide how it is to be measured. A variety of methods have been proposed over the years for this task. Gagné, Forster, and Crowley (1948) reported at least four transfer formulas then in wide usage. Given the same data, each yielded somewhat different results, making the interpretation and comparison of different studies difficult. Indeed, failure to reach consensus on this methodological point may have hindered early scientific progress on transfer (Ellis, 1965). Even today, different researchers use different formulas to compute transfer.

The use of a particular formula is often dictated by the use of a particular experimental design. Table 1.3 shows the prototypical transfer design and some of its variants. In the prototypical design (design 1), to determine the amount of transfer from task

Table 1.3. Transfer designs.

Design	Group	Training task	Transfer task
1	Experimental	A	B
	Control	—	B
2	Experimental	A	B
	Control	B	B
3	Experimental (Pretest B')	A	B
	Control (Pretest B')	B	B
4	Experimental$_1$	A	B
	Experimental$_2$	B	A

A to task B, one simply presents an experimental group with practice on task A followed by task B. The performance of this group is compared with that of a control, which has no training task and starts directly with task B. If the performance of the experimental group on task B is better than the control, then there is positive transfer from task A to task B; if it is worse, then there is negative transfer.

Two formulas are possible with such a design. The first, called the *raw score* formula by Gagné et al. (1948), is simply the difference between scores of the experimental group (E) and control group (C) on the transfer task (B):

$$(1.1) \ T_{raw} = C_B - E_B$$

This version of the formula is used for dependent measures like time on task, where higher scores mean worse performance. For those dependent measures where the reverse is true (e.g., percent correct), the control score should be subtracted from the experimental score. This ensures that positive transfer is denoted by positive values and negative transfer by negative values.

The strength of this formula is its simplicity and precision of meaning. The magnitude of transfer is expressed directly in terms of the units used to measure performance, like seconds or percent correct. The major weakness of this formula, however, is that comparisons of transfer among different kinds of tasks are often impossible.

This deficit is remedied somewhat by a formula that normalizes the amount of savings by the level of performance of the control:

$$(1.2) \ T_{\%\ improvement} = \frac{C_B - E_B}{C_B} \times 100$$

This formula is quite popular (e.g. Reed, Ernst, and Banerji, 1974; Thomas, 1974; Hayes and Simon, 1977; Smith, 1986). However, the problem of comparison across tasks is not really solved by this formula, because no provision is made for the fact that different amounts of improvement are possible in different tasks. As an absurd example, take the comparison of transfer between the tasks of (1) finding a book in a strange library and (2) finding the same book in the same location and then reading it aloud. We make these assumptions in this somewhat bizarre example:

1. Reading the book takes much longer than finding the book.
2. The reading component, being highly practiced in adult subjects, shows little improvement, whereas the finding component, which makes use of knowledge acquired specifically in this experimental situation, shows much improvement.
3. There is total transfer from finding the book the first time to finding the book the second time.

Given such a situation, formula (1.2) would show virtually no transfer from the task of finding the book to the task of finding and reading the book, yet nearly total transfer in the reverse direction. This case of asymmetric transfer is spurious, because the longer task is dominated by a highly automated component which shows negligible improvement. In fact, there is total transfer in the learned component between the two tasks. Generally speaking, comparisons using formula (1.2) are misleading whenever the tasks being compared differ in terms of the proportion of compiled subcomponents. A more meaningful formula, then, would express the amount of savings exhibited by an experimental group as a percentage of the total amount of *learning possible* in the transfer task, not the gross level of performance of the control.

There have been two approaches to measuring the amount of learning possible in the transfer task. The first, advocated by Katona (1940) and used extensively in this book, is to compare the savings resulting from practice on the training task with an equal number of trials of direct practice on the transfer task. This necessitates a slightly different transfer design (design 2). The control group, in essence, gets the designated transfer task as both a training and a transfer task. The resultant formula is:

$$(1.3) \ T_{\% \ learning} = \frac{C_{B1} - E_{B1}}{C_{B1} - C_{B2}} \times 100$$

The numerator is the difference between the control and experimental groups on the first set of trials on the transfer task ($B1$). The denominator is the improvement of the control groups on the transfer task over two sets of trials ($B1$ and $B2$). This formula implies that total positive transfer results when the benefit derived from practice on some training task equals the benefit derived from the same amount of practice on the transfer task. The measure varies sensibly from 0 to 100, although negative values and values greater than 100 are possible. The former values represent negative transfer, and the latter values a kind of supertransfer, where practice on task A results in better eventual performance on task B than the same amount of direct practice on task B. Such a situation is rare but occasionally arises when Task B is quite difficult and cannot be attempted directly, as is the case in certain part-to-whole training situations (Fitts and Posner, 1967).

The second approach to measuring the amount of improvement possible in the transfer task is to determine the *total* amount of improvement possible rather than simply the amount of improvement associated with a certain number of trials. This approach, advocated by Gagné et al. (1948), was used occasionally in verbal learning research (Murdock, 1957). With this approach, the formula becomes:

$$(1.4) \ T_{\% \ total \ learning} = \frac{C_{B1} - E_{B1}}{C_{B1} - performance \ limit} \times 100$$

With dependent measures like percent or number correct, the performance limit is defined quite naturally as 100 percent or the total number of items. However, with other dependent measures like time on task, the performance limit is often impossible to determine and in fact may be undefined. Classic studies of practice have shown that improvement, however slight, is still possible after thousands of trials (Rosenbloom and Newell, 1986). Another weakness of this formula is that it is misleading to compare studies where different amounts of practice are given on the training task. The savings realized by the experimental group (the numerator) is divided by a term which in a sense is constant and is insensitive to the amount of practice. Formula (1.3) does not suffer from these problems and, on balance, seems to be the superior measure for the study of cognitive skill.

Other variations on the prototypical design have been used widely (Gagné et al., 1948; Woodworth and Schlosberg, 1954; Ellis, 1965). Design 3 involves adding a pretest on task B prior to the experimental manipulation. Groups are matched in terms of this pretest score. Design 4 involves having both experimental groups act as each other's control. Of course, each of designs 3 and 4 requires slight modifications to accommodate formula (1.3).

2 / Transfer in the ACT* Theory

A theory of transfer should be anchored in a theory of learning, since, at least in common elements models, the elements of transfer are simply subsets of the elements of learning. In this chapter, before discussing production rules as the identical elements, we explain how they are acquired and how they are used to perform a particular skill. Following this review of the ACT* theory of skill acquisition, we derive predictions for transfer, and review data relevant to those predictions.

To illustrate these processes of learning and transfer, we use a domain different from the text-editing and calculus domains which are the major focus of later chapters. Here, for the sake of generality, we use programming skill in the artificial intelligence language LISP as our focus. This is where the ACT* theory of skill acquisition originally had its most extensive application (Anderson, Farrell, and Sauers, 1984). The examples are deliberately chosen to use only the most basic concepts of LISP, so that lack of programming knowledge will not be a barrier to understanding. Our analysis focuses on vertical transfer, or how production rules acquired early in the LISP curriculum apply to later material. In subsequent chapters, we will focus on lateral transfer, that is, transfer among skills at roughly the same level of complexity.

Acquisition of LISP Programming Skills

Cognitive processing in the ACT* theory occurs as a result of the firing of productions. Productions are condition-action pairs which specify that if a certain state occurs in working memory, then particular mental (and possibly physical) actions should take place. Here are two "Englishified" versions of productions (P) that are used in our simulation of LISP programming:

P1

IF   the goal is to write a solution to a problem
     and there is an example of a solution to a similar
         problem
THEN   set a goal to map that template to the current case.

P2

IF   the goal is to get the first element of = list
THEN   write (*car* = list).

The first production (P1) is one of a number of productions for achieving structural analogy. It looks for a problem similar to the current problem but with a worked-out solution. If such an example problem exists, this production will fire and propose using the example as an analog for solving the current problem. This is a domain-general production and executes, for instance, when we use last year's income tax forms as models for this year's income tax forms. In the domain of LISP it helps implement the common strategy of using one LISP program as a model for writing another.

The second production (P2) is one that is specific to LISP and recognizes the applicability of *car*, a basic LISP function that returns the first element of a list. For instance, the function call (*car* '(A B C)) returns A. In P2 = list is a variable that can have different values depending on the problem. In this case it would have the value (A B C).

One important question a learning theory must address is how a system, starting out with only domain-general productions like P1, acquires domain-specific productions like P2.

Solving a novel problem

To illustrate both how productions fire in sequence to solve a problem and how domain-specific productions are derived from domain-general productions, it is useful to examine the protocol of a subject who is first learning to define new functions in LISP. Defining functions is the principle means for creating LISP programs. The problem faced by our subject BR was to define a function called *first* which returns the first element of a list. *First* does the same thing as the system function *car* and is therefore completely redundant. Thus, the problem of defining *first* is really just an exercise in the syntax of function definitions.

Prior to this problem, BR had spent approximately five hours learning some of the basic functions that come with LISP (like *car*) and becoming familiar with variables and list structures. As preparation for this particular problem, BR read the instruction in Winston and Horn (1981) on how to define functions using the LISP function *defun*. Although that description of function definition occupies nearly five pages, the only things BR made reference to in solving the problem were an abstract template showing the parts of a function definition and some example definitions in the text. The template and one of these examples are given below. In the template, those terms delimited by angle brackets denote placeholders that need to be filled in by the student. The example function, called *f-to-c*, converts a temperature (*temp*) from fahrenheit to centigrade:

> (*defun* <FUNCTION NAME>
>   (<PARAMETER 1> <PARAMETER 2> . . .
>   <PARAMETER *n*>)
>   <PROCESS DESCRIPTION>)

> (*defun* f-to-c (*temp*)
>   (*quotient* (*difference temp* 32) 1.8))

Anderson, Farrell, and Sauers (1984) reported a production system simulation of BR's protocol that reproduces the major steps. Figure 2.1 presents the goal structure generated by both BR and the simulation in solving this problem. BR begins by selecting the abstract template as an analog of the function she wants to write. A set of domain-general productions for doing analogy then try to use this template. Subgoals are set to map each of the major components of the template. Knowing that *defun* is a special LISP function which appears in all function definitions, she writes this first and then writes *first*, which is the name of the function she wants to write.

BR has trouble mapping the structure:

> (<PARAMETER 1> <PARAMETER 2> . . .
>   <PARAMETER *n*>)

The reason is that she has no idea what parameters are. However, she looks at the concrete example of *f-to-c* and correctly infers that the parameter list simply contains variable names that will be the arguments to the function. *First* has a single argument, which she chooses to call *list1*.

BR then turns to the mapping of <PROCESS-DESCRIPTION> but again has trouble. As before, she looks to the example and finds that <PROCESS-DESCRIPTION> is just the LISP code the calculates the result of the function. Consequently, she writes *car*, which returns the first element of a list. This is one of only two places in the original coding of the function where a LISP-specific production fires. We assume this production was acquired from her earlier experience with LISP. To review, her code at this time is:

   (defun first (list1) (car . . .

A major hurdle remains in this problem, namely to write the argument to the function *car*. BR again looks to the example for guidance on coding arguments to functions called within the function definition. She notes that the first argument in the *f-to-c* example is contained in parentheses—*(difference temp* 32). This is because the argument is itself a function call, and function calls must be placed in parentheses. In defining *first*, she does not need parentheses, because the argument *list1* is a simple variable. However, she does not recognize the distinction between her situation and the example. She places her argument in parentheses, producing the complete definition:

   (defun first (list1) (car (list1)))

When the argument to a function is a list, LISP attempts to treat the first element inside the list as a function call. Therefore, when BR tests *first*, she gets the error message "Undefined function: *list1.*" In the past, she has corrected this error by quoting the offending list. So she produces the patch:

   (defun first (list1) (car '(list1)))

This, then, is the second and final place where a LISP-specific (and in this case, incorrect) production fires in the simulation. When BR tests this function on the input list (A B C), she gets the answer *list1* rather than A, because LISP now returns the first item of the literal list (*list1*) (the single quote in front of (*list1*) tells LISP that this is not a function call). Eventually, after some additional thrashing, she finally produces the correct code:

   (defun first (list1) (car list1))

This problem was solved by 38 subjects in the LISP tutor (Anderson and Reiser, 1985) and a number of other subjects in informal experiments. BR's solution is typical of novice problem-solving in many ways. The two places where she has difficulty, specifying the function parameters and specifying the argument to *car*, are the two major stumbling blocks for LISP tutor subjects. Her error in specifying the argument to *car* is made by over half of the tutor subjects given the same example. An informal observation is that people with no background at all in LISP, given information about what *car* does, the function definition template, and the *f-to-c* example, tend to solve the problem in the same way as BR and make the same first error. Thus, it seems that much of the problem-solving is controlled by analogy and not by any detailed understanding of LISP. The success of the simulation also suggests that problem solving by analogy can be well modeled by a production system with a hierarchical goal structure.

Knowledge compilation

In the course of solving the problem *first*, the simulation of BR creates two new productions which summarize much of the solution process. It does so by a knowledge compilation process (Anderson, 1982, 1983) that collapses sequences of productions into single productions that have the same effect as the sequence. Typically, as in this case, the process converts domain-general productions into domain-specific productions. The two productions acquired by ACT* are:

> P3
>> IF   the goal is to write a function, = func, of one variable, = var,
>> THEN   write (*defun* = func (= var)
>>> and set as a subgoal to code the relation calculated by this function
>>> and then write).

> P4
>> IF   the goal is to code an argument
>>> and that argument corresponds to a function parameter, = var
>> THEN   write = var.

Figure 2.1 indicates the set of productions that were collapsed to produce each of these productions. The first production summarizes the analogy process that searched the template for information concerning the syntax of a function definition; this production now directly produces that syntax without reference to the analog. Similarly, the second production summarizes the

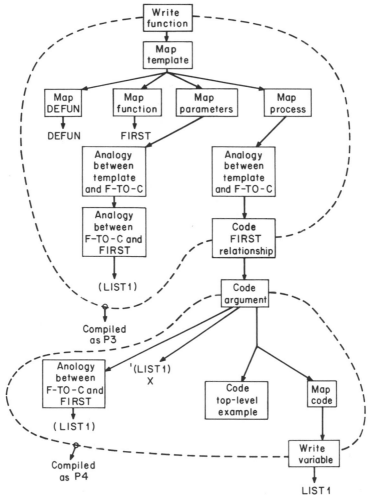

Figure 2.1. *Trace of the goals set by the simulation of BR as it tried to code a simple LISP function.*

search that went into finding the correct argument to the function and now directly produces that argument.

Armed with these two additional productions, the simulation was given another LISP problem to solve. This was to write a function called *second* which retrieved the second element of a list. Although *second* is a more complex function definition, both the simulation and the subject produced much more rapid and successful solutions to this problem. The speedup in the simulation was due to the fact that fewer productions were involved, thanks to the compiled productions. Additionally, the computationally expensive process of analogy was no longer required.

Thus, the knowledge compilation process predicts a marked improvement as one goes from a first to a second problem that involves the same productions. Substantiating the results of BR are more extensive studies with the LISP tutor, where students similarly code *first* and then *second*. The number of errors in function definition syntax (controlled by P3) drops from a median of 2 in *first* to a median of 0 in *second*, and the time to instantiate the function template drops from a median of 237 seconds to a median of 96 seconds. The number of errors in specifying the argument (controlled by P4) drops from a median of 3 in *first* to a median of 0 in *second*, and the time to enter the argument drops from a median of 96 seconds to a median of 26 seconds. By any measure, these are impressive one-trial learning statistics. This marked speedup has also been observed in the domain of geometry proof generation (Anderson, 1982). Later in this chapter we will present more comprehensive data on this one-trial learning phenomenon.

Important features of the ACT* theory

The simulation of BR illustrates three important features of the ACT* theory:

1. *Productions as Units of Procedural Knowledge.* The major presupposition of the entire ACT* theory and certainly key to the theory of skill acquisition is the idea that productions form the units of procedural knowledge. Productions define the steps in which a problem is solved and are the units in which procedural knowledge is acquired.

2. *Hierarchical Goal Structure.* ACT* production systems specify hierarchical goal structures that organize the problem solving. Figure 2.1 illustrates such a hierarchical goal structure. This goal structure is an additional control construct that was not found in many of the original production system models (Newell, 1973; Anderson, 1976) but now is becoming quite popular (e.g. Brown and VanLehn, 1980; Laird et al., 1984). It has proven impossible to develop satisfactory cognitive models that do not have some overall sense of direction in their behavior. As can be seen with respect to this example, the hierarchical goal structure closely reflects the hierarchical structure of the problem. Just as important as their role in controlling behavior, goals organize the learning by knowledge compilation. They indicate which

parts of the problem solution belong together and can be compiled into new productions.

3. *Initial Use of Weak Methods.* This simulation nicely illustrates the critical role analogy plays in getting initial performance off the ground. There is a serious question about how a student can solve a problem in the absence of domain-specific productions. This example shows that the student can in fact mimic the structure of a previous solution. However, this simulation also shows that, in contradiction to frequent characterizations of imitation as mindless (e.g. Fodor, Bever, and Garrett, 1974), the analogy mechanisms that implement this process of imitation can be quite sophisticated (for other discussions of use of analogy in problem solving, see Kling, 1971; Winston, 1979; Carbonell, 1983). While analogy is one way of getting started in problem solving, it is not the only way. It is an instance of weak problem-solving methods (Newell, 1969), which are characterized by their generality and broad applicability across domains. They are called weak because they do not take advantage of domain characteristics. Other examples of weak problem-solving methods are means-ends analysis and pure forward search. In our discussion of the calculus simulation in Chapter 6, we will show how the weak methods of analogy and means-ends analysis combine to translate declarative encodings of skill into action.

4. *Knowledge Compilation.* All knowledge in the ACT* theory starts out in declarative form and must be converted to procedural form (i.e. productions). This declarative knowledge might be encodings of examples, instructions, or general properties of objects. The weak problem-solving methods can apply to the knowledge while it is in declarative form and can interpret its implications for performance. The actual form of the declarative knowledge determines the weak method adopted. For instance, in the simulation of BR, analogy was used because the declarative knowledge was almost exclusively in the form of templates and examples. In a geometry simulation discussed by Anderson (1982), the declarative knowledge largely came in the form of statements about how to prove conclusions. This tended to evoke a working-backward problem-solving method. When ACT* solves a problem, it produces a hierarchical solution generated by productions. Knowledge compilation is the process that creates efficient domain-specific productions from this trace of the problem-solving episode. The goal structure is critical to the knowledge compilation process in that it indicates which steps of the original solution belong together.

Outlined here is a fairly complete theory of how new skills are acquired: knowledge comes in declarative form, is used by weak methods to generate problem solutions, and as a by-product, new productions are formed. The key step is the knowledge compilation process, which produces the domain-specific skill.

These are the major factors that influence the acquisition of productions. However, two additional factors influence their execution. These might be viewed as performance factors that modulate the expression of competence, except that these factors can be improved with learning:

1. *Strength.* The strength of a production determines how rapidly it applies, and production rules accumulate strength as they successfully apply. While accumulation of strength is a very simple learning mechanism, there is good reason to believe that strengthening is often what determines the rate of skill acquisition in the limit (i.e. after much practice). The ACT* strengthening mechanism accounts for the typical power-function shape of learning curves following production compilation (Anderson, 1982).

2. *Working Memory Limitations.* In the ACT* theory there are two reasons why errors are made: the productions are wrong, or the information in working memory on which they operate is wrong. This latter reason implies that even perfect production sets can display errors due to working memory failures. In fact, the only way "slips" can occur in the ACT* theory is through the loss of critical information from working memory. Consequently, the wrong production fires or the right production fires but produces the wrong result. Just as learning has an impact on production strength, it has an impact on working memory errors. Working memory capacity for a domain can increase with practice, reducing the number of such errors with expertise (Chase and Ericsson, 1982).

Conspicuous by its absence in this discussion is any mention of the ACT* mechanisms of generalization and discrimination which create new productions by inductive, syntactic transformations of existing productions. More recent research and theorizing has led us to the conclusion that such inductive mechanisms are not part of the process of production acquisition (Lewis and Anderson, 1985). Rather, we can get the effect of generalization of productions by compiling the analogy process as summarized in Figure 2.1, where we analogized to a set of examples and compiled the process into a set of generalized production rules. Thus, the ACT* processes of generalization and discrimination do not figure in our analysis of skill acquisition.

Productions as Identical Elements

In the simulation of BR, there were two kinds of domain-specific knowledge that contributed to the coding of *first*. First, there were declarative encodings in the form of templates and example functions. These were used by the weak methods. Second, there were two productions (one correct, one buggy) which had been previously compiled. By the time the simulation coded *second*, all knowledge was in the form of LISP-specific productions. In this chapter and the next few, we are going to focus on this production-based transfer and ignore the declarative-based transfer, which plays only a short-lived role during the early stages of skill acquisition.

Our basic proposal is that productions, once learned, can serve as the identical elements of Thorndike's theory. In saying this, we are asserting that productions have four desirable features that make them quite suitable for this purpose:

1. *Independence.* Productions are learned independently and transfer independently. Thus, one does not have to worry about possible interactions among productions as they occur in new combinations in transfer tasks.

2. *All-or-None Learning.* The knowledge compilation process is characterized by all-or-none, one-trial learning. One moment there is no production, and the next there is. If one is going to count productions to predict transfer, it is useful that they have this property.

3. *Strength Accrual.* Although the existence of productions has a discrete, all-or-none quality, there must be some basis for predicting the effect of amount of practice on degree of transfer. Production rules do continue to accumulate strength after their initial formation. Increased strength of productions means more rapid and reliable performance.

4. *Abstractness.* The major difficulty with Thorndike's proposal was his tendency to tie the elements to the surface structure of the behavior. ACT* productions, because of their variables and goal structures, achieve a desired level of abstraction.

Studying Skill Acquisition in the LISP Tutor

To support our claims that LISP programming skill can be analyzed in terms of ACT* productions, that productions defined by such an analysis exhibit the critical properties outlined, and that productions as identical elements account for the vertical transfer of programming skill, we draw on the data base of student performance with the LISP tutor. The LISP tutor has been under development for several years in our laboratory and currently teaches a full-semester self-paced course at Carnegie-Mellon University. While the tutor has been shown to have a positive impact on students (Anderson, Boyle, Corbett, and Lewis, in press), that is not our concern here. We study performance on the LISP tutor because it exposes in exquisite detail the microstructure of a complex skill and its acquisition.

Students working with the tutor sit down in front of a terminal with a textbook on LISP (Anderson, Corbett, and Reiser, 1987). They first read a few pages of the text describing several new LISP concepts and then turn to the terminal to write a number of programs involving those concepts. The tutor monitors their interactions at the terminal and tries to provide corrective instruction. If a student has difficulty with a particular concept, the tutor will provide additional problems until the student has achieved a certain level of mastery.

Our view of the learning process in this situation is that from reading the textbook, students acquire a declarative knowledge base from which they can compile the necessary productions to perform the skill. The text was written with just this in mind: each section contains just enough information and examples from which to compile a few additional productions. Thus, the transition from the textbook to the tutor provides an example of declarative transfer in that the declarative knowledge derived from the text greatly facilitates the compilation of the correct productions for writing LISP code. However, the transition from the textbook to the tutor is not a well-analyzed portion of the students' history nor the focus of concern here. Our focus is on students' interactions with the LISP tutor as they write code. This allows us to consider transfer of productions from problem to problem over the course of the curriculum. Any extended learning history has the potential for this kind of transfer in that skills learned earlier in the course are applied to the solving of problems later in the course. Our prediction is that individual productions transfer totally from lesson to lesson as the identical elements model would predict.

Sample dialogue

Table 2.1 contains a dialogue between the LISP tutor and a hypothetical student coding a recursive function to calculate factorial. Recursive programming is a fairly advanced topic in LISP which involves the use of functions that call themselves in the solution of a problem. A recursive function is usually structured as a conditional with one terminating case, where the recursion stops and the problem is solved directly, and one or more recursive cases, where the problem is decomposed by additional calls to the recursive function. In this case, the recursive function calculates the factorial of an integer.

The dialogue in Table 2.1 does not present the tutor as it really appears to students. Instead, it shows a "teletype" version of the tutor where the interaction is linearized. In the actual tutor the interaction involves updates to various windows. In the teletype version the tutor's output is given in normal type while the student's input is shown in bold characters. These listings present "snapshots" of the interactions; each time the student produces a response, we list his input along with the tutor's response (numbered for convenience). The total code as it appears on the screen is shown, although the student has added only what is different from the previous code (shown in boldface type). For instance, in line 2 he has added **zero** as an extension of *(defun fact (n) (cond ((* . . .

To illustrate the functioning of the LISP tutor, we will briefly trace the dialogue between tutor and student on this problem. Coding in the LISP tutor involves the instantiation of tutor-provided templates. For example, in the first line of the dialogue, when the subject typed *(defun*, there appeared the template:

(defun <NAME> <PARAMETERS> <BODY>)

The terms in angle brackets (<>) denote placeholders that the subject replaces with pieces of code. The subject is required to first fill in the <NAME> slot, then the <PARAMETERS> slot, and finally the <BODY> slot. At all points parentheses are balanced and syntax is checked by the tutor.

Although the student initially has some difficulty with the syntax of the conditional tests in lines 1 and 2, he manages to code the terminating case for the factorial function correctly. Typically, we find that students have little difficulty with terminating cases but have great difficulty with recursive cases. The

Table 2.1. Sample LISP tutor dialogue.

Define the function fact. It takes a number argument, *n*, and computes the factorial of *n*, which is the result of multiplying $n \times n-1 \times n-2 \ldots \times 1$. For instance, (fact 3) = $3 \times 2 \times 1 = 6$. By definition, the factorial of 0 is 1.

1. **(defun fact (n)**
      (cond ((equal) <ACTION>)
            <RECURSIVE-CASE>))

I assume that you are trying to test if the number argument is equal to the number zero. There is a special function for testing equivalence to zero. Try to use that function instead of EQUAL.

What code can you write to test if the condition for the terminating case is true? Try writing a predicate.

2. *(defun fact (n)*
      *(cond ((***zero** <ACTION>)
            <RECURSIVE-CASE>))

Did you mean zerop (*y* or *n*)? *y*

3. *(defun fact (n)*
      *(cond ((***zerop** n) 1)
            <RECURSIVE-CASE>))

Is the value of fact in the recursive cases calculated by:

PRESS:	IF YOU WANT TO:
1	Calling fact recursively with *n*
2	Multiplying *n* by fact of *n* minus 1.
3	Getting 1 2 . . . *n* and then multiplying the results.
4	Have the tutor choose.

Menu choice: **3**

That is a reasonable way to think of doing factorials, but it is not a plan for a recursive function. Since you seem to be having trouble with the recursive cases, let us work through some examples and figure out the conditions and actions for each of these cases.

The recursive relationship is the relationship between fact called with *n* and fact called with:

PRESS:	IF YOU WANT TO:
1	*n* minus 1
2	*n* equal to 0
3	*n* plus 1
4	Have the tutor choose

Menu choice: **1**

We will consider some concrete examples. We will characterize the recursive relationship between fact called with 1 and fact called with 0.

What is the value of (fact 1)?
Answer: **1**
What is the value of (fact 0)?
Answer: **1**   (continued)

Table 2.1. (continued)

EXAMPLES

fact (*n*)	fact (*n* − 1)
A. (fact 1) = 1	(fact 0) = 1

We will consider some more concrete examples. We will characterize the recursive relationship between fact called with 3 and fact called with 2.

What is the value of (fact 3)?

Answer: **6**

What is the value of (fact 2)?

Answer: **2**

EXAMPLES

fact (*n*)	fact (*n* − 1)
A. (fact 1) = 1	(fact 0) = 1
B. (fact 3) = 6	(fact 2) = 2

Since there is only one recursive case characterized by the examples you have just worked out, the condition in this case can be coded simply as T. We will focus on characterizing the action in this case.

In examples A and B what do you have to do to get the result of fact called with *n*?

PRESS: IF YOU WANT TO:

1   Multiply *n* by one less than *n*.

2   Multiply *n* by fact of one less than *n*.

3   Add *n* to the result of fact called with one less than *n*.

4   Have the tutor choose.

    Menu choice: **2**

We have worked through a series of examples that illustrate the recursive relation. We will now return to the goal of trying to produce LISP code that specifies the recursive relation.

4.   *(defun fact (n)*

      (cond ((zerop n) 1)

         (t (fact)))

You will have to use fact at some point but right now you want to multiply.

5.   *(defun fact (n)*

      (cond ((zerop n) 1)

         *(t **(times** n **(fact n)))))*

You cannot just code *n* at this point. What you want to do is subtract 1 from *n*.

6. *(defun fact (n)*

      (cond ((zerop n) 1)

         *(t (times n (fact **(difference)))))*

Difference would work in this case, but it is more appropriate to use the function SUB1 when you are substracting 1 from a number.

7.   *(defun fact (n)*

      (cond ((zerop n) 1)

         *(t (times n (fact **(sub1 n))))))*

You are done. Type NEXT to go on after testing the function you have defined.

dialogue after line 3 illustrates how the tutor guides the student through the design of the recursive case. It does this by first leading the student through a couple of examples of the relationship between *fact n* and *fact n-1* and then getting the student to identify the general recursive relationship. Figure 2.2 shows the actual screen image at a critical point in the design of this function.

The dialogue after this point shows two of the common errors students make in defining recursive functions. The first, in line 4, is to call the function directly without combining the recursive call with other elements. The second, in line 5, is to call the function recursively with the same argument rather than a simpler one.

After the student finishes coding the function, he goes to the LISP window and experiments. He is required to trace the function, and the recursive calls embed and then unravel. Figure 2.3 shows the screen image at this point with the code on the top and the trace on the bottom.

The tutor works by a method called *model tracing*. Residing in the tutor are a set of productions which, when applied in dif-

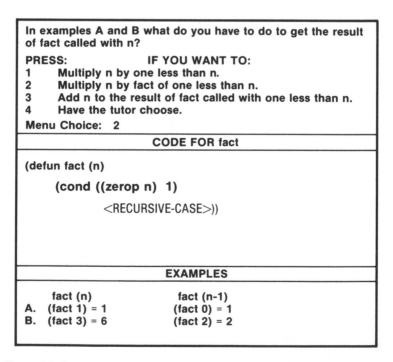

Figure 2.2. *Representation of the screen image after line 3 in Table 2.1.*

```
--- YOU ARE DONE. TYPE NEXT TO GO ON AFTER ---
--- TESTING THE FUNCTIONS YOU HAVE DEFINED ---

(defun fact (n)
    (cond ((zerop n) 1)
          (t (times n (fact (sub 1 n)))))))
```

THE LISP WINDOW
= > (trace fact)
(fact)
= > (fact 3)
1 <Enter> fact (3)
|2 <Enter> fact (2)
| 3 <Enter> fact (1)
| |4 <Enter> fact (0)
| |4 <EXIT> fact 1
| 3 <EXIT> fact 1
|2 <EXIT> fact 2
1 <EXIT> fact 6
6

Figure 2.3. *Final screen image at the end of the dialogue in Table 2.1.*

ferent combinations and orders, are capable of generating a wide range of correct solutions to a particular problem. We analyze the students' behavior by putting it into correspondence with a sequence of productions in the tutor. We can decompose the students' behavior by taking an interaction that begins with a prompt from the LISP tutor and ends with a correct symbol in the code and assign it to the production that generates the code. Thus, in the case of the earlier protocol, there was a point where the code had the form:

(defun fact (n)
    (cond ((zerop n) 1)
          (t <ACTION>)))

The next interaction with the tutor ended when the student typed *(times* to replace the <ACTION> slot above. That period of time was associated with the firing of the following production in the LISP tutor:

     IF   the goal is to multiply one number by another
THEN   use the function *times*
           and set as subgoals to code the two numbers.

We can compute the time associated with this segment and the number of errors (in this case, one) and assign these dependent measures to this production. Our analysis will be concerned with these dependent measures calculated for individual productions.

Vertical Transfer in the LISP Tutor

Typically, programming problems posed by the LISP tutor involve several new productions and many productions learned earlier. Corresponding to the four features of productions as identical elements are four predictions we want to make about student performance:

1. *Independence.* The production rules learned in earlier lessons transfer totally to the current lesson. Specifically, production performance should be solely a function of the level of strength accumulated in earlier lessons. Also, except for general subject ability factors, performance on one production should not predict performance on another.

2. *All-or-None Learning.* The new productions compiled from declarative knowledge should show a marked discontinuity in their learning curves corresponding to the compilation process.

3. *Strength Accrual.* Subsequent to the compilation discontinuity, productions should show a slow power-law improvement in performance characteristic of the ACT* strengthening mechanism.

4. *Abstractness.* Access to rules should not depend on problem context. Specifically, the time or likelihood of a production firing should not depend on where it appears either within a particular problem or across problems.

Student interactions with the LISP tutor provide a data base that allows us to put these predictions to test. As described earlier, the interactions with the tutor can be easily transformed into a sequence of productions that we assume have fired in the students' heads and the times associated with each. This is a level of analysis that graduate students used to spend years achieving for a few subjects solving a few problems. We can achieve it automatically for a full class of students doing a semester's worth of work.

A key feature of the LISP tutor is that it keeps students on one of many correct solution paths. The tutor is often prepared to follow a student along hundreds of different paths, but this is much less than the thousands of paths, mostly incorrect, that students have been observed to follow. At any point in solving a problem, there is a limited set of correct productions that the tutor is prepared to fire next. Depending on the student's input, one of four things can happen:

1. The student generates an action that matches the action of one of the correct productions. The tutor assumes that this production is the one that fired in the student's head and simply waits for the next production to fire.

2. The student makes an error, the tutor responds to that error with feedback, and then the student generates an action that corresponds to a correct production. The tutor assumes that, with the help of the feedback, the student figured out the correct answer and is now back on track.

3. The student asks for help either immediately or after an error. The tutor provides the student with an explanation of the next step in the problem and then provides the piece of code that corresponds to that step. The assumption is again that this explanation was sufficient to get the student back on track and the student is in the same mental state as the tutor.

4. The student generates three errors in the execution of a single production. In this case, the tutor offers help as if it had been requested directly and provides the next correct step.

The underlying assumption in these interactions is that before doing the next part of the problem, the student and the tutor are in the same mental state. From informal observations we know there are occasions when this is not true. A mismatch occurs when the student either misunderstands the problem statement or the feedback given by the tutor. This means that there is a certain amount of noise built into our error attribution. We attribute an error to a production applying in state x whereas a different production might be applying in state y. It is difficult to know the extent of this "noise" in the data and how it compares with noise in other sorts of data. As always, the final indicator is the reliability and interpretability of the results.

Given our methodology, there are two basic categories of data to collect from the LISP tutor, error measures and time measures. The data we will analyze come from 34 students who were taking our LISP course in the spring of 1985. The students were humanities and social science majors, and this was their first programming course. While they went through 12 lessons with the LISP tutor, we will analyze data from only the first six (see Conrad and Anderson, 1988, for analysis of a full semester). These lessons involved (1) basic LISP functions, (2) function definition, (3) conditionals and logical predicates, (4) helping functions, (5) input-output, and (6) iteration. Following these first six lessons, students took a paper-and-pencil test which provides an external validation of the LISP tutor results.

Results

The data are organized by lesson and aggregated over production. Figures 2.4 and 2.5 plot the performance on the new productions for several lessons. Figure 2.4 plots the times for correctly applied productions, and Figure 2.5 plots the mean number of errors per application (this measure has a maximum of three). We plot times for correct applications only, to get a measure that is independent of errors (we also analyzed time aggregated over correct applications and errors, but this measure does not seem to reveal any additional insights). We chose to analyze total number of errors per application in Figure 2.5 rather than probability of error because we believe it is a better measure of student difficulty. Students often make single errors and correct them as slips. Repeated mistakes are strong evidence that a student has a fundamental problem. Lesson 1 has been excluded from this analysis because measures are unreli-

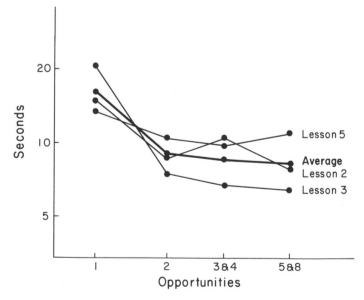

Figure 2.4. *Mean times for correct coding of the actions corresponding to nine productions introduced in lesson 2.*

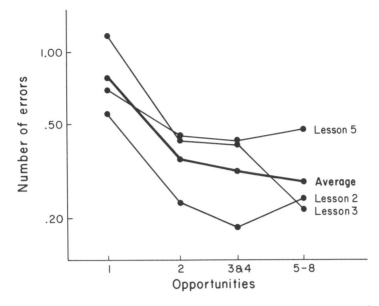

Figure 2.5. *Mean number of errors in coding the actions corresponding to nine productions introduced in lesson 2.*

able as students learn the interface; lessons 4 and 6 have been excluded because they introduce very few new productions.

We plot these measures as a function of the number of times a production is tested in the lesson. Both scales are logarithmic. Both time and errors show a marked drop-off from first to second application and a very modest decline after that. The average improvement from first to second trial is almost 50 percent for time and over 50 percent for accuracy. We plot this on a log-log scale to make the point that this drop-off is not just part of the power-law improvement normally seen for a skill.

The rate of improvement after the first trial is basically linear in these two logarithmic measures. This implies a power function relating either time or errors to amount of practice. This result is typically found in studies of practice. However, the clear discontinuity from trial 1 to trial 2 has not been examined in detail until now. It is consistent with the knowledge compilation mechanism in ACT*, which is basically a one-trial learning mechanism. This result shows up in times for errorless trials as well as number of errors.

Perhaps our most important question concerns the transfer of productions across lessons. Figure 2.6 examines the relative per-

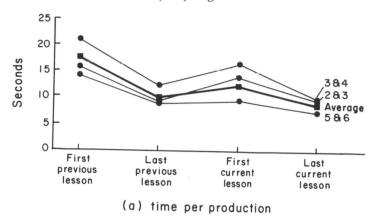

(a) time per production

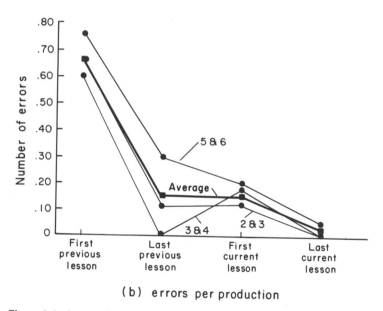

(b) errors per production

Figure 2.6. *Average times and errors for old productions across lesson boundaries.*

formance of shared productions across lesson boundaries. We plot the performance of shared productions on the first trial in lesson *n*-1, the last trial in lesson *n*-1, the first trial in lesson *n*, and the last trial in lesson *n*. Plotted are the transitions between lesson pairs 2 and 3, 3 and 4, and 5 and 6 (there are very few shared productions between lessons 4 and 5). However, the pattern in these results emerges most clearly in the average of these lesson transitions. There is nearly total transfer of shared productions between lessons and considerable improvement within lessons. The slight decrement in performance at lesson boundaries can be attributed to forgetting (lessons are approximately one week apart). These results are evident in both time and accuracy measures.

One might wonder how much support these analyses really offer for the existence of the production rules used in the LISP tutor. The apparent regularity of the data is consistent with the view that the LISP tutor provides the psychologically correct decomposition of the skill. However, an alternative interpretation arises from the fact that the production rules tend to correspond to pieces of code in LISP. For instance, the production CODE-CAR corresponds to typing *car* and the production CHECK-ARG corresponds to typing a variable name. What if we simply monitored how accurately students wrote these pieces of code and ignored the production rule analysis? Although correlated, a code-based analysis is not identical to a production-based analysis. This is because in some cases there is a many-to-one relationship between production rules and types of LISP code. For instance, while CODE-CAR usually is responsible for generating *car* there is a special production CODE-SECOND which generates CAR when we are composing a *car-cdr* sequence.

We examined a number of instances where multiple productions corresponded to the same coding action. For the sake of discussion, let us assume that productions P1 and P2 have the same overt action and further that P1 was introduced first. One test of the production-based view is to look at the error rate on the first trial for P2 and compare it with the error rate on the most recent preceding trial for P1. To summarize the results, the average error rate for 6 such cases were as follows: the first trial for P2 was 1.3 errors, whereas the most recent trial for P1 was .3 errors. This difference is highly significant ($t_5 = 4.09$; $p < .01$) and represents a dramatic reversal of the general trend of better performance with practice. The conclusion is that subject performance is better defined in terms of the LISP tutor productions than surface code.

In sum, the overall pattern of data displayed in these graphs is quite consistent with the ACT* learning mechanisms. There is the discontinuous point of learning from the first trial to the second due to knowledge compilation, a power-law growth in strength with practice, and total transfer mediated somewhat by forgetting (loss of strength) between lessons.

Effects of problem context

A critical question is whether there is any systematic effect of the context in which a product on is firing. For example, are productions slower or faster to fire, the more embedded they are in the code? Does time to fire a production depend on the production that has immediately preceded it? Our prediction is that problem context should have little effect on production performance.

Conrad and Anderson (1988) did a series of regression analyses to see if they could detect any effect of contextual variables. There was only one such variable which seemed to have an effect, and this was serial position in the code. Time to execute a production decreases as one progresses through the code as a power function of serial position within the code. Through multiple regression analysis, it was determined that this effect is due to serial position per se and not potentially correlated variables like depth of the code or a confound of production identity with serial position. Our explanation of this effect is that subjects are getting faster as they rehearse the problem statement as well as their plan for solution. As they commit this information to long-term memory, their working memory load decreases, information is maintained more reliably, and performance improves.

Interproduction Correlations

Another question is how well performance on one production correlates with performance on another. Once again, our claim is that productions are completely independent of each other in terms of acquisition. We used number of errors as our dependent measure in calculating interproduction correlations because it proves to yield the largest numbers.

In our initial pass over the data, we divided the entire set of productions into those that dealt with list operations and those that did not, which to us seemed like an intuitively plausible clustering. We looked at correlations within and between these disjoint sets. The average correlation was .17 both within and between sets. This is somewhat surprising, because it indicates that there is no tendency for productions of the same type to cluster. Intuitively, one might have suspected that some subjects would do well on all list operations and others would not. However, it appears that correlations between productions of this type are not higher than those found between apparently unrelated productions. Both correlations are quite significantly different than zero, indicating some systematic individual differences among subjects. Thus, there appears to be a general ability factor, but not one associated with list operations.

We also calculated correlations among productions within the same lesson, excluding the correlation of a production with itself, which would be one. The average within-lesson correlation is .23, which is significantly higher than the earlier .17 correlation. This indicates a tendency for subjects to have good lessons and bad lessons, which is not surprising. Again, if we divide the set of productions within a single lesson into list and nonlist sets and compare the correlations within and between sets, there is no difference.

It would be premature at this point to conclude that productions do not break up into thematic clusters. One possibility is that we simply did not intuit properly the factors that would define the clusters. To check this possibility, we subjected the data from the six lessons to factor analyses. We took the matrix of subject-by-production performance means for each lesson and submitted it to a standard factor analysis program. We then looked at the first two factors extracted for each lesson. As before, the measure of total errors consistently accounted for the most variance, so we restrict our discussion to analyses performed on this measure (for detailed reports of the factor analysis, see Anderson, in press).

At first, we could not make a great deal of sense out of the factor analyses. Productions were not clustering according to any semantic feature we could discern. In addition, the compositions of the factors were changing from lesson to lesson. For example, certain productions loaded on different factors for earlier lessons but the same factor for later lessons. In a further attempt to make sense of the situation, we took each subject's scores on the two factors for each lesson and subjected these to a factor analysis to determine which lesson factors would cluster together. Two "metafactors" emerged. The first metafactor accounted for 36 percent of the variance, and the second metafactor 16 percent of the variance.

What defines these metafactors became apparent only after considerable inspection. Twenty-two of the 34 productions organized under metafactor 1 are new productions in the lessons associated with the factors, whereas 20 of the 23 productions organized under metafactor 2 are old. Thus, the first metafactor is essentially an acquisition factor, while the second is a retention factor. This helps explain why the previous clustering of productions seemed arbitrary and why the clusters did not stay constant across lessons. Each production changes its status from new to old across a particular lesson boundary and coincidentally switches factors.

It seemed worthwhile to see how well these metafactors would do at predicting performance on the paper-and-pencil midterm. We took subjects' scores on the two metafactors and classified them as above or below the median. This gave us ten subjects in both the high-high and low-low categories, and seven in both the high-low and low-high categories. A 2 × 2 between-subjects analysis of variance (ANOVA) using midterm grade as the dependent measure yielded significant effects for both the acquisition factor ($F(1,30) = 5.1$) and the retention factor ($F(1,30) = 6.4$). The interaction was not significant ($F(1,30) = 2.8$). These results provide additional support for the psychological validity of the metafactors.

Anderson, Conrad, and Corbett (in preparation) did find some thematic clustering in later lessons with the LISP tutor. The clearest case concerned the first lesson in which recursion was introduced. They found one factor composed of operations concerned with terminating cases and another factor composed of operations concerned with recursive cases. It seems a bit implausible to propose some people are better predisposed to deal with terminating cases while others are better predisposed to deal with recursive cases. Upon reinspection of the LISP textbook, however, it became apparent that discussion of terminating cases occurred in one place while discussion of recursive cases occurred in another. Perhaps a more plausible explanation for these two factors is that subjects read one of these sections carefully and the other haphazardly. Interestingly, these two factors did not reappear in later lessons. Presumably, by the time subjects had gotten through the first recursive lesson, they had mastered both sets of material.

Conclusion

Prior to the data analysis, we articulated the four fundamental properties that define productions as the identical elements in a Thorndikelike analysis. Here is a summary of the results relevant to those properties:

1. *Independence.* Productions do appear to transfer totally from one lesson to the next. The only factors producing interdependence among productions are general subject abilities (the ac-

quisition and retention factors) and variation in subject effort (this latter factor explains the higher within-lesson correlations and also the distinction between terminating and recursive cases).

2. *All-or-None Learning.* New productions do have a qualitative transformation from the first trial to later trials.

3. *Strength Accrual.* Productions do seem to accrue strength according to the gradual power-law functions predicted by ACT*.

4. *Abstractness.* Except for the nonspecific effects of working memory load, production performance does seem to be independent of problem context.

The confirmation of these assumptions with data from the LISP tutor constitutes a significant justification for carrying them forward in further analyses of transfer. In particular, we would like to use these assumptions to analyze lateral rather than vertical transfer. Our identical elements model should be capable of predicting transfer fairly well in many lateral transfer situations.

3 / Lateral Transfer

We are now in position to launch into a study of lateral transfer, transfer between skills at the same level of complexity. From an applied perspective, lateral transfer is a key issue, in that the debate about general transfer is largely a debate about lateral transfer. We start with a rather thorough analysis of a study of transfer between various text editors. This study (Singley and Anderson, 1985) provides our first evidence that an identical productions model might do well at predicting transfer among skills. Later research forces complications and elaborations on the picture that emerges from this study, specifically the importance of the declarative component in certain transfer situations. However, the basic points of this text-editing study remain unchanged, providing the framework for those later studies.

Lateral Transfer in Text Editing

We chose text editing as our domain for a variety of reasons, but perhaps most important was the existence of a well-specified theory of expert performance. Card, Moran, and Newell (1976, 1980, 1983) put forth a series of information-processing models at various levels of detail that account for an impressive percentage of error-free, expert behavior. These models are useful in that they serve as a well-defined end point for skill acquisition in text editing. In particular, their research largely solved the skill representation problem which is always a thorny issue in attempts to provide theoretical analyses of transfer. All predictions about transfer turn critically on the representation chosen for the skill. To avoid the danger of circularity, it is preferable to have the representation decided on grounds other than the transfer data at hand. Card, Moran & Newell's GOMS model provides that representation independently for us.

The GOMS model supplies us with a representation of text-editing skill that can be used to identify the elements common to different editors. More specifically, the model provides us with the abstract goal structures which underlie and organize the production of keystrokes in the editors. Our predictions of transfer between the editors hinge on the fact that, even though the specific commands used to accomplish edits in the various systems may be different, the underlying goal structures are largely the same and provide the basis for positive transfer.

While their GOMS model is not an ACT* production system model, it is easily converted into one. A major assumption in our work is that single production rules are the units of cognitive skill, the elements that Thorndike was searching for. What we are proposing is essentially a modern version of the theory of identical elements based on productions rather than stimulus-response bonds. Unlike Thorndike's superficial elements, productions are versatile and powerful computational entities. It is widely known that production systems have the computational power of Turing machines. Productions are abstract and can be used to represent many different problem-solving methods at various levels of generality. Productions are often used to represent cognitive processes which have no direct impact on the external world yet nonetheless play an important role in skilled behavior, like planning and problem decomposition (or subgoaling). Therefore, not only external but also internal "actions" are considered in calculations of transfer. In our models, all the components of text-editing skill identified by Card et al. (goal structures, methods, operators, decision rules, and sequences of user actions) are represented as productions.

The experiment reported here involved teaching groups of computer-naive subjects one or two line editors and then a screen editor. Three questions were of particular interest:

1. *Magnitude of Transfer among Different Editors.* Would transfer be positive, negative, or nonexistent? How would transfer among the line editors compare with transfer from the line editors to the screen editor? A production system analysis of the structural similarity of the editors suggested that, whereas the line editors were quite similar, the line editors and the screen

editor shared few features. Perhaps the magnitudes of transfer would reflect this difference.

2. *Identification of Learning and Transfer Components.* Could transfer effects be localized to particular subskills and pieces of knowledge? What would be the nature of these components? These questions are crucial to the development of the identical productions theory of transfer.

3. *Advantage of Learning Two Line Editors Instead of One.* We thought subjects might show greater transfer to a screen editor after having learned two line editors rather than one. This speculation was founded on the belief that those who learned two line editors would have a more generalized skill that would apply more broadly to a new editor (Anderson, 1982). This prediction is somewhat dated. As noted in the review of ACT*, such a generalization process no longer exists in the theory.

Method

Subjects

Subjects were 24 women between the ages of 18 and 30 from a local secretarial school. None of the subjects had any computer experience, but all could type proficiently. Subjects were balanced across various conditions of the experiment for typing speed ($M = 41$ wpm) and performance on a standardized cognitive test of spatial memory, the building memory test (Ekstrom, French, and Harman, 1976). This test was found to be a fair predictor ($r = -.58$) of initial performance on a text editor (Gomez, Egan, and Bowers, 1986).

Materials

Subjects learned from a set of three commercially available text editors. Two of these editors, UNIX ED (Kernighan, 1980) and VMS EDT (Digital Equipment Corporation, 1982) belong to the genre known as line editors, whereas the third editor, UNIX EMACS (Gosling, 1981), belongs to the genre known as screen editors. Line editors differ from screen editors in basic editing strategy. Line editors display the contents of the file only upon request and force users to enter abstract commands that specify edits on a line-by-line basis. Screen editors, however, fill the screen with the contents of the file and allow users to edit the contents explicitly by moving to a particular location by means of a cursor. Screen editors are generally seen as a significant advance over the older line editors and in fact have been found superior on measures of learnability and expert performance (Roberts, 1979; Gomez, Egan, Wheeler, Sharma, and Gruchacz, 1983).

Subjects were taught a minimum core set of commands for each editor. These commands were totally sufficient for the kinds of edits our subjects had to perform. In the line editors (ED and EDT), the core set included commands for:

1. Printing, deleting, inserting, and replacing lines.
2. Substituting strings within lines (the substitution command also provided for string insertion and deletion).

In the screen editor (EMACS), the core set included commands for:

1. Moving the cursor forward, backward, and up and down.
2. Deleting characters, words, and strings.

Of course, the character of the commands differed markedly between the line editors and the screen editors. The majority of EMACS commands pertained to moving the cursor and involved special terminal keys. In all editors, subjects were spared from learning the procedures for reading and writing files and were instead fed files automatically by experimental software. Table 3.1 lists the core set of commands for each of the editors.

Subjects edited sections of a book on cognitive psychology that resided on a local computer system. The book was sectioned into 18-line files, and each file was randomly mutilated by a text mutilation program. The program performed six of 12 possible mutilations on each file. The 12 mutilations were defined by crossing the editing operations insert, delete, and replace by the data objects character, word, string, and line. It took two files to cover all 12 mutilations; the same mutilations occurred on every other screen. Each file constituted a single trial.

The subjects' task was to correct the errors introduced by the mutilation program. They worked from a marked-up copy of the files placed in a loose-leaf binder. Figure 3.1 shows a sample page of the binder, which sat flat on the table just beside the terminal. Each page corresponded to a single file.

Design

The study used a 2 × 2 between-subjects design with two control groups. The first factor was number of line editors

Table 3.1.   Command summary for three editors: ˆ denotes a control
character and] denotes an escape character.

Command type	Editor	Command	Action
Locative	ED	1,$p	Prints all lines of the file
		3p	Prints the third line
		.p	Prints the current line
		. =	Prints the line number of the current line
		CR	Prints the line following the current line
	EDT	t whole	Prints all lines of the file
		t 'dog'	Prints the first line following the current line that contains 'dog'
		t – 'dog'	Prints the first line before the current line that contains 'dog'
		t	Prints the current line
		CR	Prints the line following the current line
	EMACS	ˆf	Moves cursor forward one character
		]f	Moves cursor forward one word
		ˆb	Moves cursor backward one character
		]b	Moves cursor backward one word
		ˆa	Moves cursor to beginning of line
		ˆe	Moves cursor to end of line
		ˆp	Moves cursor to previous line
		ˆn	Moves cursor to next line
Mutative	ED	.a	Inserts lines after the current line (type '.' to exit the insert mode)
		.d	Deletes the current line
		.c	Replaces the current line (type '.' to exit the insert mode)
		s/a/b/p	Substitutes the first occurrence of 'a' with 'b' on the current line
	EDT	i	Inserts lines after the current line (type ˆz to exit the insert mode)
		d	Deletes the current line
		r	Replaces the current line (type ˆz to exit the insert mode)
		s/a/b	Substitutes the first occurrence of 'a' with 'b' on the current line
	EMACS	ˆd	Deletes the character marked by the cursor
		]d	Deletes the word marked by the cursor
		DEL	Deletes the character to the left of the cursor
		ˆk	Deletes from the current cursor position to the end of the line
		a	Inserts the character 'a' at the current cursor position (EMACS is in insert mode by default)

not only will the unit nodes in these traces
accrue strength with days of practice, but also

the element nodes will accrue strength. As will

be seen, this power function prediction

corresponds to the data about practice. A set of

experiments was conducted to test the prediction

about a power-law increase in *the* strength with

extensive practice. In one experiment subjects

studied subject-verb-object sentences of the form

(The lawyer hated the doctor). After studying
these sentences they were transferred to a
1 furthermore, the thought prevents the study

sentence recognition paradigm in which they had to

discriminate these sentences from foil by the mind

sentences made of the same words as the *target* illustrates

sentence but in new combinations. There were 25 days of

tests and hence practice. Each day subjects were tested

on each sentence 12 times (in one group) or 24

times in the other group. There was no difference

Figure 3.1. *Sample page of corrections.*

learned (one vs. two), and the second was initial line editor (ED vs. EDT). The two control groups learned no line editors; their first exposure to text editing was EMACS. One of the control groups spent the entire experiment editing with EMACS (this control would reveal whether transfer to EMACS from the line editors was positive or negative). The other control group practiced typing at the terminal prior to editing with EMACS. This group typed for the amount of time the experimental groups spent learning the line editors (this control would reveal the perceptual-motor component of transfer).

Procedure

Several days prior to the experiment, subjects were pretested on the Building Memory Test and assigned to conditions based on this score and also typing speed. On this same days, subjects received a brief orientation to computing and the computer terminal. No explicit instruction on text editing was given.

The experiment itself consisted of six consecutive days of text editing. Each day consisted of a three-hour session interrupted by two ten-minute breaks after the first and second hours. Subjects were run in pairs in a quiet experimental room.

On the first day of the experiment, all subjects except those in the typing control condition were given a brief introduction to the set of commands they would be using that day. This introduction consisted of a brief description of each command followed by a demonstration on the terminal. This introduction lasted approximately 30 minutes.

The subjects than began editing at the terminals. An experimenter was present in the room at all times to answer any questions or help with particularly difficult problems. Experimenters were told not to intervene unless a subject asked for help. A single tutor was designated for each editor, so that all subjects' experiences with a single editor would be similar. As experimenter was totally confounded with editor in the experiment, the results should not be regarded as a totally valid comparison of the editors.

The subjects spent the first two days practicing their first editor. On the third day, those subjects in the two-line-editor conditions switched to their second editor (either ED or EDT), whereas the other subjects remained on their first. All subjects, however, received a second introduction to the set of commands they would be using (which constituted a review for the subjects who did not switch). In this way, the amount of formal instruction received by subjects was constant across conditions.

On the fifth day of the experiment, all experimental subjects and the typing control group transferred to EMACS. After receiving formal instruction on the commands, these subjects spent the last two days practicing EMACS. The EMACS control group spent all six days learning EMACS. They received formal instruction on the first, third, and fifth days.

Those subjects in the typing control group spent the first four days typing the manuscript that the experimental groups were editing. In addition to incorporating all the corrections marked on the manuscript, subjects had to correct typing mistakes as they were made. This rule was enforced by a program that checked the stream of keystrokes against a target file and deactivated the keyboard once a difference was detected. Subjects could reactivate the keyboard only by pressing the delete key, which erased the mistake. This practice resulted in a level of frustration similar to that experienced by subjects in the experimental conditions. In sum, the typing control had experience reading the manuscript, interpreting the edits, and interacting through the terminal.

Keystroke data accurate to within one second were collected for all subjects. In addition, the edited versions of the mutilated files were saved to allow for error checking.

Macroanalysis of Learning and Transfer

There are two major levels of data analysis. One level describes subjects' performance in terms of gross measures, such as time per edit and keystrokes per trial. This macrolevel of analysis gives us a general understanding of what is happening and encourages us to explore certain phenomena further. The other level of analysis is a detailed examination of the keystroke data, designed to localize the components of learning and transfer intimated at the coarser level. This microlevel of analysis provides the most rigorous test of the identical productions theory of transfer.

The macroanalysis has three parts. The first presents learning data for the three editors. The second analyzes transfer between the line editors, and the third analyzes transfer from the line editors to the screen editor.

Learning in three editors

Figure 3.2 shows learning curves for the three editors used in the experiment. The curves were derived from the two experimental groups that spent four days on a single line editor and the control group that spent six days on EMACS (only the first four days are presented here). The results are expressed in terms of a measure that approximates the number of seconds spent per correct editing operation. The measure was calculated by first adjusting the total time on a trial (t) by incrementing the time by one-sixth for every error (e) committed:

$$(3.1) \quad t_{adj} = t + (e/6) \times t$$

This adjusted total was then divided by six to arrive at time per correct editing operation (similar results are obtained just using raw time). Errors were defined as mismatches in character sequences between the subject's edited file and the target file. Errors were scored in an all-or-none fashion, with a maximum of six errors per trial.

The learning curves show that, on all four days, EDT is the

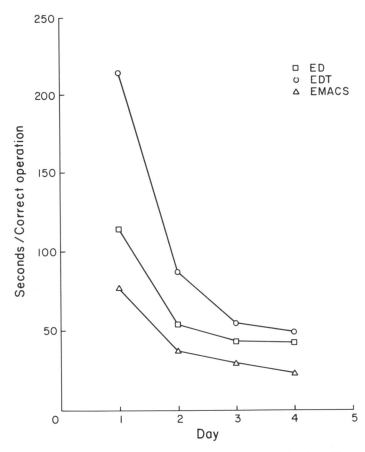

Figure 3.2. *Learning curves plotting seconds per correct edit for three editors.*

slowest editor and EMACS is the fastest. Also, EMACS appears to be leveling off at a much lower asymptote than the two line editors (an advantage of approximately 20 seconds per edit, or 2 minutes per trial). A two-way repeated measures analysis of variance yielded main effects for editor ($F(2,9) = 8.6, p < .01$), day ($F(3, 27) = 23.4, p < .01$), and also an interaction ($F(6,27) = 3.0, p < .05$). The interaction implies that the editors are being learned at different rates. Subsequent Newman-Keuls multiple range tests revealed that, across days, EDT was significantly slower than both ED ($F(9) = 3.68, p < .05$) and EMACS ($F(9) = 5.8, p < .05$). The ED-EMACS difference was nonsignificant ($F(9) = 2.13$).

The reasons for the advantage of a screen editor such as EMACS over line editors such as ED and EDT have been discussed elsewhere (Roberts, 1979; Gomez et al., 1983). A popular view is that screen editors off-load spatial memory by providing a static display of text and a method of addressing characters by cursor position. More generally, differences among editors have been ascribed to differences in the number of keystrokes required to perform edits (Card et al., 1983). Subjects did edit in EMACS using significantly fewer keystrokes than in the line editors.

Having generated possible reasons for the EMACS advantage, how do we explain the apparent superiority of ED over EDT? In our experiment, the difference between these line editors is most likely due to different procedures for locating lines. Specifically, lines are addressed by line number in ED and by content in EDT (in fact, both line addressing methods are available in both editors, but we chose to teach only one in each). So, to locate line 12 in ED, one merely types *12p;* whereas in EDT, one types *t 'string'*, where *string* is some sequence of characters unique to line 12. In most cases, the latter method involves not only more keystrokes but also more mental preparation time, especially in novices. This may explain the observed differences in both initial and asymptotic performance in the two line editors. Further analysis of the keystroke data should be instructive on this point.

In a complex skill such as text editing, the exact shape of the learning curves is most likely determined by a variety of interacting factors. Two of these factors might be fewer episodes involving error recovery and the acquisition of more efficient editing strategies. Both of these factors would not only combine to reduce total time but also reduce the total number of keystrokes. Figure 3.3 plots the average number of keystrokes per trial for the three editors on each day. A two-way analysis of variance yielded main effects for editor ($F(2,9) = 8.7$, $p < .01$) and day ($F(3,27) = 4.9$, $p < .01$). The pattern of keystroke data mirrors almost exactly the pattern of timing data presented in Figure 3.2. Such a correspondence suggests that, in learning as well as in expert performance (Card et al., 1983), the number of keystrokes correlates highly with total time.

Can the decrease in the number of keystrokes account for all the learning that is taking place? If the decrease in the number of keystrokes is solely responsible for the shape of the learning curves, then seconds per keystroke should be constant across days. Figure 3.4 shows that seconds per keystroke decreased markedly across days, suggesting that subjects were either becoming faster typists or spending less time thinking and planning. Given the magnitude of the effect and the fact that subjects were already skilled typists, the latter hypothesis seems more plausible. An analysis of variance for this data revealed that

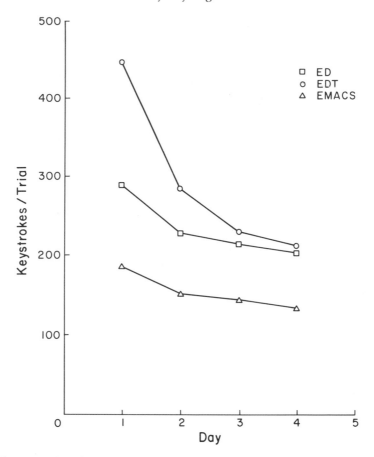

Figure 3.3. *Learning curves plotting number of keystrokes per trial for three editors.*

seconds per keystroke did not differ significantly among the editors. Thus, the difference among editors appears to be a function of the complexity of the editing operations, which is reflected in the different number of keystrokes required to successfully execute commands. Speedup, however, is due to a decrease in both number of keystrokes and time per keystroke (for a similar pattern of results in a geometry theorem-proving task, see Neves and Anderson, 1981).

Transfer between line editors

Transfer between line editors is measured in both directions: from EDT to ED and from ED to EDT. Figure 3.5 shows the massive amount of transfer from EDT to ED. Two of the curves

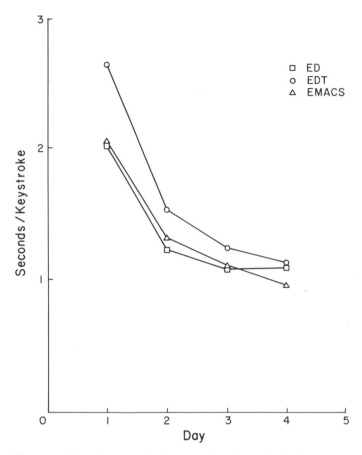

Figure 3.4. *Learning curves plotting seconds per keystroke for three editors.*

compare data for subjects who spent four days learning ED (ED practice curve) with those who spent two days learning EDT and then two days learning ED (transfer from EDT to ED). Exposure to EDT prior to ED results in a substantial improvement in performance on day 1 of ED, a savings of approximately 70 seconds per edit (7 minutes per trial). Indeed, it appears that the transfer subjects' performance on days 1 and 2 is nearly equivalent to the practice curve points for days 3 and 4. This means that those subjects who spent the first two days learning EDT are performing just as well on days 3 and 4 as those subjects who spent the first two days learning ED, a case of near total transfer.

Figure 3.5 also shows the transfer from ED to EDT. The remaining two curves compare data for subjects who spent four

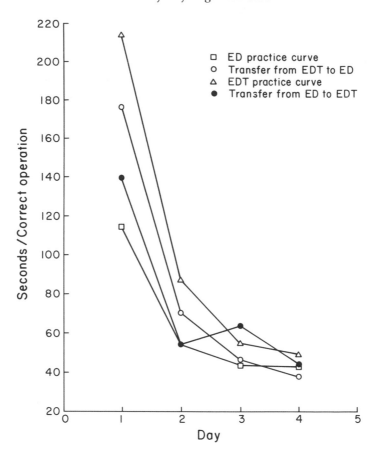

Figure 3.5. *Transfer between the line editors in terms of seconds per correct operation (days 1-2 of the transfer curves represent performance on the training editor, and days 3-4 performance on the transfer editor).*

days learning EDT (EDT practice curve) with those who spent two days learning ED and then two days learning EDT (transfer from ED to EDT). The savings on the first day are even greater than in the previous case (150 vs. 70 seconds per edit). Once again, the data from days 1 and 2 of the transfer group align fairly well with the data from days 3 and 4 of the practice group, indicating near total transfer.

To characterize further the positive transfer between the line editors, we compared the number of keystrokes per trial for the various training and transfer conditions. These comparisons were based on data from the first and second days of editing with a particular line editor (thus, the data is from the third and fourth days of the experiment for the transfer subjects). Although the transfer groups saved an average of 38 and 118 keystrokes on ED and EDT respectively across days, neither result yielded a significant main effect.

Although the difference in total keystrokes was nonsignificant, analyses of variance using seconds per keystroke as the dependent measure showed that transfer subjects were keying at a higher rate than the practice subjects in both ED ($F(1,6) = 10.3$, $p < .05$) and EDT ($F(1,6) = 13.8$, $p < .01$). On average, transfer subjects were spending less than half the time (1.1 vs. 2.3 seconds) per keystroke on day 1 than practice subjects. Once again, this savings is almost certainly due to a decrease in mental preparation time rather than an increase in keying rate.

Transfer from line editors to EMACS

Figure 3.6 shows the transfer from the line editors to EMACS. Curves are plotted for control subjects who saw nothing but EMACS (EMACS practice curve), control subjects who typed at the terminal for four days prior to EMACS (transfer from typing), experimental subjects who learned one line editor, and experimental subjects who learned two line editors (different orderings of the editors were collapsed in the two-editor condition). The most noticeable result is that, on the whole, those subjects who had four days of prior line-editing experience showed substantial transfer on the first day of EMACS (a savings of approximately 35 seconds per edit). On average, however, this is less than half the amount of transfer observed among the line editors.

A two-way analysis of variance yielded a main effect for experience prior to transfer ($F(3,20) = 5.8$, $p < .01$). As expected, subsequent Newman-Keuls tests revealed significant differences between the group that had no prior experience (EMACS practice curve) and the groups that had prior line-editing experience (one line editor, $F(20) = 5.25$, $p < .01$; two line editors, $F(20) = 5.74$, $p < .01$). No other differences were significant, including the difference between the typing and EMACS control groups.

Examining the data in finer detail, we see that the prediction concerning the advantage of two line editors over one is supported to only a modest degree. Those who learned two line editors had an advantage of about 2 seconds per edit (12 seconds per trial) on both the first and second days. However, this difference was not significant.

Figure 3.7 shows that, compared with the control groups who had had no prior line-editing experience, the experimental

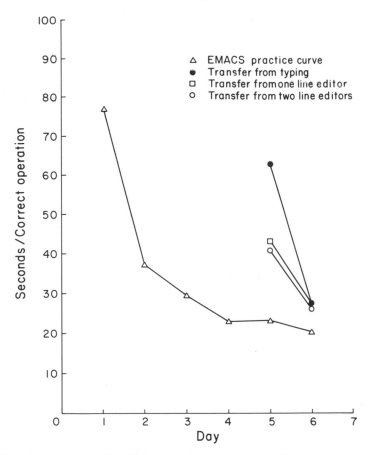

Figure 3.6. *Transfer to EMACS in terms of seconds per correct edit (transfer curves are plotted to facilitate comparisons of performance on day 1 of EMACS).*

groups made substantially fewer keystrokes per trial on the first day of EMACS (a difference of approximately 30 keystrokes). A two-way repeated measures analysis of variance produced a significant interaction between prior experience and days ($F(3,20) = 3.83$, $p < .05$). Newman-Keuls tests yielded significant differences for all four comparisons between the control groups and the experiment groups on day 1 (all $F(20) > 3.4$, $p < .05$). There were no significant differences between groups on the second day of transfer.

In addition to fewer total keystrokes, the experimental subjects were keying at a higher rate than the control subjects (1.2 vs. 1.5 keystrokes per second). Figure 3.8 presents the pattern of results. An analysis of variance of the keying rates yielded a significant

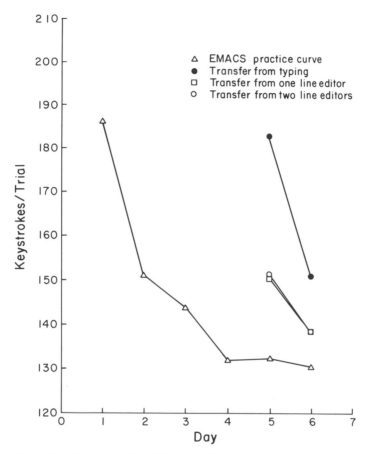

Figure 3.7. *Transfer to* EMACS *in terms of number of keystrokes per trial.*

interaction between experience prior to EMACS and day of transfer ($F(3,20) = 4.83$, $p < .01$). Subsequent Newman-Keuls tests revealed that on the first day of transfer, the two experimental groups were indeed keying significantly faster than the EMACS control group (both $F(20) > 4.7$, $p < .05$) but not the typing control group. As in the earlier keystroke analysis, there were no significant differences on the second day of transfer.

Summary of macroanalysis

At present our results are expressed in terms of rather global measures. However, the basic outlines of the phenomena of learning and transfer are beginning to emerge. So far, we have observed:

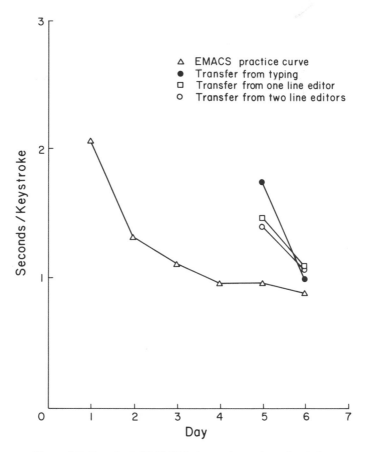

Figure 3.8. *Transfer to* EMACS *in terms of seconds per keystroke.*

1. Consistent rank ordering of the editors in terms of learn-ability and ease of use, with EMACS being the easiest and ED the hardest.

2. Near total transfer between the two line editors. For exam-ple, two days of practice on ED were nearly as good as two days of practice on EDT in terms of preparation for further editing with EDT.

3. Moderate amount of transfer from the line editors to the screen editor.

4. Slight transfer from the typing control condition to the screen editor.

5. No sign of negative transfer. All transfer at the macrolevel was overwhelmingly positive.

Learning and transfer manifested themselves in a number of ways, including:

1. Reduction in total time
2. Reduction in total keystrokes
3. Increase in keying rate

Our results so far seem to be consistent with some type of common elements theory of transfer. However, if productions are the elements, as we claim, our measures to date have been too coarse to identify specific transfer sites. Although in practical terms it is impossible to identify the firing of individual productions in this data, we can provide firmer support for our common elements theory by doing analyses at a finer grain size. Our task at this point is to perform an in-depth analysis of the keystroke data to localize the learning and transfer effects.

Microanalysis of Learning and Transfer

The goal of the microanalysis is to isolate and independently measure the acquisition and transfer of the various elements of text-editing skill. To do this, we need some theory of performance in text editing to identify the theoretically significant components. We use the extensive task analysis of text editing that already exists in the work of Card et al. (1983). According to their GOMS formulation, text editing consists of a series of largely independent unit tasks, each of which is accomplished through the satisfaction of three subgoals as shown in Figure 3.9: encode the edit from the manuscript (acquire unit task), move to the line requiring modification (locate line), and modify the text (modify text). These three subgoals are instances of goals, one of the four components of skill in the GOMS model. The other components are operators, methods, and selection rules.

We set as an initial goal of the microanalysis to trace the acquisition and transfer of the various unit tasks of text editing and their major subgoals: acquire unit task, locate line (LL), and modify text (MT). We do this by taking a detailed look at the stream of keystrokes executed by subjects over the course of the experiment. The keystroke data can be viewed as a series of keystroke bursts separated by pauses. These bursts and pauses have psychological significance in that the pauses represent the mental preparation time for an operation, and the bursts its execution. Presumably, as a person becomes more skillful at text editing, the frequency and duration of the bursts and pauses

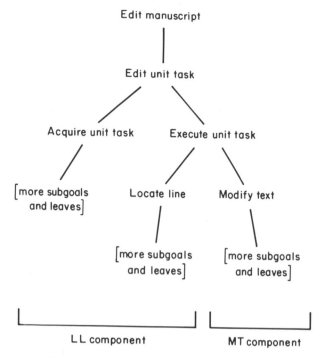

Figure 3.9. *Top-level goal structure of text editing.*

change, reflecting the acquisition and compilation of the various components of text-editing knowledge.

Keystroke parsing

In order to make sense of the nearly 500,000 keystrokes collected in this experiment, we developed a keystroke parsing algorithm that was instantiated in several data analysis programs (see Singley and Anderson, 1988). The goal of the parsing algorithm is to identify each burst and pause in the keystroke data and attribute it to the planning or execution of some text-editing operation. The general strategy is to simulate the editors by parsing commands and updating the contents of the file while collecting statistics on each interaction.

The parsing algorithm first segments the keystroke data from a single trial into six unit task episodes corresponding to the six edits on the page. The algorithm further subdivides these six segments into their LL and MT components. The LL component includes not only the time and keystrokes spent moving to the site of the modification but also the time spent acquiring the unit task from the manuscript (see Figure 3.9). The MT component is composed simply of the time and keystrokes spent modifying the text. Finally, these two components are split into planning and execution subcomponents. Operationally, we defined the execution subcomponent as the time from the first to last keystroke minus any interkeystroke pauses of greater than 2 seconds. Likewise, we defined the planning component to be the sum of all pauses of greater than 2 seconds. Typically, an LL or MT component begins with a long pause followed by keystroke bursts separated by short pauses.

Critical to the success of the parsing algorithm is that subjects move in an orderly fashion from unit task to unit task in the manuscript. Although the parser has certain methods for dealing with backtracking and skipped goals, in many cases the parser simply refuses to attribute pauses and keystrokes that fall outside of its expectations.

Table 3.2 shows one measure of the success of our parsing algorithm, the percentage of total time attributed to the satisfaction of goals. Generally, parsing efficiency ranges between 85 and 95 percent in the learning and transfer data in all three editors, but interesting subpatterns do exist. First, there is a learning effect in that parsing efficiency is lowest on day 1 and rises on days 2 and 3. The slight dip on day 4 is due to the unusually poor performance of the EDT subjects; the other editors seem to have reached asymptotic levels. Second, there is a

Table 3.2. Parsing efficiency: percentage of time attributed to the satisfaction of goals by the parsing algorithm.

Editor	Day				M
	1	2	3	4	
Learning conditions					
EMACS	94	94	95	95	95
ED	82	89	92	92	89
EDT	78	90	93	86	87
M	85	91	93	91	90
Transfer conditions					
EMACS	93	95	—	—	94
ED	94	91	—	—	93
EDT	96	94	—	—	95
M	94	93	—	—	94

transfer effect in that the transfer percentages are generally higher than the learning percentages. Finally, parsing efficiency is highest for EMACS and lowest for EDT, which is consistent with earlier results concerning learnability and ease of use.

The general sensibility of these results points to the fact that, apart from the more substantive output of the parsing analysis, parsing efficiency is an interesting and valid dependent measure in itself. Indeed, the parsing algorithm embodies a simple model of text-editing behavior. Adherence to the algorithm is in some sense a measure of a subject's goal directedness and rationality. Subjects' behavior seems to become more rule-governed with experience, as Robertson (1984) speculated.

The primary yield from the parsing analysis is a set of learning and transfer curves for the 12 subgoals corresponding to the 12 kinds of modifications in the editing task. Each of these curves is further subdivided into its LL and MT components, which are in turn split into planning and execution components. Given such a multilevel analysis, it should be possible to localize the learning and transfer effects observed at the macrolevel. As we describe these microresults, we move from the coarser to the finer levels of analysis. We start with three learning analyses and conclude with two transfer analyses.

Planning time versus execution time in learning

In this first analysis, we collapse across LL, MT, and the 12 subgoals and simply split total time per edit into its planning and execution components. One of the first discoveries is that, apart from minor differences, all learning curves decomposed in this way have a characteristic shape, regardless of editor. Figure 3.10 shows this characteristic shape, averaged across the various methods in all three editors. The two curves plotted are total time per edit and execution time per edit; planning time is merely the difference of these two.

Most striking is the fact that, whereas total time per edit drops from 48 seconds on day 1 to 16 seconds on day 4 (a 3-to-1 decrease), the execution time curve is relatively flat. Apparently, most of what a subject learns manifests itself as a reduction in planning time. Also, as we shall see shortly, the slight decrease in execution time can be attributed totally to a decrease in keystrokes rather than an increase in keying rate.

The ratio of planning time drops from 3.0 on day 1 to 1.2 on day 4. This means that subjects spend about 75 percent of their time planning on day 1 and 54 percent on day 4. This 54 percent

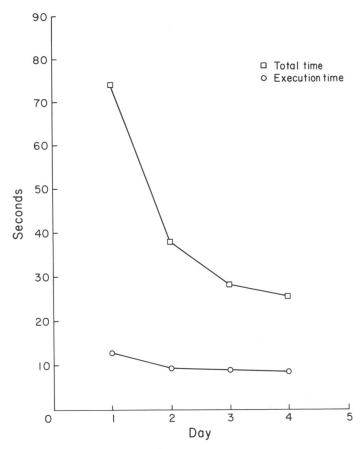

Figure 3.10. *Aggregate subgoal learning curve broken down into planning and execution components (planning time is the difference between total time and execution time).*

figure compares favorably with the results of Card et al. (1983), who reported that the seasoned experts in their studies spend about 60 percent of their time planning. Our number is somewhat lower because a full third of the subjects used in our analysis were editing with EMACS, which requires substantially less planning time per keystroke than the line editors used here and also those in Card et al. (1983). Specifically, the ratio of planning time to execution time on day 4 for our EMACS subjects was .9, which is well below the line editor average of 1.3.

Learning in LL and MT

This analysis again collapses across the 12 subgoals but partitions the keystroke data into two additional components: LL and MT. Although the dramatic reductions occur in planning time, modest reductions occur in execution time as well. The number of keystrokes per edit also decreases over the course of the experiment. The question naturally arises as to whether the reduction in execution time is due solely to the reduction in number of keystrokes. Table 3.3 presents in the first row correlation data that establishes the connection between execution time and keystrokes in each of the editors. Separate data points were entered for each of the twelve subgoals on four days of learning, making a total of 48 data points per correlation (for this analysis, data was averaged across subjects). The correlations are remarkably high (an average of .96), giving strong evidence for an airtight linkage between these two variables. This lawful pattern of results attests to the soundness of our original decision to regard pauses of greater than 2 seconds as a part of planning time. The fact that execution time can be computed by multiplying the number of keystrokes by typing speed indicates that our parsing procedure successfully segmented the planning and execution subcomponents.

To remove any doubt whatsoever concerning the exclusive relationship between reductions in execution time and keystrokes, we considered a plausible alternative hypothesis: that subjects were becoming better typists and were keying faster over the course of the experiment. To test this hypothesis, we performed six multiple trials ANOVAs for the LL and MT components of the three editors, using execution time per keystroke as the measure of keying rate. As expected, none produced a significant main effect for days, which meant that subjects were keying at the same rate throughout the experi-

Table 3.3. Correlation of dependent measures in the three editors.

Correlation	Component	Editor		
		EMACS	ED	EDT
Execution time vs. keystrokes	LL	.97	.86	.98
	MT	.99	.97	.98
Planning time vs. keystrokes	LL	.46	.83	.73
	MT	.59	.72	.65

ment, a sensible result given that they were already skilled typists. Subjects averaged .47 seconds per keystroke, or approximately 2 keystrokes per second; there were no significant differences between editors. We conclude, then, that the speedup observed in the execution subcomponent is solely a result of subjects' using fewer keystrokes to perform edits and not a result of faster typing.

Having isolated the source of speedup in execution time, we must now consider what causes subjects to use fewer keystrokes. There are at least two possibilities. First, subjects' methods may be becoming more efficient because of either the acquisition of new operators or the more judicious use of existing operators. Second, subjects may be making fewer errors, requiring fewer corrections. Fortunately, we can discriminate between these two possibilities with two new dependent measures. If subjects are acquiring more efficient methods, the numbers of keystrokes per command should decline over the course of the experiment. Likewise, if subjects are executing fewer errorful commands, requiring fewer resubmissions, the number of commands per edit should decline.

Table 3.4 shows the results of 12 multiple trials ANOVAs performed on the two dependent measures for the MT and LL components of the three editors. Five of the six commands per edit ANOVAs yielded a main effect for days, but only one of the six keystrokes per command ANOVAs did. This pattern of results strongly suggests that most of the reduction in keystrokes is due to fewer error episodes and not to more efficient methods.

Table 3.4. Summary of ANOVA results for keystrokes per command and commands per edit. The ● denotes a significant reduction in the marked component over the course of the experiment.

Dependent measure	Component	Editor		
		EMACS	ED	EDT
Keystrokes per command	LL		●	
	MT			
Commands per edit	LL		●	●
	MT	●	●	●

Given our success at reducing execution time to number of keystrokes, we are tempted to propose that planning time can be similarly reduced. If this were possible, a very simple model of learning and performance would emerge that associates some fixed amount of overhead with each keystroke and explains all speedup in terms of reductions in keystrokes. However, the results strongly suggest that the estimation of planning time is a much more complex undertaking. First, correlations between planning time and number of keystrokes are too low. Table 3.3 shows that, whereas number of keystrokes predicts over 90 percent of the variance in execution time, it predicts only 40 percent of the variance in planning time. Of course, since both number of keystrokes and planning time are decreasing, we would expect some correlation. Second, we performed six repeated-measures ANOVAs, using planning time per key-stroke as the dependent variable, and found that both MT and LL components in all three editors were significantly decreasing on this measure (all $F(3,9) > 5.0$ all $p < .05$). Also, significant main effects and interactions were found for the various unit tasks. This is additional evidence that planning time per key-stroke is not a constant in the experiment.

Unit task learning

So far in this microanalysis we have been concerned primarily with the acquisition of four components: LL and MT planning and execution. We now increase the complexity of the analysis by a factor of 12 by decomposing the LL and MT components into their 12 constituent subgoals. These subgoals correspond to the 12 kinds of edits found in the manuscript and are derived by crossing the editing operations (insert, replace, and delete) by the data objects (character, word, string, and line). The purpose of this analysis is to gain a better understanding of the micro-structure of text editing and therefore set the stage for microanal-yses of transfer.

As it is difficult to grasp separately the independent contribu-tions of the dozens of learning components, we propose a sim-ple model to summarize the results. This model attempts to account for the MT and LL planning and execution times for 9 of the 12 subgoals over the course of the experiment, or a total of 36 components per editor. We have excluded those subgoals concerned with manipulating lines (insert line, replace line, and delete line) from the analysis for reasons to be discussed shortly. The model claims that:

1. All execution times are based solely on the number of keystrokes required to perform edits.

2. LL planning times vary only as a function of days of practice.

3. MT planning times vary not only as a function of days of practice but also as a function of editing operation (insert vs. replace vs. delete) and data complexity (character vs. word vs. string).

Our strategy for supporting the model is:

1. Use correlations to show that execution time is strictly dependent on the number of keystrokes.

2. Use ANOVAs to show that LL planning time decreases over days but is independent of subgoal.

3. Use ANOVAs to show that MT planning time decreases over days but also varies as a function of subgoal. The model predicts main effects for both editing operation and data complexity but no interaction.

As for these three lines of evidence, the first has already been established. Table 3.3 presents a series of correlations that demonstrate the strong link between number of keystrokes and execution time. Subsequent analyses confirmed the exclusive relationship between these two variables. As for the second line of evidence, 3×3 repeated measures ANOVAs, using LL planning time as the dependent measure, confirmed that in all three editors LL planning time varies only as a function of practice (all $F(3,9) > 12.08$, all $p < .001$) and not as a function of subgoal.

As for the third line of evidence, that concerning MT planning time, the pattern of results is slightly more complicated. Table 3.5 presents matrices of means for the 9 subgoals in the line editors and EMACS. Because of high variability, data from the first day of learning are excluded from this analysis. Data were

Table 3.5. Matrices of planning time means for the line editors and for EMACS.

Data object	Line editors				EMACS			
	Insert	Replace	Delete	M	Insert	Replace	Delete	M
Character	11.8	13.0	11.3	12.0	4.2	4.8	2.9	4.0
Word	16.0	15.1	13.0	14.7	3.2	6.8	4.4	4.8
String	21.6	15.7	14.9	17.4	6.2	7.8	4.7	6.2
M	16.4	14.6	13.1	14.7	4.5	6.5	4.0	5.0

collapsed across the line editors after an ANOVA comparing ED and EDT in terms of MT planning time yielded neither a main effect nor an interaction for editor. This again confirms the hypothesis that line editor MT components are virtually identical.

Table 3.5 shows the gross disparity between line editor and EMACS MT planning times, first observed in the LL/MT analysis. On average, it takes subjects less than half the time to plan their modifications in EMACs than in the line editors. Hidden within the line editor and EMACS matrices are interesting differences in fine structure as well. As predicted, two 3 × 3 repeated measures ANOVAs yielded main effects for editing operation and data object in both the line editors and EMACS. However, the EMACS ANOVA also yielded an interaction, a result inconsistent with the predictions of our simple model but apparently an anomoly due to an unnaturally low entry for the insert word cell.

Ignoring for a moment the EMACS interaction and focusing on just the row and column means, we see that, in both the line editors and EMACS, MT planning time increases monotonically with data complexity, going from 12 seconds for characters to 17.4 seconds for strings in the line editors and from 4 seconds for characters to 6.2 seconds for strings in EMACS. This result suggests that there is an effect of mental load arising from differences in amount of data on the time to plan operations that manipulate the data.

The editing operations have different relative difficulties in the line editors and EMACS. Specifically, the operations are ordered delete, replace, and insert in the line editors but delete, insert, and replace in EMACS. In EMACS, replace operations are not primitive but rather consist of a combination of insert and delete, so naturally replacement requires the most time and keystrokes. In fact, a strong prediction is that the number of replace keystrokes is simply the sum of insert and delete keystrokes. Figure 3.11 shows the EMACS keystroke data that nearly confirms this prediction, although the actual number of replace keystrokes (14.4) is somewhat lower than the sum of insert and delete keystrokes (15.7). In the line editors, the keystroke difference between insert and replace operations is negligible, but both operations are substantially higher than delete operations. Delete operations require fewer keystrokes because the second argument to the substitute command is the null string.

Line operations are excluded from our simple model because they necessarily disrupt the main effects found for editing operation and data complexity by introducing a strong interaction.

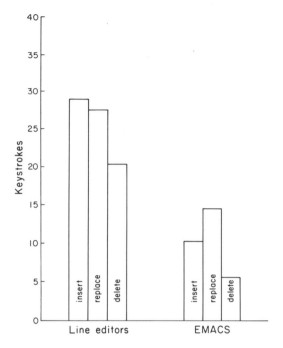

Figure 3.11. *Number of keystrokes for the three editing operations in the line editors and* EMACS.

This interaction has two sources. First, in all three editors, the predominant method for delete line operations requires just two keystrokes (*d* followed by [CR] in the line editors and ^k^k in EMACS). Therefore, the delete line operation was much lower in both MT planning time and keystrokes than the model predicted. Second, insert line operations take more planning time than replace line operations in EMACS, which is inconsistent with the general pattern. This reversal is most likely due to the difficulty subjects had "making space" for the line to be inserted, a problem documented by Mack, Lewis, and Carroll (1983).

LL and MT transfer

We observed at the macrolevel near total transfer between the line editors and moderate transfer from the line editors to EMACS. We now ask whether it is possible to localize any of these macroeffects to either the LL or the MT component. Besides shedding light on the sources of transfer, this analysis provides our first opportunity to study the intimate relation between learning and transfer in text editing. In order to guide our understanding of the empirical results, we make rough predictions based on sketchy descriptions of the underlying models. Once the basic outlines of the phenomena are understood, we compare the observed results with precise quantitative predictions.

We now compare the editors in terms of both LL and MT components to make our predictions. All three editors use different methods to locate lines. However, the LL component spans not only locate line procedures but also acquire unit task procedures and the upper-most nodes of the text-editing goal tree (see Figure 3.9). Since traversing the top nodes in the goal tree and encoding the edits are the same regardless of editor, we would expect moderate and equal degrees of transfer among the three editors in the LL component based on these rules. However, the line editors share several additional rules pertaining to the selection of LL method and also specification of the secondary carriage return method. Therefore, LL transfer between the line editors should be somewhat higher than that between the line editors and EMACS.

The degree of similarity in the line editors is even greater in the MT component. Although the surface features of the MT commands in the two line editors are largely different, their underlying conceptual structures are nearly identical. This means that the line editor MT procedures share many high-level and intermediate-level nodes in their goal trees. For example, to insert a line in ED, one moves to the line above the line to be inserted and types *a* for *append*. In EDT, one moves to the line below the line to be inserted and types *i* for *insert*. To exit the insert mode in ED, one types a period by itself on a line immediately followed by a carriage return. To exit the insert mode in EDT, one presses ^z. Although these methods are quite different in surface symbols typed, they have the same underlying logical structure. This common structure is a likely source of positive transfer in the MT component.

Although line editor MT procedures are quite similar, line editor and EMACS MT procedures are largely different. However, they do share several rules for generating the top MT nodes in the goal tree and for inserting text. Therefore, in the MT component we predict nearly total transfer between the line editors but substantially less transfer from the line editors to EMACS.

Transfer between Line Editors. Table 3.6 presents line editor learning and transfer data for LL and MT planning time. We focus on planning time because it is not affected by such factors

Table 3.6. LL/MT planning time transfer. The raw numbers from which the transfer score is calculated are second, to plan an operation.

Transfer condition	Locate line		Modify text	
	To ED	To EDT	To ED	To EDT
Between line editors				
Transfer(3)	10.0	17.4	13.1	14.8
Learning(1)	19.0	44.7	45.9	53.3
Learning(3)	9.2	13.5	12.8	16.5
Transfer score (equation 3.2)	91%	87%	99%	105%
	From line editors	From typing	From line editors	From typing
To EMACS				
Transfer(5)	14.0	19.6	12.9	20.7
Learning(1)	27.0	27.0	27.6	27.6
Learning(5)	5.7	5.7	4.0	4.0
Transfer score (equation 3.2)	61%	35%	62%	29%

as typing speed and is therefore our purest measure of higher-level cognitive processing. Data are averaged across the first two days of learning and transfer for additional reliability.

To characterize the magnitude of transfer, we use a transfer score introduced by Katona (1940) which measures the savings on a transfer task relative to a theoretical upper limit derived from learning data. This formula has the useful property that it is insensitive to the amount of training prior to transfer, since the transfer savings (the numerator) is modulated by the degree of learning (the denominator). If subjects transfer to a new editor on day n of the experiment, the percentage of transfer is given by the following equation:

$$(3.2) \quad T_{\%learning} = \frac{M_{lrn}(1) - M_{tran}(n)}{M_{lrn}(1) - M_{lrn}(n)} \times 100$$

This is simply transfer equation (1.3).

The major result in the top half of Table 3.6 is that the MT component exhibits more transfer than the LL component, with means of 102 percent and 89 percent respectively. This is what an identical productions models would predict, given that the line editor MT procedures have more in common than the LL procedures. Although MT transfer is slightly larger, LL transfer is still quite substantial.

Both editors have as a secondary LL method the use of the carriage return to move forward one line in the file. It may be that a source of positive transfer is this secondary method. To test this hypothesis, we characterized the LL methods used in the line editors as either primary, that is, line addressing (*10p*) in ED and string searching (*t 'unique'*) in EDT, or secondary, that is, the carriage return method. Figure 3.12 presents the results of this analysis. The use of the secondary method is more common in the transfer subjects, although a two-way ANOVA confirming

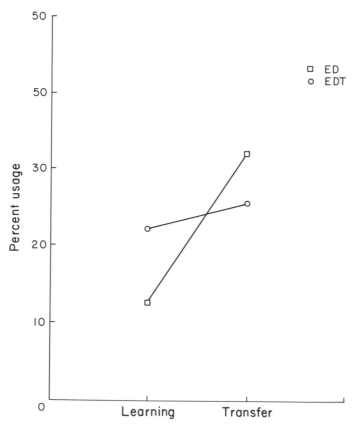

Figure 3.12. *Frequency of use of the secondary carriage return method for locating lines in the line editors.*

the difference was only marginally significant ($F(1,12) = 2.1$, $p <$ .2). It appears, however, that subjects transferring to a new line editor rely more on a secondary but familiar procedure for locating lines. This result suggests a general rule that, when more than one method is available, known methods assume an unnaturally prominant role in transfer tasks.

Another source of LL transfer from ED to EDT lies not in ED's LL component but rather in its MT component. It turns out that the specification of unique search strings when locating lines in EDT is very similar to the specification of unique replacement strings when substituting text in ED. Although these subprocedures run in service of quite different high-level goals, in our model the upper nodes rewrite to identical subgoals that involve the same subprocedures. In this way, the MT string specification subprocedure in ED can be transferred whole cloth to service an LL goal in EDT.

Transfer to EMACS. The bottom half of Table 3.6 summarizes LL and MT planning time transfer from the line editors and typing to EMACS. As with the line editor data, means are averaged across the first two days of learning and transfer. LL transfer from the line editors to EMACS is somewhat smaller than that between the line editors themselves, as predicted. The additional LL transfer sites in the line editors explain this difference. The amount of LL transfer from typing is less than that from the line editors, but is still greater than zero. To understand planning time transfer from typing, recall that subjects in the typing control group were required to type the edits that were marked on the manuscript. This means that they had practice encoding the edits from the manuscript. However, they had no exposure to the text-editing goal tree, as they were typing continuous text and not locating lines and modifying text. This explains the difference in LL transfer between the line editor and typing control groups.

The average MT transfer from the line editors and typing control to EMACS is 46 percent, definitely less than the 102 percent observed between ED and EDT. However, this still seems rather high, given that EMACS MT procedures share very little with line editor MT procedures, and there is no text modification per se in the typing manipulation at all. Here, then, is an interesting challenge to the identical elements model. Possible sources of transfer include such low-level operations as glancing at the manuscript and using the proper keying action on control and escape keys, but our data are unable to provide support for such claims. An additional candidate is the encode edit component proposed as a source of LL transfer. Unlike the experts observed by Card et al. (1983), our subjects often required more than one look at the manuscript to represent edits, especially those manipulating strings and lines. Often these additional looks occurred after the modification had been located, that is, during the period attributed to MT planning. More efficient encoding procedures gained through experience with the line editors and the typing manipulation would thus contribute to MT transfer. Although this and the other proposed sources might contribute to transfer, as a group, they seem insufficient to account for the magnitude of transfer observed. We therefore suspend any firm conclusions at this time. A better understanding of this perplexing result must wait for the results of the last and most detailed analysis.

MT unit task transfer

The outstanding question concerning transfer from the LL/MT analysis involves the source of the rather substantial transfer in the MT component from the line editors and typing to EMACS. Currently, the candidates include portions of the upper-level goal tree (good only for line editor subjects) and subskills for encoding the edit from the manuscript (good for both sets of subjects). Analysis of the differential transfer of all 12 MT unit tasks can help to localize the transfer of particular operators.

Table 3.7 presents transfer scores expressing MT planning

Table 3.7. MT planning time transfer to EMACS. All numbers are expressed as percentages (equation 3.2).

Data object	Training condition	Editing operation		
		Insert	Replace	Delete
Character	Line editor	90	77	90
	Typing	26	−39	89
Word	Line editor	48	77	83
	Typing	28	50	74
String	Line editor	64	43	28
	Typing	71	35	−98
Line	Line editor	33	58	77
	Typing	−8	12	29

time transfer from the line editors and typing to EMACS. Once again, the scores are based on data from the first two days of learning and transfer. There is no evidence for any general trend of the type observed in the unit-task learning data. Overall, the transfer data is much more variable and irregular. To facilitate its interpretation, we plot the savings scores along number lines which show the relative orderings of the various subgoals. Figure 3.13 shows this representation of the data.

Rather than attempt to understand the entire continuum of subgoal transfer data, we focus on those subgoals at either end of the distribution, that is, those that exhibit the most and least transfer. Interestingly, the delete character subgoal shows the most transfer and the delete string subgoal the least in both line editor and typing distributions. Another strong performer for both groups is the delete word subgoal, whereas the delete line subgoal is strong for only line editor subjects.

What might explain such a pattern of results? Most compelling is the fact that these extreme sites are all instances of delete operations. Furthermore, in both the line editors and the typing control, subjects do learn a deletion operator that could transfer to EMACS: the delete key. The delete key is used to edit malformed commands in the line editors and to correct typos in the typing control. So, although the delete key is not used as part of any text-editing method that can be transferred whole cloth to EMACS, it nevertheless might be available for use as the termi-

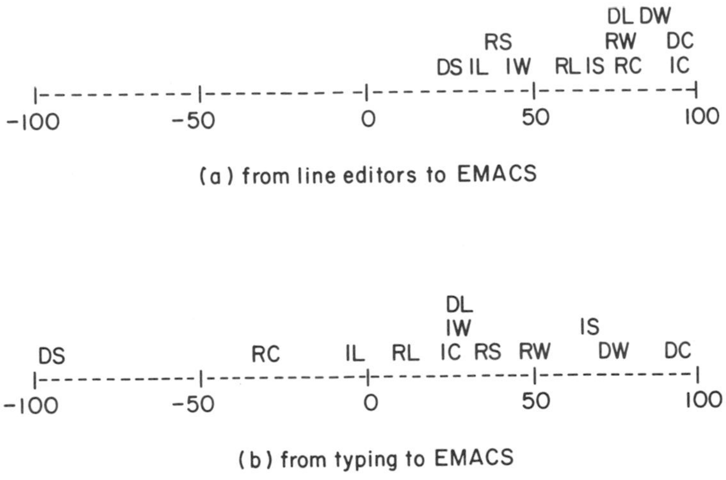

(a) from line editors to EMACS

(b) from typing to EMACS

Figure 3.13. *Number line showing ordering of unit tasks in terms of MT planning time transfer.*

nal node in the goal tree of some new method. This would explain not only the high level of positive transfer for the delete character and delete word subgoals, but also the low-level and even negative transfer for the delete string subgoals. There are much more efficient methods for deleting strings in EMACS than the repetitive use of the delete key.

An earlier analysis of the transfer of LL methods between the line editors suggested that, if many methods exist for accomplishing a goal, and most are new but one is familiar, the familiar method will be favored. When this general rule is applied to the present situation, if the delete key is in fact a source of transfer to EMACS, line editor and typing control subjects should use the delete key more often in EMACS than should EMACS control subjects. Examining the deletion methods used on the first day of learning and transfer, we found that, whereas EMACS control subjects used the delete key in 50 percent of their methods, line editor and typing control subjects used it in 68 percent of theirs. This result suggests that the delete key is being transferred.

This does not explain why the delete line subgoal shows a high level of positive transfer in the line editor group but not the typing control. In EMACS, the delete line operation is distinguished from other deletion operations by a specialized method so efficient it precludes the use of the delete key. This method has the same goal structure as the delete line method in the line editors but involves different keystrokes. In all three editors, one moves to the line requiring deletion and types the delete line operator. (In the line editors the operator is *d,* and in EMACS, it is ^k^k.) There is no such goal structure in the typing control; hence the difference in delete line transfer.

Here, then, in the delete operations are two additional sources of MT transfer to EMACS. The first, the delete key, contributes to either positive or negative transfer, depending upon its interaction with unit task. The second, the delete line goal structure, exists in only the line editor group and thereby contributes to the difference between line editor and typing control transfer. These specific cases illustrate the general point that, although text modification procedures in the line editors and EMACS are quite different in terms of overall goal structure, the two do share a number of leaf components.

Summary of microanalysis

Our microanalysis of the data provides support for two general conclusions. First, degree of transfer does seem to be a function of the overlap in number of elements. Information-processing models like GOMS help to define shared goal structures which serve as a basis for positive transfer. For instance, the massive transfer in MT between the line editors was mediated by identical goal structures underlying the different physical commands. Alternatively, in cases where tasks do not share goal structures, there can still be considerable transfer at the level of leaf nodes. This is the kind of superficial transfer that Thorndike would have identified.

Second, a complex task like text editing can be decomposed into parts, and each part seems to be learned separately. For instance, components like LL are performed and learned independently of the context in which they occur. Also, time to perform highly practiced components such as typing do not speed up while the planning components show very rapid speedup. Finally, various components of the task seem to decompose cleanly into planning and execution time.

In short, while the task of text editing is complex, under the right analyses the underlying behavior is not. In line with Simon's (1969) long-standing claims, the complexity of behavior *simply* reflects the complexity of the task.

Simulation Models and Quantitative Predictions

Up to now, we have been content to make transfer predictions based on rather qualitative analyses of similarity. We now make quantitative predictions of transfer based on detailed task analyses of text-editing skill in the three editors. The product of these task analyses is a set of production system models which simulate skilled, error-free text-editing behavior in each of the editors. The underlying goal structures used in our models are based largely on the GOMS keystroke level analysis of Card et al. (1983). The GOMS model uses a strict hierarchical control structure to model expert, error-free text-editing behavior. With such a restricted goal structure, the GOMS model is not a true instance of a production system, although it can be easily adapted to one. To recast the GOMS model as a production system, we assume that several productions fire to create the top-level goal structure shown in Figure 3.9. In response to each of these major goals, additional productions fire to create subgoals and eventually actions. This production system analysis is essentially identical to the GOMS formulation. In our simulations, we use the GRAPES production system language (Sauers and Farrell, 1982), which supports the construction of hierarchical goal trees and restricts production firings to those relevant to the current goal.

Using such production system models, a first approximation to a transfer prediction involves comparing two sets of productions for different editors. To the extent that the production sets overlap, transfer is positive from one skill to the other. To get a somewhat more accurate prediction, we assign weights to the productions according to their frequency of use in the transfer task. A production which fires frequently in the transfer task contributes more to the time estimate than one that fires seldomly. This point figures prominently, because the productions which generate the upper-level goal structures common to all editors are relatively high-frequency productions, firing in service of every unit task.

A total of 107 distinct production rules are used to simulate behavior in the three editors. A good proportion of these rules do double-duty, applying in more than one editor. Table 3.8 summarizes the rules and categorizes them in terms of whether they contribute to the LL component or the MT component. Furthermore, these rules are categorized according to their range of application. The categories are:

1. *General.* Rule applies in all three editors.
2. *Line.* Rule applies in both line editors, ED and EDT.
3. *ED.* Rule is specific to ED.
4. *EDT.* Rule is specific to EDT.
5. *Screen.* Rule is specific to EMACS.

Table 3.8. Categories of rules and their frequencies in the text-editing simulations.

Component	Category	Number of rules	Total frequency
LL	General	6	96.0
	Line	10	55.4
	ED	5	49.7
	EDT	7	73.4
	Screen	20	151.0
MT	General	3	32.0
	Line	24	105.3
	ED	6	23.0
	EDT	5	14.0
	Screen	22	88.0

There are no rules that are common to a specific line and screen editor, such as EDT and EMACS.

Table 3.8 also shows estimates for total frequencies of occurrence for each set of rules. These estimates were derived by simulating each production set on 10 randomly selected trials from the experimental manuscript. The numbers reflect the average number of firings of a rule on any two trials that contain the 12 kinds of edits subjects had to perform. Thus, for a rule that fires once on every unit task, such as the rule that sets the subgoals of locate line and modify text, the frequency of occurrence is 12. The numbers in the table are simply summations over all rules in the set.

Four rules common to all editors are not represented in Table 3.8 and make no contribution to our calculations. Two of these are rules for typing, and it has been shown in the learning analyses that there is virtually no speedup in the execution (that is, typing) component. It is a general principle that a component which exhibits no learning can have no impact on transfer. Therefore, we exclude typing productions from the analysis. The productions shown in the table contribute solely to the various planning components, so we restrict ourselves to predictions of planning time in these transfer analyses. The other two excluded rules concern failing to acquire the next unit task and terminating with success when the acquire unit task goal fails. These rules fire in succession at the very end of each trial, and the associated pause is not included in any of our measurements. Since it is impossible, given space limitations, to describe each rule in detail, we give brief descriptions of each category and one or two examples.

LL General contains rules for generating the upper levels of the goal tree in Figure 3.9 and rules for acquiring edits from the manuscript. An Englishified version of one rule is:

execute-unit-task-General

    IF   the goal is to execute-unit-task
THEN   set as subgoals to
          1. locate line
          2. modify text.

These are all relatively high-frequency rules and therefore make strong contributions to LL transfer among the editors.

LL Line contains rules for deciding between primary and secondary LL methods in the line editors, terminating commands with carriage return (this rule also appears in MT Line), recognizing when movement is and is not required, and determining whether a string search is successful and how to pad the string to make it unique. These rules apply only in EDT, since ED uses number rather than string addressing methods for locating lines. However, these rules appear in the MT component of ED, since unique strings must often be selected as arguments to the substitution command. Therefore, these rules appear in the LL Line category rather than in the LL EDT.

An Englishified version of a rule from this set is:

choose-LL-secondary-Line

IF   the goal is to choose a command
       and the supergoal is to locate line
       and the current line is = line1
       and the target line is = line2
       and = line2 is immediately after = line1
THEN   use the secondary carriage return method.

This rule implements the decision rule to select carriage return to move down a single line. This secondary method is of course common to both line editors.

LL ED contains rules which specify the primary LL method in ED and rules which court lines of the manuscript in order to supply the line number argument. The rules that specifies the method is:

LL-primary-method-ED

IF   the goal is to enter a command
       and the command is LL-primary
THEN   set as subgoals to
       1. specify the line number
       2. specify the command symbol.

This rule ultimately leads to the generation of a command such as *10p,* which positions the user on the tenth line of the file.

LL EDT contains rules which specify the primary LL method in EDT and rules for iterating through lines of the manuscript to test the uniqueness of a search string. The rule that specifies the primary LL method in EDT is:

LL-primary-method-EDT

IF   the goal is to ender a command
       and the command is LL-primary
THEN   set as subgoals to
       1. specify the command symbol

2. specify the search string delimiter
3. specify the search string
4. specify the search string delimiter.

This rule leads to the generation of a command such as *t 'hello'*, which positions the user on the first line containing the string *hello* following the current line.

LL Screen includes rules for choosing among the various LL operators in EMACS (such as forward-word, backward-word, beginning-of-line) and special-case rules for stopping in position depending upon the direction of movement. For example, the user stops immediately to the right of certain modifications when coming from the right, but immediately to the left when coming from the left. Two distinct rules are required to model this behavior. Generally, the locate line methods in screen editors like EMACS are much more precise than those in the line editors, since both horizontal and vertical positions are specified.

The rule that chooses to apply the forward-word operator is:

choose-forward-word-Screen

> IF   the goal is to move horizontally on a line
> and the cursor is to the left of the modification
> and one or more words separate the cursor and the
> site of the modification
> THEN   choose forward word.

A separate rule retrieves the command symbol associated with the forward-word operator. For example, this rule retrieves the binding for forward-word:

forward-word-Screen

> IF   the goal is to specify the command symbol
> and the command to be executed is forward-word
> THEN   set as a subgoal to type]f.

MT General contains rules for setting the upper-level goal structure for modifying text, inserting text within a particular method, and verifying the location of an edit. This last operation is technically part of LL but is counted as part of MT by our parsing algorithm.

This rule sets the goal structure for modify text:

modify-text-General

> IF   the goal is to modify-text
> THEN   set as subgoals to

1. choose a method
2. use the chosen method
3. verify the edit.

MT Line contains the many rules shared by the line editors for MT . Some of these are rules for selecting a particular MT operator; others concern the specification of string arguments to the heavily used substitution command. In the latter category, many rules deal with the management of space. For example, one rule states that if the goal is to delete text that has space on both sides, then one of those spaces should also be deleted. Similar considerations come into play for text insertion. For example, this rule deals with the insertion of a word or string of words into a line of text:

second-argument-insert-middle-space-Line

IF   the goal is to specify the second argument to the substitution command
and the modification is the insertion of a word or string of words
THEN   pad the insertion with a space on the end.

This rule ensures that all words are separated by spaces following text insertion.

MT ED rules retrieve the particular MT command buildings for ED. For example, this rules retrieves the binding for replace-line:

replace-line-ED

IF   the goal is to specify the command symbol
and the command is replace-line
THEN   set as a subgoal to type *c*.

MT EDT rules supply the command bindings for EDT and are almost completely analogous to those in MT ED. One difference is that the rule for supplying the syntactic terminator for the substitution command in ED is missing in EDT, since no syntactic terminator is required (see Figure 3.1).

MT Screen rules concern the selection of MT methods in screen editors like EMACS and also the management of space, which is also a source of common rules in the line editors. As an example of the former type, this rule selects the kill-line deletion method:

choose-kill-line-Screen

IF   the goal is to delete text
and the deletion spans the entire line
THEN   use the kill-line method.

As an example of the latter type, the next rule checks for super-fluous space following a deletion:

too-much-space-Screen

> IF the goal is to check for space following a deletion
> and the cursor is positioned on a space character
> and the character to the left is also a space character
> THEN delete the previous character.

In addition, four rules in this category specify the command bindings for the four deletion operators in EMACS. Several examples of these kinds of rules have been shown already.

This completes our description of the rule sets used to simulate behavior in the editors. One remaining task is to identify the rules that in our view are practiced by the typing control group and are transferred to EMACS. Typing control subjects must acquire edits from the manuscript and therefore practice two high-frequency rules from LL General. As for MT, subjects practice only a single rule from the MT Screen category, which states that if the goal is to insert text, then set as a subgoal to type that text (the typing interface, like the screen editors, was always in the insert mode).

Given this task analysis, we are now in a position to make quantitative predictions of LL and MT planning time transfer for all conditions. The method is simply to sum the production frequencies for a particular editor and then figure the percentage of firings that involve known rules. Of course, the known rules are defined by our various categories and differ depending on the particular transfer condition being modeled. For example, to calculate percentage transfer for LL from ED to EDT, one would use the formula:

$$(3.3)\ T_{predicted} = \frac{f_{LL\ General} + f_{LL\ Line}}{f_{LL\ General} + f_{LL\ Line} + f_{LL\ EDT}} \times 100$$

Here f_x is the sum of production frequencies for category x. In this case, the numerator represents the rules shared by the line editor LL components, and the denominator represents the entire set of rules required for LL in EDT. Instantiating this formula, we get: $(96 + 55.4) / (96 + 55.4 + 73.4) \times 100 = 67\%$.

Whereas equation (3.3) generates our theoretical predictions, we use a different equation, equation (3.2), to measure transfer empirically. At first blush, the equivalence of equations (3.3) and (3.2) is not apparent. However, in Chapter 9 we will show that equation (3.2) can be reduced to equation (3.3) under a certain set of assumptions:

1. All productions take roughly the same amount of time to learn and execute.

2. Exposure to the training task does not affect the structure of the transfer task.

3. Common elements occur with roughly the same frequencies in the training and transfer tasks.

4. Measures of subject performance are aggregated over roughly the same number of trials in training and transfer tasks.

Violations of these assumptions may account for certain discrepancies between predicted and observed values.

Table 3.9 presents predicted and observed transfer percentages for the various conditions from both experiments in tabular form, and Figure 3.14 presents that same data in graphic form. Generally, we see a remarkably good fit between predicted and observed values; the correlation between these sets of points is .98. This represents an almost perfect linear relationship between the production overlap predictions and empirical measures of transfer. This linear relationship is:

$$(3.4)\ T_{obs} = .26 + .88T_{pred}$$

Here T_{obs} is the observed transfer and T_{pred} is the theoretical prediction. Unfortunately, this equation is less than perfect, because it predicts greater than 100 percent transfer when

Table 3.9. Predicted and observed transfer percentages (equations 3.3 and 3.2, respectively) for all transfer conditions in the text-editing experiment.

Component	Training editor	Transfer editor	Predicted transfer	Observed transfer
LL	ED	EDT	68%	87%
	EDT	ED	75	91
	Line	EMACS	39	61
	Typing	EMACS	19	35
MT	ED	EDT	90	105
	EDT	ED	85	99
	Line	EMACS	27	62
	Typing	EMACS	7	29

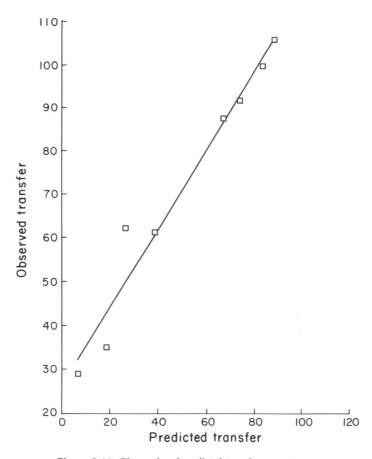

Figuer 3.14. *Observed and predicted transfer percentages.*

$T_{pred} = 1$, that is, when there is total production overlap. It appears that in all eight cases we are underpredicting the amount of observed transfer.

One simplifying assumption (assumption 1 above) made throughout this analysis is that all productions have equal cost in terms of learning and therefore contribute equally to transfer. However, given the systematic bias in our predictions, we may be assigning inappropriate weights to the components of transfer. Specifically, we are apparently underestimating the contribution of the general components and overestimating the contribution of the specific components. Looking at the low extreme case, we find ourselves predicting about 13 percent transfer in the case of typing to EMACS and observing about 32 percent. The typing condition and EMACS share a high-frequency production that encodes edits from the manuscript. It is perhaps reasonable that there is more to a production that interprets the edit marks on a line than many of the productions specific to EMACS, such as a production that issues the ^f keystroke. Looking at the high extreme case, we predict 79 percent transfer between the line editors and observe 96 percent. This suggests that the productions specific to the line editors are being overweighted. Again, it is not unreasonable to suppose that a production which issues the *p* command is less costly to learn than a production which decides among methods.

To identify the appropriate weightings, we could rewrite the linear transfer equation as:

$$(3.5) \quad T_{obs} = \frac{T_{pred} + G}{1 + G - S}$$

Here the $+G$ represents the extra emphasis needed for the general productions, and the $-S$ represents the lesser emphasis needed for the terminal productions unique to an editor. Without these adjustments, equation (3.5) reduces to the simple equation $T_{obs} = T_{pred}$. When $G = .3$ and $S = .16$, equation (3.5) reduces to equation (3.4).

In summary, we are encouraged by the close linear relationship between observed and predicted transfer. The fact that we do not get the simple equation $T_{obs} = T_{pred}$ probably reflects the fact that different productions deserve different weightings in the transfer equation.

Conclusion

The analysis of transfer in the text-editing experiment has implications for the identical productions model of transfer. The very high level of positive transfer observed between text editors that shared few commands reinforces the position that superficial identical elements models of the type that Thorndike advocated are inadequate. The fact that most of the transfer was localized in the planning components provides further support for an abstract representation of elements, as in our ACT* production system models.

Our ability to predict magnitudes of positive transfer is further evidence not only for the identical productions model of transfers but also for the GOMS model of text-editing skill upon which it is based. Transfer predictions are most likely to be correct when based upon the kind of thorough rational and empirical task analysis provided by GOMS. However, although our GOMS-based identical elements model was quite successful at making relative predictions, it was less able to predict the magnitude of transfer in absolute terms. Putting aside the difficulties resulting from inaccurate task analyses, quantitative predictions are still quite difficult when studying a complex skill such as text editing in full-blown form. One reason for the difficulty is that, in an editor with close to full functionality, subjects are confronted with many choices concerning methods for accomplishing particular edits. One subject may fixate on a method in a training editor which figures prominently in a transfer editor, whereas another may fixate on a method which has no role in the transfer editor at all. As a result, the first subject exhibits more transfer than the second. This difficulty arises whenever methods and strategic knowledge play a prominent role in a skill. Unless subjects are forced to practice certain components, transfer will be indeterminate to some degree.

Our observation that subjects tended to carry over methods adds a qualtitative dimension to transfer as well as a quantitative one. Specifically, transfer subjects relied more heavily on the secondary carriage return method for locating lines in the line editors and the delete key to modify text in EMACS. In such cases, the application of the known method may yield positive or negative transfer, depending on whether the method is optimal in the transfer task. Of course, transfer of methods is just another case of transfer of productions, but it clearly complicates using production overlap to make quantitative predictions of certain performances measures like time.

The sharp discrepancy between the amount of improvement in planning time versus typing time reinforces the methodological point that transfer of a complex skill involves the independent contributions of many components at different levels of learning. Those components that exhibit little learning in the training task have negligible effect on performance in the transfer task.

4 / Negative Transfer

At first glance, our identical elements theory seems to make a rather counterintuitive prediction concerning negative transfer, namely that it does not exist. Our simple prediction is that transfer is a function of overlap in productions between two tasks. One might conclude that the worst possible transfer situation is when there is no overlap between two sets of productions, in which case transfer is zero, not negative.

However, claims of negative transfer abound. For instance, a considerable amount of folklore surrounding the use of computers concerns the negative transfer suffered in moving from one system to another. We can personally testify to the negative transfer we suffer between different dialects of LISP. We are often confused, for instance, about the names of certain functions and the order of arguments. However, complaints such as ours are not convincing as evidence against identical elements theories. Presumably, by any aggregate measure, we perform much better in one dialect of LISP as a consequence of learning another, as measured against a naive control. The few loci of negative transfer require refined measurements to identify and are dominated completely by the positive effects. It turns out that negative transfer at the aggregate level is quite difficult to observe experimentally.

Upon closer inspection, however, we see that there are two possible sources of negative transfer in our simple identical-productions model. One is the transfer of nonoptimal methods, which we observed at least once (the use of the delete key) in the text-editing experiment. In this case, the transfer of productions is perfect and complete. However, even though the productions apply in the transfer task, they are nonoptimal relative to what control subjects would acquire through a more direct exposure.

The second possible source of negative transfer is the transfer of productions whose conditions match but whose actions are completely inappropriate in the transfer task. In this case, a subject has failed to discriminate properly between training and transfer tasks and mistakenly applies productions which are overly general. To remedy the situation, subjects must learn new productions whose conditions are more specific and whose actions are suited to the transfer task.

These first two types of negative transfer are relatively easy to detect in that they lead to behaviors that deviate in a qualitative way from optimal behavior. In both cases, subjects mistakenly believe that they know what is appropriate in certain situations and fail to realize that new productions must be learned. For this reason, we characterize the interference in these cases as *acquisition interference*. This simply means that old productions are interfering with the acquisition of new productions.

There is a third type of negative transfer, however, whose origin is more subtle and whose presence is more difficult to detect. This final type may be thought of as true procedural interference in that the presence of one production may actually disrupt the *performance* of another, rather than simply the acquisition of another. True procedural interference is a logical consequence of the implementation of pattern matching in the ACT* theory (see Anderson, 1983, ch. 4). The theory states that when a set of productions shares conditions that match the same elements in working memory, the matching of any single production from the set takes longer because it is competing with the other productions for activation from the elements.

In ACT*, productions are matched through the use of activation-based data flow networks similar to the ones used in McClelland and Rumelhart's interactive activation model (1981) and Forgy's RETE algorithm (1979). In the network, activation spreads from source nodes, which are active elements in working memory, to intermediate-level nodes, which are individual tests and pairwise conjunctions of tests from the left-hand sides of productions, and finally to top-level nodes, which represent individual production rules. When the level of activation exceeds some threshold at a top-level production node, the production fires. Interference in the network arises from the fact that productions sharing intermediate level nodes in the network (that is, sharing tests on the left-hand sides) are connected through inhibitory links. Through these links, strongly activated productions drive down the activation of weakly activated productions until a single production emerges as the undisputed choice on a particular matching cycle. The overall effect of the inhibitory links on performance, however, is to lengthen the amount of time it takes for any production to fire when there are multiple partial matches. The amount of interference is directly related to the number of shared tests on the left-hand sides.

It is unclear to what extent this third type of negative transfer disrupts performance in normal situations. We suspect that in most cases it is a rather subtle effect that is dominated by the other transfer sources we have enumerated, both positive and negative. True procedural interference has generally been difficult to observe experimentally, although certain well-known instances exist. One such instance is the Stroop effect (1935), where subjects are shown words printed in different colors and are asked to say the color of the word. Subjects have trouble with this task when the word happens to spell the name of a color that differs from the color of the ink. For example, a troublesome stimulus might be the word *yellow* printed in red ink. Generally, subjects take longer to say the color of the ink in these cases and sometimes mistakenly blurt out the word itself. Interestingly, Cohen, Dunbar and McClelland (in preparation) recently proposed a connectionist model of the Stroop effect which uses many of the same ideas presented here concerning shared nodes and inhibitory links.

Negative Transfer in Historical Perspective

The first two types of negative transfer, nonoptimal and overly general methods, are well documented in the classic work by Luchins (1942) on the Einstellung effect. *Einstellung* is the German word for *set* and refers to the tendency of subjects to become mechanical in their choice of methods when solving a sequence of similar problems. Luchins gave his subjects a series of waterjug problems which involved the pouring of water into and between jugs of various sizes in order to get a desired quantity. For example, if jugs A, B, and C held the quantities 15, 39, and 3 fluid ounces, respectively, and the goal was to get 18 fluid ounces, then one solution (denoted $B - A - 2C$) would be to fill B, fill A from B, and fill C from B twice ($39 - 15 - 3 - 3 = 18$). A more direct solution would be simply to combine A and C into B ($A + C$). Luchins gave his subjects five training and five transfer problems. The training problems could be solved only by the B − A − 2C method. The first two transfer problems could be solved by both B − A − 2C and a more direct method (such as A + C), the third problem could be solved only by the direct method (A + C), and the last two problems could once again be solved by both methods. Thus, Luchins encouraged the acquisition of a method which was alternately nonoptimal and completely inappropriate on transfer problems.

Luchins found that training on the first five problems caused subjects to overlook almost completely the more direct solution on the first two transfer problems. In a preliminary experiment involving 11 subjects, not a single subject noticed the simpler solution. Here, then, is the case of transfer of nonoptimal methods. Luchins pointed out that mechanization in these cases is not necessarily bad and may in fact be adaptive from a cognitive economy standpoint. Subjects are spared the work of searching for a solution and are in many cases faster than control subjects.

Luchins found, however, that his subjects also performed much worse on the third transfer problem (the one not admitting a B − A − 2C solution) than control subjects who had solved no problems. In one experiment involving college seniors, only 39 percent of the experimental subjects could even find a solution to the problem, compared with a 100 percent success rate for control subjects. Thus, it appears that his subjects were fixated on a method that was not just nonoptimal but completely wrong, and this blinded them to the possibility of other methods. Luchins explains this result in terms of subjects making the mistaken generalization that all problems were of the same type and could be solved by the same method. Consequently, subjects did not confront each problem on its own merits and simply lapsed into the mechanical application of a known method.

This, then, is one of the few reported instances of negative transfer at the aggregate level. One additional instance comes from the realm of verbal learning. The classic interference experiment involved learning two lists of paired associates which had the same stimuli but different responses. The standard result was that recall of the second list was worse as a consequence of learning the first list (Postman 1971).

Although we have now cited two instances of negative transfer at the aggregate level, in most cases the effect is quite hard to capture in the laboratory (Bilodeau and Bilodeau, 1961; Hammerton, 1981; Newell 1981). In fact, Osgood's transfer surface, which represents a largely successful effort to summarize the verbal learning transfer literature, was critized primarily for the unreliability of many of its predictions concerning negative transfer (Bower and Hilgard, 1981). Part of the confusion concerning negative transfer has stemmed from the fact that the likelihood of observing the effect depended upon how transfer was measured. The standard result in studies of verbal learning and perceptual-motor skill is that negative transfer is quite short-lived, having a half-life on the order of a few trials (Lewis, 1959; Bilodeau & Bilodeau, 1961; Hammerton, 1981). Therefore, if a researcher takes a short-sighted view and measures performance on only a single or perhaps several trials on the transfer task (as in the two instances of aggregate negative transfer already reported), negative transfer is likely to be observed in certain cases. However, if one takes an extended view and measures performance over, say, dozens of trials, negative transfer rapidly convert to positive transfer (Bilodeau and Bilodeau, 1961). Thus, there is often a lack of correlation between initial performance and long-term savings.

An interesting illustration of this discrepancy comes from the study of perceptual-motor skill, specifically the study of simulators as substitutes for direct practice on complex tasks, such as flying an airplane (Holding, 1981). A large part of the skill of flying involves making the appropriate motor responses to a variety of stimuli or signals, primarily visual ones. Simulators have been designed which attempt to capture the essence of many of these stimulus-response connections but which necessarily cannot replicate the totality of the flying experience. For example, a simple simulator might involve moving a control-stick in response to the movement of a dial or pointer. Real flying is of course much more complex than this, and trainees often experience negative transfer on their first flight after practice on a simple simulator. This effect has been attributed to *stimulus compounding*, the difficulty associated with detecting and attending to the relevant training stimuli among a sea of new and distracting stimuli (Hammerton, 1981). Nonetheless, if long-term savings rather than initial performance is of primary interest, even the simplest simulators have been shown to be remarkably effective (Hammerton, 1967). For example, Flexman, Matheny, and Brown (1950) reported significant reductions in dual-control hours following practice on a simulator which presents an "artificial horizon" to trainees consisting of nothing more than a line on a board held up by an instructor. This reinforces the general point that, over time, negative transfer gives way to positive transfer.

To interpret what is happening in these situations requires a slight refinement of the identical productions model. This refinement involves consideration of the hitherto ignored declarative component out of which productions are compiled. Recall the two sources of negative transfer, one involving the transfer of nonoptimal methods and the other involving the transfer of plainly incorrect methods. Our claim is that, in most practical situations where savings measures are of primary concern, only nonoptimal methods make a lasting and nonnegligible contribution to negative transfer. Incorrect methods are quickly discerned and supplanted by new productions which have been compiled from properly discriminated declarative encodings. This process is greatly facilitated by a learning environment that is highly reactive. It is the declarative precursors which are discriminated, not the productions themselves. This position, which differs from the view put forth in Anderson (1983), arose from recent studies of skill acquisition which suggested that discrimination processes were under the conscious control of subjects and operated on declarative structures (Lewis and Anderson, 1985). Productions which produce clearly inappropriate actions contribute to poor initial performance on a transfer task but are quickly weeded out. Productions which produce actions which are merely nonoptimal, however, are more difficult to detect and persist for longer periods. Our claim is that these nonoptimal methods constitute the sole source of negative procedural transfer in the limit.

Although negative transfer is a well-established phenomenon, this fact need not disconfirm the identical productions model. That model makes no necessary prediction about performance. It says only that productions will transfer wholly and completely from one task to another when they can. Whether this results in improved performance depends on whether the productions are optimal for the task.

One might conclude that these caveats concerning negative transfer take away some of the predictive power of an identical productions model. However, they only eliminate a program like Thorndikes's from trying to predict aggregate performance on the basis of a superficial analysis. There are a number of ways to make the theory testable:

1. Develop detailed models of the production overlap and make predictions on that basis.
2. Examine transfer of methods at specific loci.
3. Get convergent measures, such as protocols, for the hypothesis of transfer of inappropriate methods.

Negative Transfer in Text Editing

Our claim, once again, is that nonoptimal methods constitute the sole source of negative transfer after extended practice on a transfer task. Consequently, it seems clear that in most cases the identical productions theory predicts that transfer will be largely positive when there is much production overlap. The few exceptions to this rule concern those situations where some key productions apply which are very nonoptimal. Typically, these productions fire at the very top of the goal tree and force a highly unnatural decomposition of the task. In most cases, however, transfer at the aggregate level is positive.

In order to press this issue of negative transfer to the limit, we tried to create a situation where the identical productions model would be committed to predicting large positive transfer and yet where intuition told us we would get negative transfer. We accomplished this by importing a classic interference paradigm from verbal learning into the domain of text editing. For our purposes, we created a new, special kind of editor for the transfer task. This editor is identical to EMACS, with the one exception that all the control and escape keys are replaced or scrambled. For example, in regular EMACS, ^d deletes a character and ^e moves to the end of a line, whereas in this new editor, ^d moves down a line and ^e deletes a word. In all, almost half of the commands in the new editor are bound to keys used for contrary purposes in EMACS, with the remainder bound to entirely new keys. For obvious reasons, we call this new editor perverse EMACS.

Were a subject to learn EMACS first and then perverse EMACS, it would be reasonable to expect a lot of negative transfer. In fact, if we regard the functions of the keys as the stimuli and the bindings as the responses, we have an approximation to the classic A-B, A-Br interference paradigm used in verbal learning research (Postman, 1971). The important observation, however, is that an identical productions model like ours predicts strong positive transfer in this situation. Using the standard goal tree representation of skill, perverse EMACS is identical to EMACS, except that the terminal nodes executing specific EMACS keystrokes have been replaced. In other words, EMACS and perverse EMACS share all the internal nodes of their goal trees and differ only in the leaves.

The basic plan of our experiment was to teach subjects EMACS, then perverse EMACS, and finally EMACS again. Our major prediction was that each of the transitions would be marked by strong positive transfer. Not only would subjects' initial training on EMACS transfer to perverse EMACS, but also their continued training on perverse EMACS would serve to improve their performance on EMACS when they returned to it. Aside from these general predictions, we claimed that transfer would be localized primarily to the various planning components in the editors, since the areas of overlap lie mainly in the underlying goal structures and not the surface procedures.

Our experiment had one other feature which serves as an additional source of transfer predictions. We compared the performance of one group that passed through the basic EMACS–perverse EMACS–EMACS cycle with another group that passed through the same cycle except that it learned one of the line editors first. The crucial manipulation here is that we controlled the amount of practice the second group got so that, with its combination of line editor and EMACS training, it was performing as well on EMACS prior to transfer to perverse EMACS as was the first group that had EMACS training alone. Although the groups performed equivalently on EMACS, we predicted that they would show differential transfer to perverse EMACS. This is due to the fact that the two groups had different learning histories and therefore different compositions of text-editing skill. Our specific prediction was that the transfer task would favor the group with the combination of line editor and EMACS training.

This prediction was based on the analysis that the group with prior line editor experience would achieve equal overall performance by having the components common to EMACS and the line editor better practiced and the components unique to EMACS less well practiced. Presumably, any component general to a line editor and EMACS would transfer completely to perverse EMACS, whereas those components specific to EMACS might not. Thus, the line editor group would show more transfer, reflecting a stronger general component.

Method

Subjects

Subjects were 8 women from the same population as in the text-editing experiment from the previous chapter (experiment 1). As before, they were balanced across groups for typing speed and performance on the building memory test.

Materials

Three editors were used in this experiment: EMACS, perverse EMACS, and EDT. The decision to use EDT instead of ED as the line editor was entirely arbitrary. The functionalities of EMACS and EDT were identical to those in the first experiment (see Table 3.1). Table 4.1 presents a full comparison of the commands in EMACS and perverse EMACS. Although in the context of regular EMACS perverse EMACS is certainly a treacherous editor, every effort was made to make the commands sensible in their own right. In fact, we tried to preserve many of the more user-friendly design features of EMACS. For example, command names are mnemonic: ˆu moves the cursor up one line and ˆd moves it down. In addition, commands are grouped in pairs:]e deletes a character, and ˆe a word. In the latter case, however, just to add to the confusion, the functionality of the escape and control keys within the pairs are reversed, so that the escape version of the command operates on characters and the control version operates on words (just the opposite is true in EMACS). Finally, we designed perverse EMACS to approximate regular EMACS in its proportion of control to escape key commands and also left-handed to right-handed commands. Our purpose in all of this was to make the new version of EMACS as learnable and usable as the old, so that

Table 4.1. Screen editor command summary. The ˆ denotes a control character and] denotes an escape character.

Command type	Action	EMACS binding	Perverse EMACS binding
Locative	Forward character	ˆf	]r
	Forward word	]f	ˆr
	Backward character	ˆb	]l
	Backward word	]b	ˆl
	Beginning of line	ˆa	ˆf
	End of line	ˆe	ˆb
	Previous line	ˆp	ˆu
	Next line	ˆn	ˆd
Mutative	Delete character	ˆd	]e
	Delete word	]d	ˆe
	Delete previous character	DEL	ˆa
	Delete line	ˆk	ˆw

differences in performance between the two might be attributed to something besides absolute differences in the editors.

Design

Our primary task in designing this experiment was to give two groups different amounts of general and specific practice but equate their overall performance on EMACS prior to transfer. We calculated from experiment 1 that a group with roughly two days of EMACS practice would perform as well as another group with two days of EDT and one day of EMACS practice. More specifically, we calculated that two days of EMACS practice would leave subjects with slightly better performance, and so we planned to stop the subjects in this group on day 2 when their performance had reached the criterion level. This was our method for matching the two groups.

The full design for the experiment was as follows. One group, called the *line-and-screen* group, started with two days of EDT followed by one day of EMACS, two days of perverse EMACS, and one day of EMACS. The second group, called the *screen-only* group, started with two days of EMACS, followed by two days of perverse EMACS, and two days of EMACS.

Procedure

The procedure was nearly identical to that used in the first experiment. Subjects spent three hours per day editing the standard manuscript. With each new editor, subjects were given a half-hour introduction by the experimenter which included both a description of the commands and a demonstration of two trials. The only difference in the procedure was that, on day 2 of the experiment, members of the screen-only group were stopped prematurely by the experimental program if their performance dipped below a target level. We determined this target level by yoking each subject from the screen-only group to another subject run earlier in the line-and-screen group. Pairings were based on rank orderings of subjects from performance on the first day of EMACS. As expected, all screen-only subjects attained their target levels on the second day of the experiment.

Macroanalysis of Transfer

As in experiment 1, there are two levels of data analysis. The macroanalysis describes transfer in terms of aggregate measures

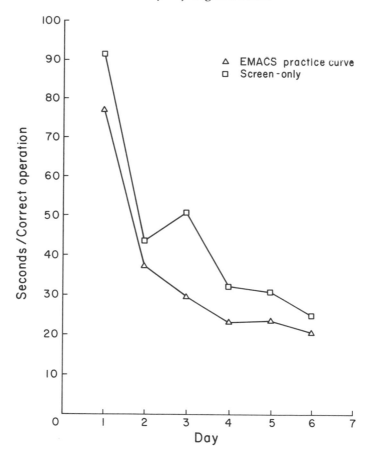

Figure 4.1. *Comparison of the screen-only group from experiment 2 with the* EMACS *control group from experiment 1 in terms of time per correct edit.*

like time per correct edit and keystrokes per trial; the microanalysis describes attempts at localizing transfer through the application of the parsing algorithm. In the macroanalysis, the
relative performance of the screen-only group enables us to
assess whether there is negative transfer at the aggregate level.
Since, as editors, EMACS and perverse EMACS are practically
equivalent on all objective measures, we can use the EMACS
learning curve from the first experiment as a rough approximation to a perverse EMACS leaning curve and thereby gauge
whether the screen-only group experiences positive or negative
transfer overall.

    Figure 4.1 compares the screen-only and EMACS control
groups on time per correct edit over six days of editing. The

screen-only group spent days 3 and 4 of the experiment using perverse EMACS; all other data points in the figure represent performance on EMACS. The two curves follow each other fairly closely. In fact, *t*-tests revealed that the two groups are not statistically different on five of the six days. On only day 3, the first day of transfer to perverse EMACS, do the groups differ significantly ($t(6) = 2.9, p < .05$). The perverse EMACS subjects, however, are still 41 seconds faster on day 3 than they are on day 1. The EMACS control group is only 49 seconds faster. Thus, transfer is 41/49, or 84 percent. These results highlight the overwhelming similarity and positive transfer between the two editors. First, compared to day 1 using EMACS, there is large positive transfer to perverse EMACS for the screen-only group on day 3. The difference between the two groups on day 3 represents the temporary deficit suffered by the screen-only group while learning the specific rules of perverse EMACS. By day 4, this deficit has largely disappeared, and on day 5, when the screen-only group returns to EMACS, it picks up at the same point on the learning curve as the group that stayed with EMACS all along.

To characterize further these transitions between editors, we examined the keystroke data for intrusions. For present purposes, instrusions are defined as keys that are bound to commands in the training editor but are nonfunctional in the transfer editor. For example, in transfer to perverse EMACS these keys are defined as ˆk, ˆn, ˆp,]b,]d,]f, and *DEL* (see Table 4.1). This measure represents only a conservative lower bound on the actual number of intrusions, since approximately half of the keys are bound in both EMACS and perverse EMACS, in accordance with the A-B, A-Br paradigm. Undoubtedly, subjects confused these bindings and struck these keys at inappropriate times. However, the identification of intrusions of this type would have required uncertain inferences about subjects' goals on our part. We chose to look at a more conservative measure which nonetheless reveals the approximate magnitude of the effect.

On day 1 of perverse EMACS, subjects average only .28 intrusions per trial. To put this in perspective, subjects average 165 keystrokes per trial across an average of 19 trials on this day. Thus, intrusions amount to only .002 percent of the total keys struck. Additionally, the vast majority of these intrusions occur in the first few trials. This is in accordance with our analysis of the rapid extinction of blatantly incorrect productions. By the second day of perverse EMACS, intrusions are down to .08 per trial, or approximately one intrusion for every 1,800 keystrokes. Therefore, even though we use a rather conservative measure, we are fairly confident in concluding that the firing of incorrect, EMACS-specific productions plays a short-lived and altogether negligible role in transfer to perverse EMACS.

We return now to our prediction concerning differences between the screen-only and the line-and-screen groups in terms of transfer to perverse EMACS. Figure 4.2 presents data that allow us to compare the two groups. Plotted is time per correct edit for the two days of perverse EMACS as well as for one day before and after (we plotted days 2–5 of the experiment for the screen-only group and days 3–6 for the line-and-screen group,

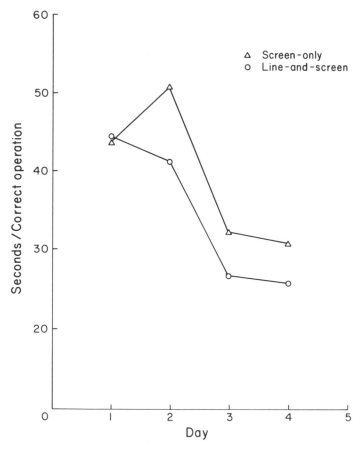

Figure 4.2. *Transfer to* perverse EMACS *in terms of time per correct edit (the curves are aligned so that day 1 represents performance on EMACS prior to transfer, days 2-3 performance on* perverse EMACS, *and day 4 the return to EMACS).*

so as to align the perverse EMACS data and to facilitate comparisons). The two groups are matched quiet well on EMACS prior to transfer (43.5 and 44.2 seconds per edit for the screen-only and line-and-screen groups, respectively). However, these functionally equivalent groups are separated by transfer to perverse EMACS. A one-tailed matched-groups t-test confirms that the average performance on perverse EMACS of the screen-only group is significantly worse than that of the line-and-screen group ($t(3) = 2.3$, $p < .05$). Interestingly, the last day plotted, which represents the return to EMACS, shows that the two groups never quite recover their former equivalence: the screen-only group continues to lag behind.

As might be expected from the results of experiment 1, the pattern observed in the time data is duplicated almost perfectly in the keystroke data. Our matching procedure inadvertently matched groups on keystrokes as well as time per edit, giving further credence to the position that number of keystrokes is a major predictor of performance in text editing. Once again, the two groups are separated by the transfer task, but this time the matched-groups t-test is only marginally significant ($t(3) = 1.7$, $p < .09$). If we accept the keystroke difference as real, however, it sheds an entirely new light on our interpretation of the results. Until now, we have explained the screen-only group's inferior performance in terms of a weaker, less-practiced general component that runs more slowly in perverse EMACS. This kind of explanation is based on a strong identical elements model of transfer that makes no appeal to negative transfer. However, the disadvantage in keystrokes raises the possibility that the screen-only group's strong specific component is playing a role as well. The group's well-practiced EMACS-specific methods may be interfering with the acquisition and use of efficient methods in perverse EMACS. With this kind of explanation, the screen-only group is in a kind of double jeopardy: both its general and its specific components are liabilities. The general component is weaker and therefore contributes less to positive transfer, whereas the specific component is stronger and therefore contributes more to negative transfer.

Microanalysis of Transfer

The microanalysis provides further interpretation of the results. We focus on the screen-only group, since its poorer performance makes it a more likely victim of negative transfer. Once again, we proceed from coarser to finer levels of analysis.

LL and MT transfer

We have pointed out previously that, using the standard goal tree formulation, EMACS and perverse EMACS differ in only their terminal nodes. In other words, both MT and LL planning components overlap completely, but the execution components are largely different. Whereas the LL execution component is completely different in the two editors, the MT execution component overlaps somewhat because insert operations make use of the standard alpha-numeric keys which have not been re-bound. Given this analysis, one would expect large and equal amounts of transfer in the LL and MT planning components, less transfer in the MT execution component, and essentially none in the LL execution component. Of course, if execution components are somehow interfering with one another, transfer could be negative.

To measure LL and MT transfer, we devised a new transfer formula which is similar in spirit to the formula used in experiment 1. The goal once again is to measure transfer relative to the amount of learning that takes place with the same amount of practice. Since we did not make an independent assessment of learning in perverse EMACS, we use regular EMACS learning data from experiment 1 to estimate learning rates. This approximation is quite good, given the fact that the two editors are functionally and structurally equivalent. The new transfer score is given by the equation:

$$(4.1) \quad T_{\% learning} = \frac{M_{lrn}(1) - M_{tran}(n)}{M_{lrn}(1) \times r} \times 100$$

As in equation (3.2), the numerator represents the speedup due to transfer, and the denominator the speedup due to learning. The day 1 learning mean ($M_{lrn}(1)$) is taken from the screen-only group's performance on day 1 of the experiment. To calculate the speedup due to learning, we multiply this mean by a fraction r, which represents the proportion of speedup observed in experiment 1 for the component in question. In this way, the learning baseline is supplied by the screen-only group, but learning rates are supplied by experiment 1. This allows for a more sensitive within-subjects measure of transfer, which behaves identically to the between-subjects measure used in experiment 1.

Table 4.2 presents LL and MT transfer scores for both planning time and keystrokes. Our predictions concerning LL and

Table 4.2. LL/MT transfer from EMACS to perverse EMACS.

Measure	Locate line	Modify text
Planning time (sec.)		
$M_{tran}(3)$	16.0	17.7
$M_{lrn}(1)$	29.4	34.8
r	.67	.78
$T_{\%learning}$ (equation 4.1)	68%	63%
Number of keystrokes		
$M_{tran}(3)$	10.7	20.8
$M_{lrn}(1)$	8.7	18.8
r	.10	.17
$T_{\%learning}$ (equation 4.1)	−234%	−61%

MT transfer are largely confirmed. Planning time transfer is substantial (an average of 66 percent) and virtually identical for LL and MT components. Keystroke transfer (namely execution component transfer) is much less than planning time transfer, and LL is much worse than MT. Most striking is that the keystroke transfer is not small or zero but negative. On average, subjects strike an extra 2 keystrokes per edit on day 1 of perverse EMACS, compared to day 1 of EMACS on both LL and MT components. Thus, it appears that EMACS-specific methods are somehow interfering with the acquisition of new methods in perverse EMACS. The exact nature of this interference remains to be seen.

Unit task transfer

Although transfer at the macrolevel is overwhelmingly positive, we have now identified two sources of negative transfer in the LL and MT execution components. In this second transfer analysis, we attempt to localize further the sites of negative transfer by examining individual unit tasks. The analysis is restricted to the MT component, since LL procedures are essentially the same for all unit tasks and did not differ in terms of transfer. In addition, the three unit tasks involving line operations are excluded, since MT procedures for these three share nothing with the others and add unnecessary complexity to the analysis.

Insert operations are identical in the two editors, but delete operations are grievously different. This means that, even though the transfer observed in the LL and MT analysis for the MT execution component was negative overall, that subset of unit tasks involving insertion should show substantial positive transfer. Negative transfer should be restricted to those unit tasks that involve deletion. Since replacement involves both insertion and deletion, transfer scores for those unit tasks should lie somewhere between the other two.

To dramatize further the fact that positive transfer dominates the planning components and negative transfer is restricted to a subset of execution components, we first examined MT planning time for each time of the nine unit tasks. As expected, a 3 × 3 ANOVA using the transfer score in equation (4.1) as the dependent measure yielded no main effects or interactions, thereby confirming that MT planning time transfer for all nine unit tasks was equally positive.

When we performed the same ANOVA using keystroke transfer as the dependent measure, a main effect for editing operation emerged ($F(2,12) = 123.6$, $p < .001$). As predicted, insertion operations exhibited substantial positive transfer (110 percent) and deletion operations exhibited massive negative transfer (-240 percent). Finally, replace operations were in the middle (-100 percent). Here is strong support for the view that deletion operations are the source of negative transfer in the MT execution component.

MT methods transfer

We now know that the acquisition of EMACS deletion methods somehow interferes with the acquisition of perverse EMACS deletion methods. Critical to the status of our identical elements model of transfer is the nature of this interference. In experiment 1, the one case of negative transfer was characterized in terms of the positive transfer of a nonoptimal method. No real evidence was found for procedural interference in the classic sense (namely slower and more errorful performance), and a fairly strong version of our identical elements model was retained.

The pressing question now is whether the rather substantial negative transfer observed in this experiment can be similarly explained. To answer this question, we performed a qualitative analysis of the methods used for the deletion of characters, words, and strings in both EMACS and perverse EMACS by screen-only subjects on the first four days of the experiment. As shown in Table 4.1, there are four deletion operators in each editor: delete character marked by cursor (del-char), delete word marked by cursor (del-word), delete character to left of cursor (del-pre-char), and delete from current cursor position to the end of the line. This last operator will be ignored, because it was not used in any of the three unit tasks in either editor. Table 4.3 shows the distribution of the remaining three operators in the deletion unit tasks of both editors.

In EMACS, the operator of overwhelming preference is del-char ($\hat{}d$). Subjects adjust their operator selections somewhat by the amount of text to be deleted, as evidenced by the increased use of del-word (]d) on words and strings. However, even in the delete string unit task, $\hat{}d$ enjoys a 2-to-1 advantage over the more optimal]d. The perverse EMACS results show that del-char (now bound to]e) is again the runaway favorite, but now its dominance is even greater. The del-pre-char operator, which played a minor role in EMACS, has all but disappeared in perverse EMACS. Interestingly, of the three deletion operators used in perverse EMACS, only one,]e, did not have a previous binding in EMACS. This is a possible reason for its enhanced role in perverse EMACS.

Thus, it appears that negative transfer can once again be explained in terms of the positive transfer of a nonoptimal method. Transfer is negative because, whereas the use of del-char in EMACS involved a single keystroke, its use in perverse EMACS involves two (the escape key in the]e operator must be struck independently and therefore counts as an extra keystroke). Thus, what was a nonoptimal method in EMACS becomes even worse in perverse EMACS. In addition, the negative

Table 4.3. Distribution of operators in deletion unit tasks for EMACS and for perverse EMACS.

	Operator					
	EMACS			Perverse EMACS		
Unit task	del-char ($\hat{}d$)	del-pre-char (DEL)	del-word (]d)	del-char (]e)	del-pre-char ($\hat{}a$)	del-word ($\hat{}e$)
Delete character	78	16	6	97	0	3
Delete word	66	22	12	81	3	16
Delete string	60	10	30	75	0	25

effects of this nonoptimal method are amplified somewhat by its increased frequency of use.

Simulation Models and Quantitative Predictions

Given our development of a simulation model for EMACS, and given our analysis of the similarity between EMACS and perverse EMACS, we find it quite easy at this point to make quantitative predictions of transfer between these two screen editors. As before, our predictions are restricted to transfer percentages for LL and MT planning times. In addition, we focus solely on the first transition between perverse EMACS and EMACS for the screen-only group, since this represents the cleanest transfer situation in our experiment.

To recap our task analysis of EMACS, a total of 26 and 25 rules are used in the LL and MT planning components, respectively. Of the 26 rules in the LL component, six are general to all editors, and 20 apply only in EMACS. Of these 20 rules, only six pertain to the actual retrieval of EMACS-specific command bindings, and the rest are shared by both EMACS and perverse EMACS. As an example of an LL rule that is used in EMACS but not in perverse EMACS, the following rule retrieves the binding for the operator that moves the cursor ahead one character:

forward-character-EMACS

    IF   the goal is to specify the command symbol
          and the operator is forward-character
  THEN   set as a subgoal to type ^f.

In contrast, the LL rules common to both screen editors include rules for choosing among the various LL operators (such as forward-word, backward-word, beginning-of-line) and special-case rules for stopping in position, depending upon the direction of movement. This example of a shared rule selects the forward-word operator:

choose-forward-word-Screen

    IF   the goal is to move horizontally on a line
          and the cursor is to the left of the modification
          and one or more words separate the cursor and the
             site of the modification
  THEN   choose the forward-word operator.

Once this rule fires, a separate rule retrieves the command symbol associated with the forward-word operator. Once again, these rules are different in the two screen editors, since forward-word is *]b* in EMACS and *^r* in perverse EMACS. Thus, as we have stated repeatedly, the two screen editors are identical in terms of their internal goal structures and differ simply in terms of their leaf nodes.

Of the 25 rules used for MT, three are general to all editors, 18 apply in both screen editors, and only four are specific to EMACS. Once again, these four rules pertain to the retrieval of the bindings for the four deletion operators in EMACS. MT rules shared by the screen editors concern the selection of MT methods and also the management of space. As an example of the former type, this rule selects the delete-word operator:

choose-delete-word-Screen

    IF   the goal is to delete text
         and the deletion spans a single word
  THEN use the delete-word operator.

As an example of the latter type, the next rule checks for a lack of space between words following an insertion:

insert-space-between-words-Screen

    IF   the goal is to check for space following an insertion
         and the cursor is positioned on an alpha-numeric
            character which marks the beginning of a word
         and the character to the left is not a space character
  THEN hit the space bar.

Table 4.4 summarizes the number of rules in each category and

Table 4.4. Categories of rules and their frequencies in the screen editor simulations.

Component	Category	Number of rules	Total frequency
LL	General	6	96
	Screen	13	89
	EMACS	7	62
	Perverse EMACS	7	62
MT	General	3	32
	Screen	18	70
	EMACS	4	18
	Perverse EMACS	4	18

their total frequencies. Applying equation (3.3), we find that our predicted transfer for LL and MT from EMACS to perverse EMACS is 75 percent and 85 percent, respectively. Interestingly, the transfer we observed was only 68 percent and 63 percent, respectively. Thus, we have overpredicted the amount of transfer between these two editors. This contrasts sharply with the eight cases of underprediction in the first experiment. It is tempting to conclude that here in the quantitative analysis is our first evidence, however slight, of true procedural interference between the screen editors in the planning components. We discussed how true procedural interference might be produced by interference in pattern matching. This is negative transfer only in the relative sense, however. The overwhelming effect is positive, just not as positive as we had predicted.

Summary of Text-Editing Experiment

At the aggregate level, the transfer observed in this experiment was overwhelmingly positive. Subsequent microanalyses identified the planning components as a major source of positive transfer, which corresponds to our production rule analysis of the skill. Negative transfer was restricted to the deletion components, where a nonoptimal method was imported from the training editor. Thus, our analysis of negative transfer as the positive transfer of nonoptimal methods is largely supported.

Negative Transfer in Programming

Given our claim that negative transfer is largely restricted to nonoptimal methods, we might reasonably ask how it is possible to observe negative transfer at the aggregate level. The magnitude of the negative effect is determined by the centrality of the productions which implement the nonoptimal methods. Negative transfer at the aggregate level is possible when nonoptimal productions fire high in the goal tree and force a particularly bad decomposition of the task. An experiment by Kessler and Anderson (1986) found just this phenomenon in the domain of programming.

The Kessler and Anderson experiment represents one of the few well-documented instances of negative lateral transfer at the aggregate level. It involves learning to program recursively versus iteratively. Kessler and Anderson studied this phenomenon in a LISP-like language, but it has been studied in other programming languages as well (Anzai and Uesato, 1982; Kurland

and Pea, 1983). The basic result is that, while there is large positive transfer from iterative programming to recursive programming, there is negative transfer in the opposite direction. This phenomenon was first noted by Anzai and Uesato (1982), but they concentrated on the asymmetric property of the transfer rather than on the negative property. The analyses developed by Kessler and Anderson explain both.

Kessler and Anderson first taught subjects the basics of a LISP-like laboratory language called SIMPLE (Shrager and Pirolli, 1983). Subjects then learned the more advanced programming techniques of recursion and iteration. One experimental group was trained on recursion and transferred to iteration; another was trained on iteration and transferred to recursion. Two control groups programmed with either recursion or iteration in both training and transfer phases. The problems that all groups saw were identical; all that differed was the method specified for solution.

Table 4.5 shows the results in terms of mean time to solve a problem. To calculate transfer from these scores, we use the following formula, which is a simple variation of the standard formula:

$$(4.2) \quad T_{\%learning} = \frac{A_1 - E_2}{A_1 - C_2} \times 100$$

As an example, to measure transfer from iteration to recursion, we set A_1 as the average of experimental and control groups doing recursion in the first phase (no experimental difference between these subjects yet), E_2 as the second phase performance of experimental subjects who transfer from iteration to recursion, and C_2 as the second phase performance of control subjects who do recursion throughout. We can similarly design a transfer measure for subjects who transfer in the

Table 4.5. Mean time (sec.) to finish a problem in the Kessler and Anderson (1986) experiment.

Condition	Training	Transfer
Recursion-recursion	547	392
Recursion-iteration	530	576
Iteration-recursion	546	368
Iteration-iteration	482	277

opposite direction. With this measure, the average transfer observed from iteration to recursion was a positive 67 percent, while the average transfer from recursion to iteration was a negative 20 percent.

This aggregate negative transfer is quite dramatic, given the fact that the processes of writing iterative and recursive programs share components. The positive transfer from iteration to recursion is testimony to this fact. To explain the negative transfer in the opposite direction, Kessler and Anderson took protocols of subjects in the two experimental conditions. They found that subjects transferring from iteration to recursion developed a reasonable understanding of iteration and were able to use it as a basis for understanding recursion. In contrast, subjects who started with recursion never understood it and adopted a strategy of memorizing examples and using analogy to extend them. They carried this memorization strategy over to the iteration problems where it is definitely nonoptimal because iterative constructs tend to be rather complicated syntactically. In support of this interpretation, Kessler and Anderson found that subjects who transferred to iteration from recursion made over three times as many references to the examples as those subjects who started with iteration.

Thus, the negative transfer from recursion to iteration is apparently due to the perfect transfer of a nonoptimal, rote learning strategy. This results in negative transfer at the aggregate level because the selection of a learning strategy exerts a major influence on problem decomposition and is critical to overall task performance. It is not surprising that, when faced with a difficult task like recursion with little preparation, novice programmers adopt a rote learning strategy. As in the classic studies by Wertheimer (1945), Katona (1940), and Judd (1908), this rote strategy emerges as a liability primarily in transfer situations.

Work by Schoenfeld (1983) suggests that a poor overall approach to a task may stem less from purely cognitive factors and more from students' attitudes and beliefs about their own abilities. For example, students with math anxiety may adopt a rote learning strategy even in those situations where the mathematical material is well within their grasp. Although we have no reason to suspect that affective factors such as these were at play in the Kessler and Anderson experiment, it is quite possible that in many training situations such factors play an important role and may account for what is commonly perceived as negative transfer.

Conclusion

In general, the results of our analyses of negative transfer are extremely supportive of our identical productions model. All sustained cases of negative transfer seem to be explainable in terms of the positive transfer of nonoptimal methods. In the two experiments where this issue was explored in detail, ours and that of Kessler and Anderson, we were able to find independent converging evidence for this position. The text-editing studies have also shown that dominant methods become even more dominant in transfer situations. This means that if a method is nonoptimal in a transfer task, the resulting negative effect will be amplified.

The aggregate positive transfer in the text-editing experiment is our strongest evidence yet for the identical productions model. We took what would have been a massively interfering condition in verbal learning and found massive positive transfer. Studies of declarative memory have shown that the retrieval of facts is made slower and more errorful in such experimental situations. Nowhere in our microanalyses, however, do we find evidence for this kind of interference in the execution of keystrokes. All results point to the fact that the nonoptimal productions are firing in the transfer editor with no performance deficit. Indeed, the only sign of procedural interference of any kind was the slight overprediction of positive transfer based on our simulation model of text editing. Nonetheless, the level of observed transfer was massively positive. The fact that declarative interference is well documented but that procedural interference is not suggests another possible distinction between these two types of knowledge.

5 / Use Specificity of Procedural Knowledge

Our analysis of transfer has mainly focused so far on showing the high degree of transfer that occurs when training and transfer skills share an abstract structure, as was the case in the transfer observed between text editors. The text-editing results can be taken as evidence for a more abstract interpretation of an element than was the case in Thorndike's theory. These abstract elements can serve as the basis for substantial transfer, even when a superficial analysis of similarity yields no common elements. Yet the identical productions model places clear restrictions on the kinds of transfer that can take place, and in a sense it shares much of the specificity of Thorndike's model. This is due to the fact that skills using knowledge in one way share no elements with skills using the same knowledge in a different way. For instance, we would predict no transfer from a production system embodiment of English syntax for comprehension to a production system embodiment of English syntax for generation. Although an abstract characterization of the syntactic knowledge underlying competence is the same in comprehension and generation (Chomsky, 1965), the knowledge is organized differently in the productions for the two tasks. For comprehension, the productions examine strings of words on the left-hand sides and generate conceptual structures on the right-hand sides. For generation, just the opposite is true.

In the case of natural language, it is both questionable whether production systems are the right formalism for the task and difficult to put the lack of transfer hypothesis to test. One cannot easily do controlled experiments in this domain. There are abundant claims to the effect that people can comprehend a second language but not produce it. However, the degree to which comprehension is achieved in these cases through the use of extralinguistic cues is never clear. In the domain of child language, it is generally observed that there is improvement in both comprehension and generation, with generation appearing to lag behind (Huttenlocher, 1974; Rescorla, 1980). This relative independence faintly suggests that comprehension and generation may involve separate systems. However, the apparent disadvantage of generation may again reflect use of extralinguistic cues in comprehension.

The observation that children generally proceed through similar developmental sequences in both comprehension and generation might be interpreted as evidence against the use specificity view. Or the correlated order of appearance of syntactic structures may simply reflect frequency of exposure in the environment and relative complexity of the structures.

Although it is difficult to reach definitive conclusions in such a complex domain, the scant experimental evidence suggests that language comprehension and generation are at least somewhat dissociated (for a review, see Clark and Hecht, 1983). In one study, Goldin-Meadow, Seligman, and Gelman (1976) asked two-year-old children to respond to spoken words by choosing their referents from a set of pictures (the comprehension task). The children were also shown the pictures in isolation and asked to name them (the generation task). The surprising result was that the children displayed different vocabularies in the two tasks. For example, a child might successfully select a picture of a dog in response to the word *dog*, but only produce the word *woof-woof* when shown the picture. It is not uncommon for children to comprehend "adult" words but produce "baby" words in this way.

In a related study, Thomson and Chapman (1977) found that children sometimes use the same words in different ways in the two modes. For example, children may consistently choose the appropriate referents for words like *dog* and *ball* in the comprehension task, but overgeneralize the words in the generation task, such as calling all animals *dog* and all spherical objects *ball*. Similarly, Karmiloff-Smith (1977) found that young French-speaking children take one meaning of the word *same* (*même*) in comprehension (*same kind*) but take another in generation (*same one*). All of these results suggest that word usage and semantics are somewhat dissociated in the two systems.

For further evidence in the area of syntax, Schustack (1979) looked at children's ability both to recognize irregular past-tense inflections and to generate them. She found no correlation between mastery of inflections in the two modes.

One last bit of evidence is drawn from the study of brain-damaged patients, whose systems of comprehension and generation have been radically dissociated through some type of physical trauma. In these patients, it is possible to observe something that is never observed in the course of normal language development: generation ability in the absence of comprehension ability. For example, in a rare disorder called *word deafness*, a patient with normal hearing cannot understand speech but nonetheless can speak fairly fluently (Brain, 1965; Rubens, 1979; Damasio, 1981). In another rare disorder called alexia, or word blindness, a patient can write but not read (Geschwind, 1972). Clear cases of these disorders are hard to find because the kinds of severe brain traumas that cause them typically impair the functioning of all systems. Nonetheless, their rare occurrence is further evidence for the use specificity of linguistic knowledge.

Use Specificity in Calculus

In searching about for a domain in which to put this hypothesis about the use specificity of production-based transfer to careful experimental test, we hit upon freshman calculus. In a typical calculus course, students learn skills associated with integration and skills associated with differentiation. Both of these skills are based on the same abstract knowledge of calculus. Thus, as a test of the use specificity hypothesis, we can determine whether integration practice transfers to differentiation. Our prediction, as always, is that transfer should be limited to the production rules (if any) shared by the two tasks. We can also divide the problem-solving skill into components associated with the planning (selection and sequencing) of calculus operators versus the actual application of those operators. Again, we can ask whether planning transfers to application or vice versa.

Unlike natural language, calculus has the strategic advantage of being a skill we can teach fairly quickly to relatively tractable high-school populations. In our experiments, we taught students to solve standard related-rates word problems for differentiation and a variation of these that we invented for integration. The calculus-based paradigm turns out to be the paradigm that finally exposed some flaws in the identical productions model of transfer. Before describing an experiment testing the use specificity of procedural knowledge hypothesis, we will first briefly describe the problem-solving domain and a minimal computer tutor that we used to collect data.

Solving Related-Rates Word Problems

Related-rates word problems are typically the first type of word problem encountered in calculus and are usually presented in one of the first few chapters of an introductory calculus text. To solve them, one needs to know just a few simple differentiation techniques and also how to apply the chain rule, a technique that produces new derivatives not by differentiation but rather by the composition of existing derivatives. Since calculus builds on earlier mathematics courses, it is also necessary to know the standard equation manipulation routines of basic algebra (poor mastery of prerequisite algebra knowledge was in fact a major stumbling block for some of the students observed). Typically, a related-rates problem states a couple of relationships between several variables and asks the student to find the rate of change of one variable with respect to another. Finding this derivative often involves differentiating equations and perhaps chaining them together. For example, a related-rates problem drawn from the related-rates tutor used in the first calculus experiment is: "The economy of the newly founded republic of San Pedro is growing such that, in any year y, the level m of the money supply in billion dollars is 2 times the square of the number of years elapsed. The gross national product g of the economy is 4 times the money supply. How fast is the gross national product growing when y equals 2 years?" For this problem, one would write the equations:

(5.1) $m = 2y^2$

(5.2) $g = 4m$

(5.3) $y = 2$

The goal of this problem is to find a value for dg/dy (the growth of the gross national product, or GNP, with respect to time) when y equals 2. One strategy for finding dg/dy is:

(5.4) $dm/dy = 4y$ (differentiate equation 5.1)

(5.5) $dg/dm = 4$ (differentiate equation 5.2)

(5.6) $dg/dy = 16y$ (apply the chain rule to equations 5.4–5.5)

(5.7) $dg/dy = 32$ (evaluate equation 5.6 with equation 5.3)

This is the first and arguably the easiest problem given by the tutor. It is easy because the equations derived from the problems statement are differentiated and chained together to produce the solution in a very straightforward way. However, some problems require a fair amount of search once the equations have been written.

To do a systematic investigation of problem solving in this domain, it is necessary somehow to restrict the class of problems to allow for a formalization of the problem space. Consequently, it was decided that the problems would have these fixed features:

1. Three variables, referred to generically as x, y, and z. The value of the z variable is always given.

2. Two relations, one between x and y, the other between y and z. Each relation can be stated either as a regular equation (for example, $x = 3y^2$) or as a derivative (for example, $dx/dy = 6y$). These relations can also be stated either with x in terms of y (forward direction) or with y in terms of x (backward direction). By crossing these two binary features, each relation can take on four possible forms. Given two relations, this means a total of 16 possible initial states for the problems.

3. A goal, to find the value either of the x variable (an integration goal) or of dx/dz (a differentiation goal) for a particular value of z. These goals were so named because, in most cases, finding a value for x involves integration and finding a value for dx/dz involves differentiation. Crossing the 16 initial states by these two goals yields a total of 32 problems.

When the preceding related-rates problem is viewed in this framework, g stands for the x variable, m for the y variable, and y for the z variable. The initial state contains two regular equations, both in the forward direction (g in terms of m, and m in terms of y). The goal is to find the value of dg/dy when y equals 2 and is therefore a differentiation goal.

As a further expansion, eight different cover stories were generated for the 32 deep structures. Four cover stories are from the domain of solid geometry and involve squares, cones, icicles, and ladders whose dimensions (the x and y variables) are changing with time. The remaining four are from the domain of economics and involve the growth of the GNP, profits, prices, and unemployed workers. The related-rates problem given previously is an example of the economics GNP cover story.

In the formalization of the problem space, it was also determined that, for solving such problems, seven mathematical operators were sufficient:

1. *Differentiate.* This operator takes a regular equation stating x in terms of y and produces the derivative dx/dy.

2. *Integrate.* Takes the derivative dx/dy and produces a regular equation stating x in terms of y.

3. *Apply Chain Rule.* Takes two derivatives, dx/dy and dy/dz, and produces a third, dx/dz.

4. *Substitute Equations.* Takes two regular equations, x in terms of y and y in terms of z, and produces a new equation stating x in terms of z.

5. *Flip Derivative.* Takes the derivative dx/dy and produces the derivative dy/dx.

6. *Restate Equation.* Takes a regular equation stating x in terms of y and transforms it into an equation stating y in terms of x.

7. *Evaluate.* Given an equation stating either x or dx/dz in terms of z, and a value for z, returns the value of x or dx/dz, respectively.

Unlike typical related-rates problems found in most introductory calculus textbooks, the problems studied here require not only differentiation but sometimes integration as well. Integration is necessary whenever the initial state contains derivatives and the goal is to find the value of a variable. Similarly, differentiation is required whenever the initial state contains regular equations and the goal is to find the value of a derivative. The latter situation is the one normally found in textbook related-rates problems.

The calculus operators can be grouped into pairs according to the kinds of transformations they achieve. The first pair, differentiate and integrate, changes the type of the relation, either from derivative to regular equation or vice versa. The second pair, apply chain rule and substitute equations, puts previously unassociated variables in direct relation to one another. The third pair, flip derivative and restate equation, changes the directionality of the relation. The only difference between members of these pairs is that one operates on derivatives and the other operates on regular equations. The one operator that has no partner, evaluate, happens to take both derivatives and regular equations as operands.

The Related-Rates Tutor

To help collect data, we wrote a bare-bones tutor for these problems. The tutor is written in INTERLISP and runs on the Xerox Dandelion series. Figure 5.1 shows the basic goal struc-

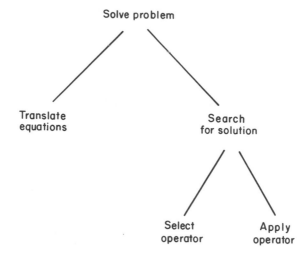

Figure 5.1. *Upper-level goal structure for solving related-rates problems.*

ture for solving related-rates problems, to which the interface of the tutor was designed to correspond. First, students translate the problem statement into a set of equations. They then alternate in the selection and application of operators until a solution is found. The interface is designed to separate out these various components of problem solving so that their acquisition and transfer can be traced independently.

Figure 5.2 shows the layout of the screen as it appears to a student solving problems. The screen consists of four windows and one menu, with these functions:

1. *Problem Statement Window.* Displays the text of the word problem.

2. *Student Workspace Window.* Displays student input as it is typed. Students must input both the equations derived from the problem statement during the translation phase and the results of operator applications during the solution phase.

3. *Equations So Far Window.* Displays a running record of all relations generated during the course of problem solving. Relations are displayed from top to bottom in the order they are generated.

4. *Prompt Window.* Displays the tutor's instructions and feedback to the student.

5. *Operations Menu.* Displays the seven operators available to students during the solution phase. To initiate an operator application, the student first selects an operator from the menu

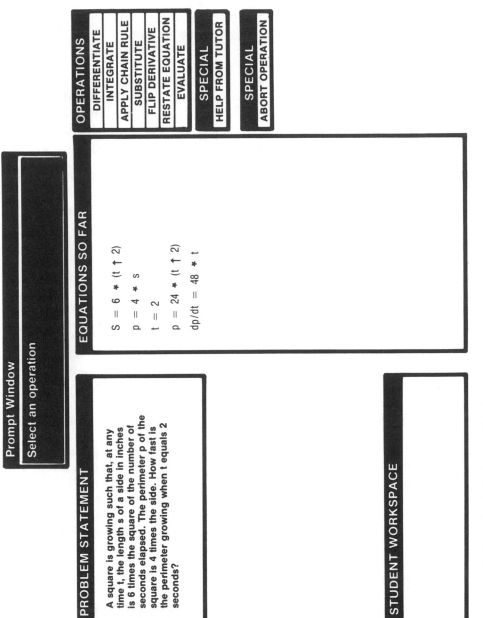

Figure 5.2. *Configuration of calculus tutor interface.*

OPERATIONS

- DIFFERENTIATE
- INTEGRATE
- APPLY CHAIN RULE
- SUBSTITUTE
- FLIP DERIVATIVE
- RESTATE EQUATION
- EVALUATE

SPECIAL
HELP FROM TUTOR

SPECIAL
ABORT OPERATION

Prompt Window

Select an operation

EQUATIONS SO FAR

S = 6 * (t ↑ 2)

p = 4 * s

t = 2

p = 24 * (t ↑ 2)

dp/dt = 48 * t

PROBLEM STATEMENT

A square is growing such that, at any time t, the length s of a side in inches is 6 times the square of the number of seconds elapsed. The perimeter p of the square is 4 times the side. How fast is the perimeter growing when t equals 2 seconds?

STUDENT WORKSPACE

with a mouse and then selects the operands from the Equations So Far window (apply chain rule, substitute equations, and evaluate require two operands). The student is then prompted to write the result of the operator application in the Student Workspace window.

At the beginning of each problem, the text of the word problem appears in the Problem Statement window, and the Equations So Far window is blank. The student's first task is to write the three relations based on the text of the problem. As each relation is written, it is checked and, if correct, displayed in the Equations So Far window (the tutor is accurate at recognizing paraphrases of relations and reduces all student input to a canonical form). Students get two attempts to write each relation. After mistakes, students get the negative feedback "Sorry, the tutor does not recognize (echoes student input) as correct. Please try again." The tutor reveals the correct relation in the Equations So Far window if students are unsuccessful after both attempts.

Once the problem has been set up, students begin the solution phase by selecting an operator and its operands. Once an operator has been selected, students get two attempts to write the correct result of its application in the Student Workspace window, as in the setup phase. Once again, they receive minimal feedback after wrong answers and are given the right answer after two unsuccessful attempts. After repeated operator selections and applications, students eventually reach the goal, at which point they are interrupted by the tutor and informed of their success.

Although by and large the tutor allows free exploration of the problem space, there are a few restrictions. First, the tutor blocks illegal operator applications and provides the feedback: "Sorry, that operator does not apply to that (those) equations(s). Please make another selection." Operator applications are illegal if the operands do not meet certain preconditions; for example, flip derivative requires a derivative as an operand, and apply chain rule requires two derivatives of the general form dx/dy and dy/dz. Second, the tutor blocks higher-order differentiation; that is, one cannot differentiate a derivative (students are not taught anything about higher-order differentiation, and higher-order derivatives are in no way required for the solution of these problems). Third, operator applications performed previously are blocked with the message: "You already have the result of that operation. It is (echoes previous result)." Finally, exploration of the problem space is restricted once students have derived the relation that states the unknown, sought-after quantity in terms of the known quantity, which is invariably one or two steps from the goal. At this point, students are focused on further transformations of this relation and are unable to regress. This restriction was added to prevent total flailing in the problem space and in fact was hardly ever invoked.

Aside from the seven operators, two additional selections are available to students in the Operations menu. One is a help facility, which, if selected, provides students with the next step along the optimal solution path from any point in the problem space. The nature of this help is quite minimal; the operator and operands are provided, but nothing else. No attempt is made to explain or justify the proposed operator application. After receiving help in operator selection, students are still required to apply the operator themselves and type the result in the Student Workspace window. The final selection is an abort operation facility, whereby students can abandon particular operation selections if deemed unprofitable at midstream.

In summary, the tutor is designed to facilitate the independent measurement of the acquisition and transfer of the major components of related-rates problem-solving skill: translation of equations, selection of operators, and application of operators. During the course of problem solving, the tutor provides minimal feedback on incorrect translations, incorrect operator applications, and illegal or poor operator selections. Furthermore, the tutor can provide optimal moves to students if they are in need of assistance. This keeps students moving and allows for successive approximations to the target skill. It is also useful for modeling purposes to see where students need help and if and how they profit from it.

Method

Subjects

Subjects were 36 high school juniors and seniors from a local private girls' school. All subjects were either taking trigonometry or precalculus concurrently with the experiment and were maintaining a B average or better. None of the subjects had had any direct calculus instruction. For example, none of them had yet learned about limits or derivatives.

Design

We set out to provide training to subjects on different types of problems and then measure transfer to a new type. As mentioned previously, we had developed four major clases of problems by crossing type of cover story to be translated (geometry vs. economics) with type of goal to be solved (differentiation vs. integration). It is possible to degrade these problems and create new classes by omitting either the translation phase or the solution phase, or both. This yields nine sets of problems in all, derived by crossing type of translation practice (geometry, economics, or none), with type of solution practice (differentiation, integration, or none). In those problems with no solution component, subjects are still given practice in applying operators drawn from the optimal solution path. Therefore, a more accurate description of the no-solution problems might be no-operator-selection problems.

Figure 5.3 shows that, given the nine problem types, the experiment falls neatly into a 3 × 3 between-subjects design. Subjects spend two days solving problems with the tutor. On day 1, subjects solve problems from one of the nine classes. On day 2, they transfer to a particular type, specifically those problems involving a geometry cover story and a differentiation goal (the choice of geometry differentiation problems as the transfer task was somewhat arbitrary, although problems of this type were identified as most representative of related-rates problems in textbooks). The group that receives two days of practice on

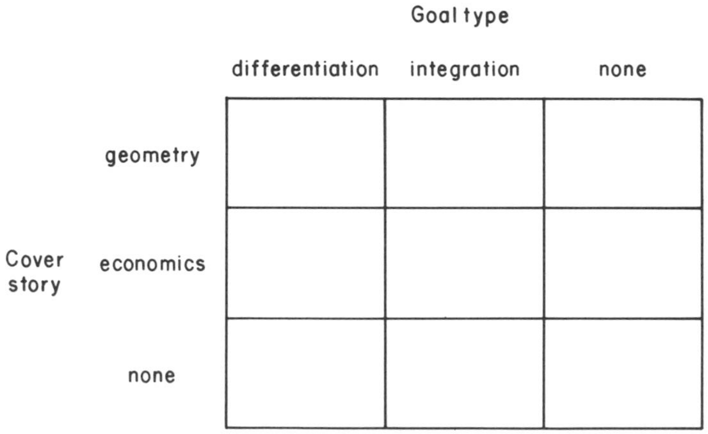

Figure 5.3. *Design of calculus experiment 1 (all manipulations occur on day 1 of problem solving).*

this type of problem serves as a control against which the performance of the others is judged. Given such a design, one can determine the degree of transfer from various combinations of translation task and solution goal.

Specifically, we are interested in three questions:

1. Does practice on one component of the skill transfer to another? For example, does practice on problem translation transfer in any way to problem solution, and vice versa? In this case, the identical productions model predicts no transfer, since no rules are shared by these skills. Similarly, the model predicts no transfer between operator selection and application.

2. Within the translation component, does practice on economics cover stories transfer to geometry cover stories? The identical productions model here predicts perfect transfer, since problem statements from the two domains have identical syntactic structures and are parsed by identical sets of rules.

3. Within the solution component, does practice on integration problems transfer to differentiation problems? In this case, the identical productions model predicts a middling level of transfer, since the two types of problems share many of the same operations. However, to preserve the model, we must show that the transfer we observe is in fact localized to these shared operations.

Materials

Unlike most experiments, no attempt was made in this experiment to counterbalance the ordering of problems across subjects. In fact, the order was fixed for all groups; that is, all subjects received problems defined by a particular initial state in the same serial position. Recall that the four types of problems differ only in terms of cover stories and goal states: As pointed out by Kieras and Bovair (1986), this kind of experimental situation is preferable when the microstructure of learning and transfer across individual problems is of major interest. Such microeffects are lost in the "statistical stew" when counterbalancing for presentation orders.

Procedure

The experiment lasted three days, two hours per day, for a total of six hours. On day 1, subjects read an introductory text which presented in very direct terms the prerequisite calculus knowledge for solving related-rates problems. The seven operators were introduced in detail, and examples were given of each. In addition, a solution trace was given for a typical related-rates problem. Following this reading of the instruction booklet, subjects worked with a stripped-down version of the tutor which presented a series of operator application exercises. At this time, a separate summary sheet was given to subjects which gave formulas and examples of operator applications (this sheet was available to subjects throughout the remainder of the experiment, although it was most useful during the first day). Subjects were given five practice exercises on each of the seven operators. Exercises for the various operators were intermixed, but the ordering for all subjects was fixed, as with the problems. The exercise was displayed in the Prompt window (e.g. "Differentiate the following equation: $y = 5x^2$"), and subjects were given two opportunities to type the correct result in the Student Workspace window. In this way, the interaction was nearly identical to that for operator applications in the regular tutor. As such, these preliminary exercises provided an opportunity not only to practice the seven operators but also to become acquainted with a critical part of the interface.

Day 2 of the experiment was the first day of problem solving with the tutor. The type of problems encountered by subjects depended upon experimental condition. On day 3 of the experiment, all subjects transferred to geometry-differentiation problems. On both days of problem solving, subjects were first given a brief demonstration of how to use the tutorial interface on two sample problems. No explicit instruction was given on either translation of problem text or solution strategies.

Results

On days 2 and 3 of the experiment, subjects solved an average of 8.3 and 10.0 problems, respectively. However, we have complete data from all subjects for only the first six problems on both days. We therefore restrict our analysis to these first six problems. All summary statistics reported here are based on averages of performance on this restricted set.

Before any substantive analyses were performed, the equivalence of the nine experimental groups was checked with a 3×3 ANOVA which used mean time per operator application on day 1 as the dependent measure. No main effects or interactions were found. Although no differences were found between the groups, further ANOVAs analyzing day 2 and day 3 data use this day 1 dependent measure as a covariate to reduce within-group variability.

The structure of the tutor's interface allowed for the independent measurement of the two major components of related-rates problem-solving skill: translation and solution. Furthermore, the solution component was subdivided into its operator selection and operator application subcomponents.

Translation

Table 5.1 compares geometry and economics cover stories in terms of translation time per equation and percentage of incorrect translations on day 2 of the experiment (the first day of problem solving). Analyses of covariance comparing these day 2 means reveal no differences on either of these dependent measures: $F(1,17) = .61$, $p = .45$ and $F(1,17) = .01$, $p = .93$ for translation time per equation and percentage of incorrect translations, respectively. This result is interesting, given that the rules used to generate the text for both types of problems are identical in terms of syntax and differ only in surface content. Despite the syntactic equivalence, it might nevertheless have been suspected that the cover stories differ in difficulty because the geometry problems involve a spatial component not present in the economics problems. Others (e.g. Larkin and Simon, 1987) have found that spatial reasoning plays an important role in the setup of certain types of problems, particularly those involving critical conservation relations not stated explicitly in the text. However, in the problems used here, all relations required are stated explicitly, so there is no real need for this kind of elaboration of the initial state.

There is no effect of the problem type factor on either trans-

Table 5.1. Translation results for both days of problem solving in the calculus experiment.

Day	Measure	Geometry translation	Economics translation	No translation
2	Translation time per equation (sec.)	50.9	46.6	—
	% incorrect	36	36	—
3	Translation time per equation (sec.)	26.3	26.8	45.3
	% incorrect	21	22	40

lation time per equation or percentage of incorrect translations on the first day of problem solving. This is preliminary evidence for the independence of the translation and solution components, but the transfer data should be more telling.

Table 5.1 also presents the results from day 3 of the experiment, when all subjects are solving problems with geometry cover stories. Focusing first on learning, we see that those subjects who translate geometry cover stories on both days of problem solving improve in terms of both time per equation (from 50.9 to 26.3 seconds) and percent incorrect (from 36 percent to 21 percent). In addition, there is virtually total transfer from economics cover stories to geometry cover stories in terms of both of these measures. This supports the position that subjects are learning generalized translation rules keying primarily on syntactic cues and not on specific content words. This type of translation was in fact first proposed as an artificial intelligence technique by Bobrow (1964) and was later found to approximate human translation processes by Paige and Simon (1966). A production system embodiment of these translation rules would show near perfect transfer from one cover story to the other. Finally, the day 3 performance of those subjects who spend day 2 solving problems but doing no translation is roughly equivalent to the day 2 translation performance of the regular groups. Thus, it appears there is very little or no transfer from the solution component to the translation component, as would be expected from a production system analysis.

Operator selection

Table 5.2 compares differentiation and integration problem types in terms of mean time per operator selection and extra moves per problem (relative to the optimal number) on day 2 of the experiment (the first day of problem solving). ANOVAs comparing these day 2 means yield a main effect for extra moves ($F(1,17) = 10.8$, $p < .01$) but not for time per selection. This means that differentiation problems are in fact more difficult in terms of number of extra moves but not time per move. There is no significant effect for cover story on either dependent measure. This is further support for the independence of translation and solution.

Table 5.2 also presents the results from day 3 of the experiment, when all subjects are solving differentiation problems. Those subjects who solve differentiation problems on both days of the experiment (the learning control group) improve in terms

Table 5.2. Operator selection results on both days of problem
solving in the calculus experiment.

Day	Measure	Differentiation selection	Integration selection	No selection
2	Time per selection (sec.)	34.9	34.7	—
	Extra moves per problem	3.4	1.7	—
3	Time per selection (sec.)	18.6	24.5	33.0
	Extra moves per problem	2.6	2.2	3.4

of both time per operator selection (from 34.9 to 18.6 seconds; $F(1,9) = 137.7$, $p < .0001$) and extra moves per problem (from 3.4 to 2.6: $F(1.9) = 6.0$, $p < .05$). This reduction in extra moves is totally accounted for, however, in the reduction of illegal moves (from 1.9 to 1.1; $F(1,9) = 14.9$, $p < .01$), illegal moves being defined as before as those that violate the preconditions of the operators. Aside from the substantial speedup, learning seems to be of a rather trivial sort (learning the preconditions of the operators) as opposed to something more insightful regarding the optimal strategy for solving these problems.

The transfer data in Table 5.2 shows that there is substantial but less than total transfer from integration to differentiation problems in terms of time per operator selection. Expressed as a percentage of the theoretical maximum improvement observed in the differentiation control group (namely our standard formula), the savings is $(34.9 - 24.5)/(34.9 - 18.6)$, or approximately 64 percent. An ANOVA performed on the day 3 data yielded a main effect for the problem type factor ($F(2,26) = 16.4$, $p < .001$), and subsequent Newman-Keuls multiple-range tests revealed that all three selection times are different from one another (all $F(24) > 3.3$, all $p < .05$). This confirms that integration subjects experience substantial but less than total transfer to differentiation problems. Interestingly, the integration group surpasses the theoretical maximum reduction in terms of extra moves and actually surpasses the performance of the differentiation control. This difference, however, is not statistically significant.

Finally, there is virtually no transfer on either measure for the group that has no operator selection practice on day 2 of the experiment (the no goal group). This group did, however, practice the translation and operator application components on day 2. This means that there is no transfer from these to operator selection. Thus, it apparently supports our implicit assumption that related-rates problem-solving skill can be decomposed into several totally independent parts. A similar simplifying assumption was made by Hayes and Simon (1974) in their UNDERSTAND model, where problem comprehension was totally disjunct from problem solution.

An interesting question is what to make of the 64 percent transfer observed from integration to differentiation. To address this issue, we first look at the strategies that subjects use to solve the two types of problems. All the problems presented by the tutor give subjects the task of trying to find an equation relating x and z given an equation relating x and y and another relating y and z. Often problem solving takes the form of preparing the two initial relations so they can be combined properly to form the final relation. It is possible to characterize the strategies used to solve these problems by the operator (either chain rule or substitute equations) chosen to combine the two initial relations. Depending upon the initial relations, one combining operator may be more or less optimal than the other. For example, in the solution trace presented earlier, a better strategy is to substitute equations first and then differentiate the result rather than to differentiate both initial relations first and then apply the chain rule. It is generally the case that those initial states composed of regular equations favor use of the substitute equations operator and those composed of derivatives favor use of apply chain rule. This bias is somewhat modulated by the goal type of the problem, with integration goals favoring substitute equations and differentiation goals favoring apply chain rule.

Table 5.3 gives a problem-by-problem breakdown of strategies used on the first six problems on both days of problem solving. Shown is the percentage of subjects using the apply chain rule operator to derive the target relation (the remaining subjects are using the substitute equations operator). On day 2 (first day of problem solving), the preferred operator for solving differentiation problems is apply chain rule. However, on problems 1 and 5 where substitute equations is optimal, subjects use apply chain rule on average only 52 percent of the time, as opposed to an average of 72 percent on other problems. Thus, initial state seems to .have some influence on choice of strategy. Interestingly, however, this sensitivity to initial state all but disappears on day 3. Those subjects who solve differentiation problems on day 2 use apply chain rule 87 percent of the time on day 3, for

Table 5.3.   Strategy analysis. The numbers represent percent usage of the chain-rule strategy; S and C stand for substitution and chain-rule strategy, respectively.

		Problem						
Day	Problem type	1	2	3	4	5	6	M
2	Differentiation	50	67	80	73	55	67	65
	Optimal strategy	S	C	C	C	S	C	
	Integration	0	0	0	0	0	0	0
	Optimal strategy	S	S	S	S	S	S	
3	Differentiation	82	75	100	83	100	82	87
	Integration	50	20	75	82	80	50	59

an increase of 22 percent. In addition, there is no difference between strategy choice on problems 1 and 5 and remaining problems. As apply chain rule becomes more dominant, a kind of Einstellung effect emerges as a secondary phenomenon.

Turning to the integration problems on day 2, we see that apply chain rule is not used by any subject on any problem. The overwhelming dominance of the substitute equations operator on these problems has at least two possible sources: First, it is in fact the optimal choice on all 6 of the integration problems. Second, substitute equations may have some a priori advantage over apply chain rule because it is an operator imported from basic algebra and is presumably already familiar to subjects.

Day 3 data for those subjects who solved integration problems on day 2 shows that use of apply chain rule is virtually identical to that of the differentiation control on day 2 (59 percent versus 65 percent). Thus, there is little evidence for the transfer of substantive strategic knowledge, and the 64 percent savings in terms of operator selection remains unexplained.

Even though we have shown that practicing the substitution strategy on day 2 on integration problems has little effect on choice of strategy on day 3 on differentiation problems, it is still the case that the substitution strategy is a source of overlap for the two types of problems. Indeed, Table 5.3 shows that integration subjects use the substitution strategy on a full 41 percent of the differentiation problems. Thus, the substitution strategy is still a possible source of transfer in operator selection. We have simply been unable to localize the effect.

In our pursuit of an explanation for the 64 percent transfer, it is useful to remember that, aside from basic strategy, many of the same operators are selected in both kinds of problems. For

Table 5.4.   Relationship between the frequency of selection of operators on day 2 and the level of transfer on day 3. The data are drawn from subjects who solved integration problems on day 2 and differentiation problems on day 3. Transfer is expressed in terms of time per selection and is based on comparisons with differentiation control subjects.

Operator	Frequency of selection (day 2)	Transfer (day 3)
Integrate	12.4	−20%
Differentiate	1.3	66%
Substitute	11.6	107%
Chain rule	1.8	65%
Restate	11.3	84%
Flip derivative	2.1	53%
Evaluate	13.5	90%

example, the evaluate operator is always the last operator selected in both integration and differentiation problems. If common operator selections are indeed a source of transfer, our identical elements model would predict that those operators selected with higher frequency on integration problems would exhibit higher levels of transfer to differentiation problems. Table 5.4 provides an analysis of the operator selections made by our integration subjects in terms of frequency of selection on day 2 and percentage transfer in terms of time per selection on day 3. All operator selections are in fact practiced to some degree on day 2. Overall, the table shows a fairly direct relationship between frequency of use and percentage transfer, except for one anomolous entry: the integrate operator. Despite the fact that integration is one of the most frequently selected operators on day 2, it shows the least transfer on day 3. In fact, the transfer is slightly negative (−20 percent), although it may be best viewed as simply zero transfer. There is a good explanation for this, based entirely on the fact that, unlike the other operators, the integrate operator is properly selected under radically different circumstances in the two types of problems. The following two production rules show the conditions for selecting the integrate operator in the integration and differentiation problems, respectively:

P select-integrate-Integration-goal

>   IF = equation is part of the initial state of the problem
>   and = equation is a derivative
> THEN integrate = equation.

P select-integrate-Differentiation-goal

>   IF = equation is part of the initial state of the problem
>   and = equation is a derivative
>   and the goal is to find an equation stating = var1 in
>   terms of = var2
>   and = equation has a variable = var3 on the right-
>   hand side
>   and = var3 does not equal = var2
> THEN integrate = equation.

The first thing to notice is that these rules are quite distinct. In the integration problems, the integrate operator applies indiscriminately to all derivatives, whereas in the differentiation problems, it applies in only rare circumstances. Specifically, integration is required in only those cases where a derivative is stated in terms of the wrong variable, so that the chain rule is blocked. Thus, different rules are responsible for the selection of this operator in the two types of problems, and this accounts for the total lack of transfer. When we exclude the integrate operator from the analysis, the correlation between frequency of selection on day 2 and level of transfer on day 3 is .87. This provides strong support for the identical elements model and does much to account for the 64 percent transfer observed in operator selection.

Operator application

Unlike the translation and operator selection components, all subjects get three days of practice on operator application. Table 5.5 shows the results in terms of time per application for the three solution conditions (integration, differentiation, and none) on all three days. There was no effect of translation condition on operator application on any day, so the table collapses across this factor. This, by the way, is further evidence for the independence of translation and solution components.

The three solution conditions are virtually identical on the first two days, but the integration condition lags behind somewhat on the third (in the none condition, subjects practice the same operator applications as in the differentiation condition, so

Table 5.5.   Time per operator application (sec.) on all three days of
              the calculus experiment.

Day	Solution condition		
	Integration	Differentiation	None
1	82.8	78.7	83.7
2	40.6	43.2	43.8
3	33.5	26.3	27.7

the total transfer observed between these two conditions on day
3 is to be expected). Expressed as a percentage of the total
improvement shown by the differentiation control subjects,
transfer from integration to differentiation in terms of operator
application is $(43.2 - 33.5)/(43.2 - 26.3)$ or 57 percent. This is in
fair agreement with the 64 percent figure observed in operator
selection. As before, the lack of total transfer may be attributed
to the fact that, in the course of solving integration problems on
day 2, subjects get most of their practice on operators that apply
less frequently on day 3. Table 5.6 shows operator frequencies
for integration subjects on days 2 and 3. Most of the high-
frequency operators on day 2 (such as integrate, substitute, and
restate) appear much less often on day 3. Once again, the identical productions model would predict a fairly high correlation
between frequency of application on day 2 and level of transfer
on day 3. The correlation observed in this instance was .48,

Table 5.6.   Operator frequencies on days 2 and 3 for the integration
              subjects. On day 2, subjects are solving integration prob-
              lems; on day 3, differentiation problems.

Operator	Day 2	Day 3
Integrate	12.4	5.2
Differentiate	1.3	7.8
Substitute	11.6	4.6
Chain rule	1.8	5.2
Restate	11.3	4.8
Flip derivative	2.1	4.3
Evaluate	13.5	6.8

somewhat lower than the .87 observed for operator selection but still fairly supportive of the model. One reason for a lower correlation is the fact that measures of transfer in this case are based on transitions from the second to the third days of practice, rather than from the first to the second, as was the case with operator selection. Such transitions necessarily involve less learning, and as a result, transfer measures tend to be less reliable.

Summary of Calculus Experiment

This experiment had three major results. First, the translation and solution components were shown to be totally independent. On day 2, translation condition had no effect on solution performance, and likewise, solution condition had no effect on translation performance. This was the first evidence that these were encapsulated components. More important, the transfer results showed that practice on translation had no effect on solution, and vice versa. Specifically, subjects who practiced solution but not translation on day 2 did no better on translation on day 3 than subjects with no practice whatsoever on day 2. Similarly, subjects who practiced translation and operator application but not operator selection on day 2 did no better on selection on day 3. This provides additional support for the encapsulation of translation and solution processes, and it suggests that the solution subcomponents of selection and application are independent as well. Since all of these components tap a common, abstract knowledge of calculus, this pattern of results is the first piece of evidence for the use specificity of knowledge.

Second, we observed 64 percent transfer from integration to differentiation in terms of operator selection, and 57 percent transfer in terms of application. Both of these cases are potential counterexamples to the use specificity principle. However, careful analysis revealed that transfer in both cases was concentrated in the selections and applications shared by the two problem types. These results provide additional support for the identical productions model.

Third, within the translation component, we observed total transfer from problems with economics cover stories to those with geometry cover stories. This suggests that subjects were using a generalized, syntactic parsing strategy. Ultimately, this result supports the view that production rules have an abstract quality not found in Thorndike's elements.

Use Specificity in LISP Programming

Kessler's (1988) research is another demonstration of lack of transfer among different uses of the same knowledge. McKendree and Anderson (1987) had reported preliminary evidence that there was little transfer from evaluating LISP code to generating LISP code. Kessler set out to perform a more thorough analysis of this issue, looking at transfer relationships between not two but three components: generation, evaluation, and debugging.

A loose parallel may be drawn between the coding and evaluation of a programming language like LISP and the generation and comprehension of a natural language. In fact, this parallel has been drawn quite explicitly and profitably by some researchers (e.g., Soloway, Ehrlich, and Gold, 1983). Thus, the results of experiments like Kessler's may have some bearing on the issue of the use specificity of linguistic knowledge.

In Kessler's experiment, subjects worked with simple LISP functions like:

```
(defun pal (x)
  (append x (reverse x)))
```

This function makes a palindrome out of the items of a list. Thus if a user types (*pal* '(*a b c*)), LISP will return (*a b c c b a*). This works by appending the list that is given with the reverse of the list.

Subjects were given training on either coding, evaluation, or debugging. In the coding condition, subjects had to write a function given the problem specification. Subjects were just learning how to write LISP functions, and so they found this a relatively difficult task. In the evaluation condition, they were asked to simulate the steps of the LISP interpreter as it stepped through the code. In the debugging condition, subjects were given a buggy version of the function and asked to correct it. For example, the buggy version of the *pal* function that Kessler used was:

```
(defun pal (x)
  (list x (reverse x)))
```

In contrast to the *append* in the correct function definition, *list* in this function definition embeds its arguments in an extra layer of parentheses. Thus, the preceding function would produce ((*a b c*) (*c b a*)) rather than the desired (*a b c c b a*).

Kessler gave subjects practice at either coding, evaluating, or debugging nine such functions. Then he looked at transfer to each of these three tasks using a 3 × 3 factorial design. Table 5.7

Table 5.7. Raw scores and percentage transfer (in parentheses) between coding, debugging, and evaluation in the Kessler (1988) experiment. Results are expressed in terms of time to finish a problem (sec.) and number of errors per problem.

Training	Measure	Transfer Coding		Debugging		Evaluation	
Coding	time	163	(100%)	182	(81%)	358	(12%)
	errors	2.0	(100%)	2.0	(71%)	8.6	(−66%)
Debugging	time	184	(92%)	146	(100%)	336	(41%)
	errors	2.3	(90%)	1.5	(100%)	6.6	(29%)
Evaluation	time	304	(47%)	283	(25%)	231	(100%)
	errors	4.3	(23%)	3.0	(29%)	5.1	(100%)
None	time	412		329		376	
	errors	4.9		3.6		7.2	

shows his transfer results measured in terms of mean time to process a function (either code, evaluate, or debug it) and mean number of errors. The table also shows the time it took subjects to do each task initially. From this data, we calculated our standard transfer measure for each condition. The results are clear. There is a high level of transfer between debugging and coding (an average of 91 percent), but rather little transfer between these two and evaluation (an average of 16 percent). The lack of transfer to and from evaluation is additional support for the use specificity position, but the high level of transfer between debugging and coding is somewhat problematic and might be interpreted as contrary evidence. However, according to Kessler's analysis, the coding and debugging tasks are not totally disjoint and in fact share a major subcomponent. In the debugging condition, after isolating the problem, subjects have to delete a fragment of the code in a structured editor and rewrite it. They have to write this same fragment of code (plus the rest of the function) in the coding condition. Thus, the writing of the fragment is common to both tasks. For instance, in our example, both coding and debugging subjects have to write the fragment (*append x* (*reverse x*)). The identical elements model predicts that transfer will be concentrated in this common component. If this is true, once again the principle of use specificity will be preserved.

Table 5.8 presents a differential analysis of the unique components and the common components in debugging and coding.

Table 5.8.   Differential transfer analysis for common and unique
components in the Kessler (1988) programming
experiment. Results are expressed in terms of time to
finish a problem (sec.) and number of errors per problem.

Training	Measure	Transfer			
		Coding		Debugging	
Common components					
Coding	time	124	(100%)	89	(98%)
	errors	1.8	(100%)	1.1	(100%)
Debugging	time	114	(103%)	87	(100%)
	errors	1.6	(114%)	1.2	(100%)
None	time	254		176	
	errors	3.2		2.7	
Unique components					
Coding	time	39	(100%)	92	(65%)
	errors	0.2	(100%)	0.9	(0%)
Debugging	time	65	(78%)	59	(100%)
	errors	0.7	(67%)	0.4	(100%)
None	time	158		153	
	errors	1.7		0.9	

The average transfer between debugging and coding on the common components is 105 percent, while it is only 52 percent for the
unique components. These results reinforce the position that the
positive transfer seen between tasks is concentrated in the shared
components. Of course, 52 percent is still high, but there is some
question as to whether all the so-called unique components in
Kessler's analysis were really unique. For example, they included
such shared processes as encoding the problem statement and
using the structured editor (actually the LISP tutor).

Conclusion

According to experimental evidence from the domains of calculus and LISP programming, transfer is restricted to the production rules shared between skills. More important, transfer is not
based on an abstract characterization of the knowledge underlying the production rules. These results are generally consistent with research on problem solving which has shown that
skills are quite use-specific and are situated in certain contexts
(Rogoff and Lave, 1984).

6 / Simulating Analogical Transfer

U p until this point we have been content to base our predictions of transfer on purely procedural embodiments of the skills under study. Our strategy has been to use production systems to model skilled performance and to compare production sets across skills. One implication of this kind of analysis is that two production sets based on the same abstract knowledge may nevertheless share no elements, because knowledge embodied as productions is in a sense directional and use-specific. Perhaps the clearest and strongest statement of this position is the largely untested prediction that there is no transfer between language comprehension and generation. However, it is certainly possible that, by adopting a strict production system view of transfer, we are glossing over some critical issues. Specifically, it may in some cases be necessary to consider the learning histories of skills and the origins of productions. According to the ACT* theory of skill acquisition (Anderson, 1982), productions arise from declarative precursors which are not committed to a specific use and are not specialized to a particular use. It may be that these declarative precursors will provide yet another basis for transfer, especially in those cases where compiled production sets share no elements yet are based on the same declarative knowledge. To explore this possibility, it seemed wise to produce at least one detailed simulation of the initial stages of skill acquisition. This simulation differs from the previous simulations in that the early stages rather than the endpoint of skill acquisition is being modeled. One of the principle functions of creating a simulation is to check one's theoretical analysis for oversights.

We decided to simulate problem solving in the calculus experiment. To help guide our development of a simulation model, we gathered verbal protocols from four additional subjects as they solved both differentiation and integration problems with the tutor. The model is implemented in the PUPS production system language (Anderson and Thompson, in press).

Theoretical Underpinnings

The model draws heavily on the ACT* theory of skill acquisition. To review, the ACT* theory breaks down acquisition into two major stages: a *declarative* stage, where a declarative representation of the skill is interpreted by general productions, and a *procedural* stage, where the skill is directly embodied in domain-specific productions. The transition from the declarative to the procedural stage is achieved by the process of *knowledge compilation.* An important recent modification to the theory has been the addition of structural analogy as a mechanism for translating initial declarative encodings into action. Extensive studies of novice LISP programmers (Anderson, Farrell, and Sauers, 1984; Pirolli and Anderson, 1985), as well as studies of subtraction and algebra instructional materials (VanLehn, 1983; Neves, 1981), have exposed the importance of example problems to the initial performance of a skill. Anderson (1986) showed how an analogy mechanism coupled with the standard knowledge compilation mechanisms could not only achieve the transition from declarative to procedural knowledge but also generalize the resultant procedural representation. This is done by abstracting common features of the source and target of the analogy. In accordance with this ACT* formulation, the current model stresses two features, the initial declarative encoding of domain knowledge and the importance of structural analogy in both operator application and operator selection.

Initial declarative encoding of domain knowledge

A serious effort has been made to develop a truly plausible representation of a subject's knowledge state at the beginning of related-rates problem solving. Presumably, after reading the instruction booklet on day 1 of the experiment, subjects have three types of knowledge which apply directly to the task:

1. Declarative encodings of the new, calculus-specific operators such as differentiate, integrate, and apply chain rule. These are what subjects derive from the instruction booklet.

2. Procedural representations of the familiar operators from algebra, such as restate and evaluate. Subjects learned these domain-specific productions in their algebra courses.

3. General productions for performing the various weak methods, specifically means-ends analysis. We assume these productions to be part of the human cognitive architecture.

A true test of the sufficiency of the ACT* skill acquisition mechanisms would be to start with these three components and see whether the entire course of skill acquisition could be approximated through practice. One of the trickier problems is to get a truly clean and principled separation of declarative and procedural knowledge before practice begins, especially in the weak methods. The overwhelming tendency when writing production systems simulating novice behavior is to embed too much knowledge in the productions themselves (that is, in compiled form) and not enough in declarative form. The result in most cases is a serious underestimation of the amount of learning that takes place.

Importance of structural analogy

The verbal protocols collected in this experiment provide further support for the critical role of structural analogy during the initial phases of skill acquisition. For example, here is an excerpt of a subject attempting to differentiate an equation for the first time (recall that the subject has a summary sheet at his side displaying the formula for differentiation):

Formula: $y = cx^n \longrightarrow dy/dx = n \times cx^{n-1}$

Given: $m = 2y^3$

Subject: Differentiate the equation *m* equals 2 times *y* to the third power. OK, let's follow the ol' formula. (Subject looks at summary sheet.) OK, *y* equals *c x* to the *n*, so you just take *dy*, which in this case is *dm* (subject begins typing answer), *dm* divided by, wait a minute, ah, *dx*, which is *dy* in this case, equals, ah, 3, which is *n*, 3 times *c*, which is 2, which is 6, 6 times *x*, which is *y*, 3 *y* to the second power, *n* minus 1 which is the second power, hit return . . .

(Typed answer: $dm/dy = 6y^2$)

Here, then, is a good example of the use of structural analogy in the application of operators. The mapping of elements is explicit, and in this case it works quite well. In all of these operator applications, the analogy is of the form:

$$\frac{formula\ input}{formula\ output} : : \frac{given\ equation}{answer?}$$

A correspondence is drawn between the formula input and the given equation, and an answer is generated which corresponds to the structure of the formula output but uses the bindings from the given equation. An interesting impasse occurs when the mapping between formula input and given equation is not obvious, as it is in this case of integration:

Formula: $dy/dx = cx^n \longrightarrow y = \dfrac{c}{n+1} \times x^{n+1}$

Given: $dw/da = 2$

Subject: OK, integrate the equation dw over da equals 2. In this case, you're just working backward. Hmmm, you don't really have a variable in this case, you just have dw over da equal to 2, and, uh, you plug in for y, which is equal to w, so the w, in this case, it's w (subject begins typing), y equals, ah, c, which is just 2, c, over, ummm, I guess we don't have a variable, so, ah, y is equal to, ah, dw over da equals 2, hmmm, it would be your y, which is just w, is equal to 2, c, which is 2, divided by n plus 1, you don't have a variable, so it would be zero, and you don't have a variable, so it would be to the zero power.

(Typed answer: $w = 0$)

Of course, the actual answer here is $w = 2a$. What this subject is lacking is a method for elaborating such equations into a form more closely analogous to the formula input:

$$dw/da = 2 \longleftrightarrow dw/da = 2a^0$$

Without this elaboration, the subject can find no binding for the term "x to the nth power" in the formula. After floundering temporarily, the subject fills in a default value of 0 as a patch, and the resultant product is 0. This particular integration exercise was in fact responsible for a large spike of errors observed in the integration learning curve.

Structural analogy plays a critical role in this model not only in the initial application of operators but also in the planning of operator selections. However, the analogy mechanism currently does not operate at the level of adapting a worked-out solution to the current problem, as is done in other systems (e.g. Carbonell, 1983). Rather, it plays a more low-level, but nonetheless crucial, role in the specification of subgoals. For example, if the goal of a problem is to find dp/dt, but no equation currently exists relating p and t, a subgoal might be set to apply the chain rule. The chain rule says $dx/dz = (dx/dy)(dy/dz)$. Subgoals must be set to find the derivatives that, when chained together, produce dp/dt. But what exactly are these derivatives? This can be answered by solving the following analogy between the chain rule and the current situation:

$$\frac{dx/dz}{(dx/dy)(dy/dz)} :: \frac{dp/dt}{(?)(?)}$$

Generally, we can characterize the analogy to be solved for operator selection as:

$$\frac{formula\ output}{formula\ input} :: \frac{goal}{subgoals?}$$

So, the analogy mechanism works much like before, except that the reasoning is in the opposite direction. In this way, the weak methods are kept free of domain-specific knowledge in our simulation.

Operator application and subgoal planning share the same declarative base; that is, both operate on the declarative representations of the formulas. However, the compiled product sets for each of these processes are completely disjoint. Early practice on one use might serve to correct or strengthen the declarative base and so facilitate early practice on the other use. Here, then, is a situation where a failure to consider the declarative component may result in an underprediction of transfer.

Components of the Model

The model contains the two major components of operator selection and operator application. No effort has been devoted to modeling the translation phase of problem solving.

Operator selection

The model derives its problem-solving power from a generic means-end analysis engine. Means-ends analysis is a weak method well documented by Newell and Simon (1972) as having extensive psychological validity and considerable general-purpose computational power. Newell and Simon used this method extensively in their classic GPS program (Ernst and Newell, 1969), which has been used to simulate problem solving in domains like logic, cryptarithmetic, tower of Hanoi, and missionaries and cannibals. Perhaps most relevant is the work of Larkin, McDermott, Simon, and Simon (1980) which documented the importance of means-end analysis as a novice strategy for solving systems of physics equations.

The informational demands of means-ends analysis are few: the system must be able to detect critical differences between the current state and the goal, index operators by the differences they reduce, and decide which difference is most important if more than one exists. The control structure of means-ends analysis is simply to examine the current state and the goal, determine the most important difference between them, retrieve an operator that reduces that difference, and apply it. Control flow is complicated by the fact that, if the chosen operator cannot be applied to the current state, the system recurses and attempts to reduce the difference between the current state and the preconditions of the operator.

The means-end analysis engine developed here has four difference detectors, one for recognizing that no relation currently contains the two variables contained in the goal relation (a *contains* difference), another for recognizing that the current relation is of a different type (derivative versus regular equation) than the goal relation (a *type* difference), a third for recognizing that the current relation is stated backward relative to the goal relation (a *directionality* difference), and a fourth for recognizing that a value has not been computed for the goal relation (a *value* difference). These four seem to be plausible rules that the student would have learned from prior algebra courses. The one difference detector for which this might not be apparent is the type difference, which detects differences between regular and derivative expressions. However, high school algebra involves numerous types of expressions which must be discriminated, such as quadratic versus factored equations and proper versus mixed fractions. The rank ordering of differences, which is required for means-end analysis in its classic conception, is somewhat problematic in this instance. We could find no a priori mathematical knowledge upon which our novices could rank order differences. However, all of our subjects had one day of operator application practice prior to problem solving and could presumably rank order the operators in terms of difficulty. Thus, our proposed control structure is:

1. Detect all differences between the current state and the goal state of the problem. Among all the operators that apply directly and reduce one of these differences, choose the operator that is easiest to apply.

2. If no operators apply directly, choose an operator whose preconditions are most closely matched. In other words, choose the operator that requires the fewest subgoals to be satisfied.

The second feature concerning the minimization of subgoals is consistent with the behavior of the physics novices observed by Larkin, McDermott, Simon, and Simon (1980). Such a control structure provides a combination of working forward and working backward which is characteristic of means-end analysis (Newell and Simon, 1972).

The operators pair off quite nicely in terms of the differences they reduce. Apply chain rule and substitute equations reduce the "contains" difference, differentiate and integrate reduce the "type" difference, flip derivative and restate reduce the "directionality" difference, and evaluate reduces the "value" difference. Discriminations between the two members of a pair are often made on the basis of goal information. In other words, if the goal is a derivative, apply chain rule is the operator of choice when a "contains" difference has been detected and two derivatives exist as inputs, differentiate is the operator of choice when a "type" difference has been detected, and so forth. This knowledge about the operators is directly told to the students and is practiced extensively on the first day of operator application. It is given to PUPS as declarative embellishments of the operators. This declarative knowledge is critical for the initial selection of operators, and it is another potential source of transfer between operator application and selection which we had previously overlooked.

To illustrate the operation of the means-ends analysis engine, we now trace its application to two differentiation problems. Table 6.1 shows a rank ordering of the seven calculus operators in terms of ease of application (these results are taken from day one of application practice in the calculus experiment). This table is used to discriminate among operators when more than

Table 6.1. Mean time per correct application for the seven operators on the initial day of operator application. The rank ordering shown here is used by the means-ends analysis engine to select among operators that both apply directly and reduce differences.

Operator	Time per correct application (sec.)
Flip derivative	28.7
Evaluate	61.6
Differentiate	90.7
Substitute	97.2
Apply chain rule	133.2
Integrate	141.7
Restate	160.4

one reduces a difference and applies directly. As shown, the operators in order of difficulty are flip derivative, evaluate, differentiate, substitute, apply chain rule, integrate, and restate.
    The initial state of problem 1 is:

(6.1) $s = 16t^2$

(6.2) $r = 4s$

(6.3) $t = 4$

The goal is to find a value for dr/dt when t equals 4. The system first examines the equations that have been written and determines that no relation currently expresses r in terms of t; that is, the system detects a contains difference between the current state and the goal. The system also determines that neither of the relations in the initial state is of the same type as the goal; that is, a type difference is detected. Neither the directionality nor the value difference is detected at this time, because these differences are only meaningful given a relation containing the goal variables. The system then consults the means-end analysis table and determines that the substitute operator applies directly to reduce the contains difference, and the differentiate operator applies directly to reduce the type difference. Since Table 6.1 shows that differentiation is easier than substitution, the differentiate operator is selected and applied to equation 6.1. This produces *ds/dt*. Once again, the system cycles through its difference detection phase, and a contains difference is detected, as well as a type difference for equation 6.2. Once again, the system chooses to differentiate equation 6.2, producing *dr/ds*. On the next cycle of different detection, the contains difference is detected once again, but this time it is the chain rule rather than the substitution operator that reduces the difference. The chain rule is selected and applied, producing *dr/dt*. Finally, a value difference is detected between this latter relation and the goal, and the evaluate operator is selected to reduce the difference. This produces *dr/dt* = 512, and the problem is solved.

This problem is relatively easy in that it is solved completely by working forward. This is because, on every cycle of difference detection, an operator was found which reduced a difference and could be applied directly. However, on the second differentiation problem, no operators apply directly at first. This requires an initial phase of working backward and the specification of subgoals.

The initial state for the second problem is:

(6.4) *ds/dt* = 32*t*

(6.5) *ds/dr* = 4

(6.6) *t* = 4

Once again, the goal is to find the value of *dr/dt* when *t* = 4. Here, the system first detects a contains difference, since no relation states *r* in terms of *t*. However, neither substitute nor apply chain rule applies directly to reduce this difference. Since apply chain rule has the fewest of its preconditions violated by the current state of the problem (both equations (6.4) and (6.5) are of the right type for the chain rule), the subgoal is set to apply the chain rule. The system at this point uses structural analogy to determine that an application of the chain rule that produces *dr/dt* would require the two derivatives *dr/ds* and *ds/dt* as input. These two derivatives are set as subgoals. At this point, the system notices that one of these subgoals, *ds/dt* is already satisfied. The remaining subgoal, *dr/ds*, is derived by first detecting a directionality difference between *dr/ds* and equation (6.5) and then selecting flip derivative to reduce the difference. In this case, no preconditions are violated, and the operator is applied. Once the subgoal *dr/ds* is satisfied, the chain rule is applied, producing *dr/dt* in terms of *t*. At this point, the system detects a value difference, the evaluate operator is selected and applied, and the problem is solved.

This mixture of forward and backward chaining does quite well at describing the sequences of moves actually made by subjects solving both differentiation and integration problems. To gather empirical support for our model, we compared the initial moves chosen by the simulation with the initial moves made by subjects in the calculus experiment. In addition to first moves, we examined the combiner operators chosen by both simulation and subjects (the combiner operators, apply chain rule and substitute, are those operators that reduce the contains difference, which is present in all problems). In each analysis, we examined the first six problems on both days of problem solving for the integration and differentiation subjects, which provided us with a total of 48 (2 × 6 × 2 × 2) moves to predict. In terms of most preferred move, the simulation agreed with the subjects in 46 out of the 48 cases (the two failures were recorded in predicting first moves). In other words, in 95 percent of the cases, the simulation chose the move most often selected by subjects. Across problems and conditions, the most preferred moves amounted to 58 percent of all moves made in the first-move analysis and 77 percent of all moves made in the combiner analysis.

Table 6.2 presents a matrix relating predicted and observed first moves in terms of individual operators (the matrix is

Table 6.2.   Observed rank orderings of predicted and unpredicted first moves in the calculus experiment.

Observed first move	Predicted first move				
	Substitute	Chain rule	Integrate	Differentiate	Flip derivative
Substitute	1.5	5.6	5.2	4.2	5.7
Chain rule	4.2	1.0	4.3	5.5	3.2
Integrate	5.5	2.6	1.2	3.7	2.0
Differentiate	4.2	5.6	4.2	1.2	5.7
Flip derivative	5.5	2.6	3.8	5.3	1.0
Restate	3.5	4.9	4.2	2.8	4.8
Evaluate	3.5	5.6	5.2	5.1	5.7

5 × 7 instead of 7 × 7 because, whereas all seven operators were observed as first-move selections, only five were predicted). For each predicted operator, we have rank ordered the seven observed operators in terms of frequency of subject selection. Presented in the matrix are the observed rank orders of the *i*th operator when the *j*th operator has been predicted, averaged across day, problem, and solution condition. The rank orderings range from 1 to 7, with a mean of 3.5. Help requests amounted to only 4 percent of the total first moves made and thus have been excluded from this analysis. On the diagonal of the matrix, which represents the observed rank orderings of predicted operators, the values are much lower than anywhere else in the matrix. Indeed, the average observed rank ordering of predicted moves is 1.1, compared with an average rank of 4.5 elsewhere in the matrix. In all five categories of prediction, the predicted operator has the highest observed rank ordering. This is additional evidence that the simulation is doing quite well at predicting the moves made by subjects.

One complication in this analysis is that, given the initial states of the six problems, not all operators are legal as first moves. Of course, all first moves predicted by the simulation are legal. Of the remaining six operators, an average of 3.3 are legal and 2.7 are illegal as first moves. It is likely that the illegal moves are seldom selected and are accentuating the differences between the rank orderings of predicted and unpredicted moves. However, if we exclude illegal operators from our analysis, we find that the simulation is still doing quite well at predicting subjects' selections. The average rank ordering of legal, unpredicted moves is 3.6, compared with 5.2 for illegal moves and 1.1 for predicted moves.

Operator application

The new calculus operators differentiate, integrate, and apply chain rule are represented declaratively in the system. As an example, Figure 6.1 shows the declarative representation of the differentiate formula. The PUPS working memory elements displayed here are framelike and allow for any number of user-defined attribute-value pairs. By cross-referencing working memory elements in the slots, one can create networks of arbitrary complexity. In this system, both operator formulas and their operands (the equations) are represented as networks that closely approximate tree structures.

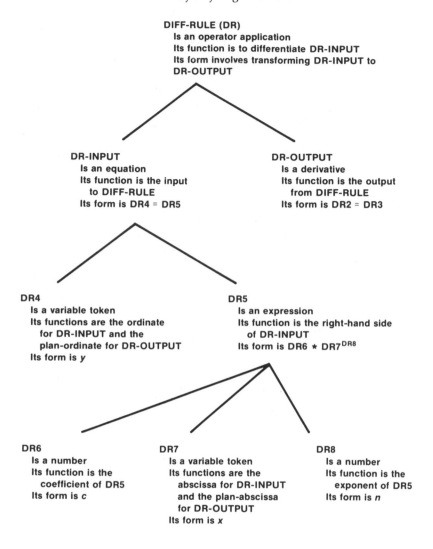

DIFF-RULE (DR)
Is an operator application
Its function is to differentiate DR-INPUT
Its form involves transforming DR-INPUT to
DR-OUTPUT

DR-INPUT
Is an equation
Its function is the input
to DIFF-RULE
Its form is DR4 = DR5

DR-OUTPUT
Is a derivative
Its function is the output
from DIFF-RULE
Its form is DR2 = DR3

DR4
Is a variable token
Its functions are the ordinate
for DR-INPUT and the
plan-ordinate for DR-OUTPUT
Its form is y

DR5
Is an expression
Its function is the right-hand side
of DR-INPUT
Its form is DR6 $\star$ DR7^{DR8}

DR6
Is a number
Its function is the
coefficient of DR5
Its form is c

DR7
Is a variable token
Its functions are the
abscissa for DR-INPUT
and the plan-abscissa
for DR-OUTPUT
Its form is x

DR8
Is a number
Its function is the
exponent of DR5
Its form is n

(a) the top-level node and the input equation $y = cx^n$

Figure 6.1. *Declarative representation of the differentiation formula.*

The working memory elements in Figure 6.1 make primary use of three attributes: isa, function, and form. For the purposes of analogy, all three are critical. Generally, the analogy mechanism expects to be given a source element, which has values for both function and form slots, and a target element, which has a value for the function slot only. The mechanism fills in the form

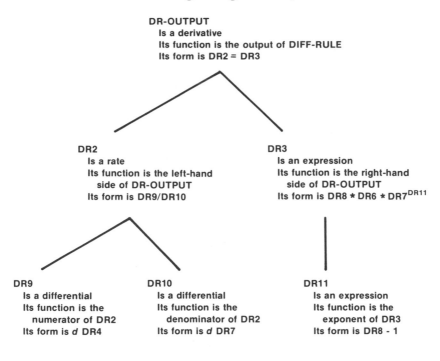

DR-OUTPUT
Is a derivative
Its function is the output of DIFF-RULE
Its form is DR2 = DR3

DR2
Is a rate
Its function is the left-hand
   side of DR-OUTPUT
Its form is DR9/DR10

DR3
Is an expression
Its function is the right-hand
   side of DR-OUTPUT
Its form is DR8 * DR6 * DR7^{DR11}

DR9
Is a differential
Its function is the
   numerator of DR2
Its form is *d* DR4

DR10
Is a differential
Its function is the
   denominator of DR2
Its form is *d* DR7

DR11
Is an expression
Its function is the
   exponent of DR3
Its form is DR8 - 1

(b) the output equation $dy/dx = n * cx^n$

Figure 6.1. (*continued*)

slot of the target by bringing elements in the functional descriptions of the source and target into correspondence. Elements can be brought into correspondence if they serve the same function in both source and target domains and have identical isa values.

If PUPS wanted to use this knowledge structure as a basis for analogy, it would try to map it onto a problem. The left-hand side of the formula (DR-INPUT in Figure 6.1) would be mapped to the equation to be differentiated. Then PUPS would try to generate a structure analogous to the right-hand side (DR-OUTPUT) using the correspondences it established mapping the left-hand side to the equation. The details of this generation process are fairly complicated and will be discussed shortly. However, the mechanism draws the same correspondences as the protocol subjects and derives the answer in a depth-first, left-to-right fashion.

Analogical errors

One pitfall in the use of analogical reasoning is the danger of drawing false analogies (Halasz and Moran, 1982). An interesting consequence of a network-matching algorithm like this one is that false analogies can be modeled by spurious correspondences between networks. For example, the networks representing the integration and differentiation formulas share many correspondences, most notably in their left-hand sides. One might reasonably expect intrusions in the application of these formulas. In fact, an examination of the error data from the first day of operator application revealed that a small but nonnegligible percentage of the errors could be explained by the confounding of these two formulas. For example, when differentiating, some subjects divide the coefficient by $n + 1$ rather than multiplying by n. Similarly, some subjects increment rather than decrement the exponent. Different combinations of these errors and their complements were observed in both differentiation and integration.

A Detailed Trace of the Simulation

In order to illustrate fully the computational properties of operator selection and application, we present a detailed trace of the simulation as it solves the third problem in the set of six differentiation problems. For the purposes of the simulation, the initial state of problem 3 is:

(6.7) $s = \frac{1}{4} \times r$

(6.8) $ds/dt = 8t$

(6.9) $t = 4$

The goal of this problem is to find the value of dr/dt when $t = 4$. The solution path generated by the simulation is:

(6.10) $ds/dr = \frac{1}{4}$ (differentiate equation 6.7)

(6.11) $dr/ds = 4$ (flip equation 6.10)

(6.12) $dr/dt = 32t$ (apply chain rule to equations 6.11 and 6.8)

(6.13) $dr/dt = 128$ (evaluate equation 6.12 with 6.9)

In all, the simulation requires 61 production cycles to solve this problem. Of these, 31 involve the use of structural analogy to interpret the declarative representations of the formulas. Structural analogy supports both operator application (forward mode) and subgoal specification (backward mode). Of the remaining 30 cycles, four involve the selection of operators from the means-ends table, which is another declarative structure. We assume that both the declarative representations of the formulas and the means-end table are acquired by our subjects by reading the instruction booklet and practicing operator applications on the initial day prior to problem solving.

The initial state

Figures 6.2–6.4 present the declarative representations of the three equations comprising the initial state of problem 3. All equations are represented as tree structures. The nodes in the tree are connected through both the function and the form slots. Generally, elements in the function slots point to nodes at higher levels in the tree, and elements in the form slots point to nodes at lower levels. In addition to values for the isa, function, and form slots, the root node of each equation has an extra "elabo-

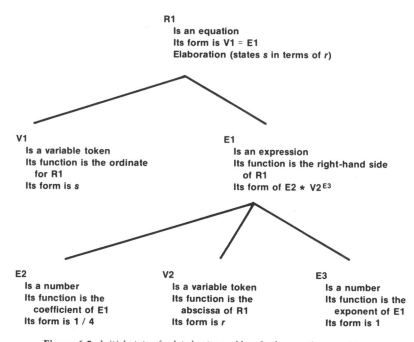

R1
Is an equation
Its form is V1 = E1
Elaboration (states *s* in terms of *r*)

V1
Is a variable token
Its function is the ordinate
for R1
Its form is *s*

E1
Is an expression
Its function is the right-hand side
of R1
Its form of E2 $*$ V2^{E3}

E2
Is a number
Its function is the
coefficient of E1
Its form is 1 / 4

V2
Is a variable token
Its function is the
abscissa of R1
Its form is *r*

E3
Is a number
Its function is the
exponent of E1
Its form is 1

Figure 6.2. *Initial state of related-rates problem 3: the equation* s $=$ ¼ $\times$ r.

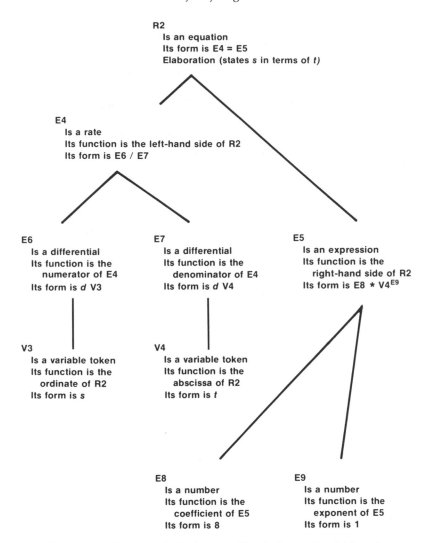

Figure 6.3. *Initial state of related-rates problem 3: the equation* ds/dt = 8t.

ration" slot, telling which two variables are related by the equation and in which direction. These elaboration slots are examined by the difference detectors and are critical for planning.

In addition to these three equations, the initial state contains a statement of the overall goal of the problem. The goal is represented simply as an equation with the right-hand side missing (in Figure 6.5 the mode representing this right-hand

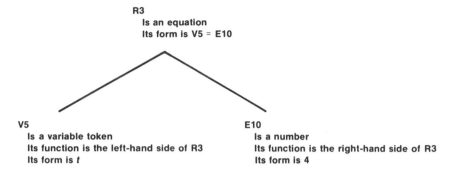

R3
Is an equation
Its form is V5 = E10

V5
Is a variable token
Its function is the left-hand side of R3
Its form is *t*

E10
Is a number
Its function is the right-hand side of R3
Its form is 4

Figure 6.4. *Initial state of related rates problem 3: the equation* t = 4.

side is A3). The purpose of problem solving, then, is to fill in this right-hand side.

The production set

Table 6.3 presents Englishified versions of the 12 productions used for planning and analogical problem solving. Not shown in the figure are 12 other productions that perform simple equation transformations and memory management. The equation transformations are used for two related purposes: to simplify the results of operator applications (increment exponents, multiply through coefficients) and to restore the results of operator applications to the canonical form used to represent equations in the formulas. This ensures a match between the equations generated by the simulation and the inputs and outputs of the formulas and thereby allows for application by analogy. This canonical form is simply cx^n; that is, the right-hand side of every equation must have a coefficient, a variable, and an exponent. Thus, the simulation was not hampered by mismatches in representation, as some of our subjects were (recall the subject who was unable to apply the integration formula to $dw/da = 2$). In this sense, the simulation represents the best of our subjects.

Productions P1 through P4 in the figure are the four productions used for difference detection. Productions P5, P6, and P7 are used to retrieve unary and binary operators respectively from the means-end table once differences have been detected. In both P5 and P6, the operators that are retrieved can be applied immediately, which leads to a kind of forward-chaining through the problem space. The existence of two productions rather than one to retrieve applicable operators is due to minor

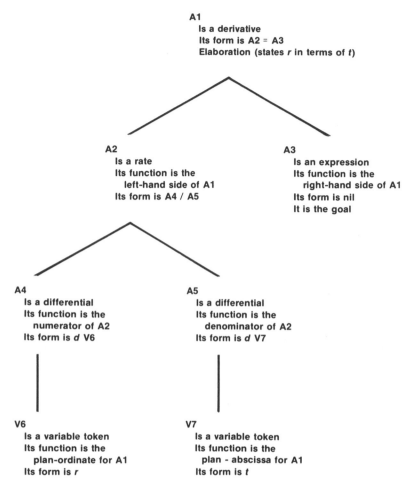

Figure 6.5. *The goal of problem 3.*

syntactic differences in representation (if PUPS had a more powerful representation language, we would have been able to write
one production that had the effect of both). Both P5 and P6 are
given higher strength than P7, which retrieves operators that do
not apply directly. The firing of P7 represents a kind of
backward-chaining, as subgoals are set to find equations which
satisfy the preconditions of the proposed operator. The simulation uses backward-chaining only as a last resort, that is, when
no operators can be found both that reduce differences and
whose preconditions are already satisfied.

Productions P5, P6, and P7 retrieve their operators from the

Table 6.3. Productions used for planning and analogical problem solving.

P1 detect-diff-contains

IF the goal is to find an equation of type =t that states variable =v1 in terms of variable =v2, and no equation already relates =v1 and =v2, and no operator application is already planned to reduce the "contains" difference,

THEN set as a subgoal to retrieve an operator from the means-ends table that reduces the "contains" difference.

P2 detect-diff-type

IF the goal is to find an equation of type =t, and there is an equation in the initial state not of type =t,

THEN set as a subgoal to retrieve an operator from the means-ends table that reduces the "type" difference and produces an equation of type =t.

P3 detect-diff-direction

IF the goal is to find an equation of type =t that states variable =v1 in terms of variable =v2, and there is an equation of type =t that states =v2 in terms of =v1

THEN set as a subgoal to retrieve an operator from the means-ends table that reduces the "directionality" difference and produces an equation of type =t.

P4 detect-diff-value

IF the goal is to find the value of =v1, and there is an equation of the form =v1 = =rhs, and expression =rhs has a form but is not simply a number,

THEN set as a subgoal to retrieve an operator from the means-ends table that reduces the "value" difference.

P5 retrieve-unary-operator

IF the goal is to retrieve a unary operator that reduces a difference of type =d and produces an equation of type =t, and the means-ends table contains an entry =operator that reduces a difference of type =d and produces an equation of type =t, and the current equation is =current,

THEN create a new root node for an operator application whose function is to apply =operator to equation =current.

(continued)

Table 6.3.   (continued)

P6 retrieve-binary-operator

IF   the goal is to retrieve a binary operator that reduces a difference
      of type = d and produces an equation of type = t,
      and the means-ends table contains an entry = operator that
      reduces a difference of type = d and produces an equation
      of type = t,
      and the current equations are = current1 and = current2,

THEN create a new root node for an operator application whose
      function is to apply = operator to equations = current1 and
      = current2.

P7 retrieve-binary-operator-no-inputs

IF   the goal is to retrieve a binary operator that reduces a difference
      of type = d and produces an equation of type = t,
      and the means-ends table contains an entry = operator that
      reduces a difference of type = d and produces an equation of
      type = t,
      and the current equations are = current1 and = current2,
      but they are not appropriate for = operator,

THEN create a new root node for an operator application whose
      function is to apply = operator,
      and set as subgoals to find appropriate inputs.

P8 goal-satisfied

IF   the goal is to find an equation = goal of type = t that states = v1
      in terms of = v2,
      and an equation = new has just been generated of type = t
      that states = v1 in terms of = v2,

THEN identify = new as an instance of = goal
      and mark = goal as satisfied.

P9 interpret-formula

IF   the goal is a = thing whose function is to do = something to
      = data1 and whose form is nil,
      and there is an element of a formula = f that is a = thing whose
      function is to do = something to = data2 and whose form is
      nonnil,
      and the current operator application involves the formula = f,

THEN try to generate the form slot of the goal from the form slot of
      the formula by analogy.

P10 functional-elaboration

IF   the goal is a = thing whose only function is to do = something
      to = data,

Table 6.3. (continued)

and there is an element of a formula =f that is a =thing whose
function slot has two values, one to do =something to =data,
another to do =something-else to =other-data,
and the current operator application involves the
formula =f,
THEN try to generate the missing function slot of the goal from the
extra function slot of the formula by analogy.

P11 states-elaboration

IF there is a variable =v1 whose function is to be the ordinate
of =equation,
and there is a variable =v2 whose function is to be the abscissa
of =equation,
and =equation currently has no "states" elaboration,
THEN =equation states =v1 in terms of =v2.

P12 supply-middle-variable

IF there is an operator application that takes two inputs,
=input1 and =input2,
and there is a variable =v1 whose function is to be the
ordinate of =input1 and whose form is =letter1,
and there is a variable =v2 whose function is to be the
abscissa of =input2 and whose form is =letter2,
and there is a variable =v3 whose function slot has two values,
one to be the abscissa of =input1 and another to be
the ordinate of =input2, and whose form slot is nil,
and there is a letter =letter3 that does not equal =letter1 or
=letter2,
THEN the form of =v3 is =letter3.

means-end table, a declarative structure shown in Table 6.4. We
assume that the means-ends table is derived by students when
they read the instruction booklet and practice operator application exercises on the first day. The entries in the table are ordered
from most to least difficult so that, when the table is loaded into
working memory, the easier operators will have greater recency
and will take precedence over the more difficult operators.

Production P7 sets subgoals to find appropriate inputs for
particular operators. One or more additional operator selections
and applications may be required to generate these inputs. Production P8 is simply a demon that examines the products of

Table 6.4.   Means-ends analysis table.

Restate-difference
    Is a unary operator
    Its function is to reduce a directionality difference
    It produces an equation

Integrate-difference
    Is a unary operator
    Its function is to reduce a type difference
    It produces an equation

Chain-difference
    Is a binary operator
    Its function is to reduce a contains difference
    It produces a derivative

Substitute-difference
    Is a binary operator
    Its function is to reduce a contains difference
    It produces an equation

Differentiate-difference
    Is a unary operator
    Its function is to reduce a type difference
    It produces a derivative

Evaluate-difference
    Is a binary operator
    Its function is to reduce a value difference

Flip-difference
    Is a unary operator
    Its function is to reduce a value difference
    It produces a derivative

operator applications to determine whether subgoals have been satisfied.

Production P9 is the one production in the system that performs function-to-form analogy, so called because the analogy mechanism uses the functional descriptions of elements in the form slot of the model to generate corresponding elements in the form slot of the target. Function-to-form analogy is the mechanism through which the declarative representations of the formulas are interpreted. The purpose of P9 is to select a working-memory element whose form slot is empty (designated the target) and a similar element whose form slot is not (designated the source). Typically, the target is some element of an equation that the simulation is trying to derive, and the source is a corresponding element from a formula. The analogy mechanism, which is implemented in LISP and is part of the PUPS architecture, attempts to write the missing form slot of the target. A short description of the analogy algorithm can be found in the Appendix to this chapter. A more complete description can be found in descriptions of the PUPS implementation (Thompson, 1986; Anderson and Thompson, in press).

Production P10 performs another kind of analogical processing, whose aim is to elaborate the functional descriptions of elements in the target domain using the functional descriptions of elements in the source domain. Anderson and Thompson (in press) call this kind of processing function-to-function analogy. The critical point here is that sometimes the functional descriptions of elements in the target domain are too sparse to allow for the standard function-to-form analogy to work. In these situations, if the functional description of the source is somewhat richer, it may be possible to elaborate the functional description of the target by the same kind of analogical processing just described. The only difference is that the writing nodes are in the function slot of the source element rather than the form slot. Once the functional description of the target is elaborated, the standard function-to-form analogy has a greater probability of success.

As an example of function-to-function analogy as a prerequisite to function-to-form analogy, consider the situation faced by the simulation as it tries to apply the differentiation formula (see Figure 6.1) to an equation. The general strategy of the simulation is to bring the equation it wants to differentiate into correspondence with the equation representing the input of the differentiation formula, and to use the correspondences generated by this process to generate the result. Initially, the equation the simulation wants to differentiate is represented as a tree structure nearly identical in structure to the equation that serves as the input to the formula. However, one critical difference is that, in the source domain (the formula), the two variables that appear in the input equation (DR4 and DR7) have elaborated functional descriptions showing that the variables play an important role in not only the input but also the output. In short, the ordinate of the input is also the ordinate of the output, and the abscissa of the input is also the abscissa of the output. In the target domain, the variables are simply described by their roles in the input (the output does not yet exist). Thus, the first step in generating the output in the target domain is to elaborate the functional descriptions of these variables. Once the ordinate and abscissa of the output have been identified, function-to-form analogy can generate the rest of the result.

Production P11 examines new equations generated during the course of problem solving and fills in their elaboration slots with information about the variables they contain. Again, this represents knowledge the student presumably has acquired from prior math courses. These elaborations are examined by the difference detectors and are critical to planning.

Rounding out the set, production P12 is a special-purpose production which plays a minor role in the reverse application (that is, decomposition) of the chain rule and substitute equations operators. By examining the outputs of the declarative representations of these operators, the analogy mechanism can determine only the ordinate of the first input and the abscissa of the second. However, to specify the inputs fully, the so-called "middle" variable (the variable shared by both inputs that disappears in the output) needs to be identified. Production P12 embodies the following line of reasoning. There are three variables involved in the problem; two have already been bound to placeholders in the formula. Since all placeholders must have different values, by process of elimination, the middle variable must be the one remaining unbound variable.

Production P12 is somewhat inconsistent with the spirit of the model in that it represents a special-purpose rather than a general-purpose rule. However, P12 might be regarded as a highly compiled version of decisions made in actuality by many more firings of general-purpose reasoning productions.

The trace

We now describe the sequence of productions that fire in the solution of problem 3. Table 6.5 shows a summary of the trace. In addition to the 12 productions from Table 6.3, Table 6.5 references the 12 productions that perform memory management and equation transformation. Their operation is only briefly noted. Once again, the initial state of problem 3 is:

(6.14) $s = \frac{1}{4} \times r$

(6.15) $ds/dt = 8t$

(6.16) $t = 4$

The goal is to find a value for dr/dt when t equals 4. In the first two cycles, the simulation detects two differences between the

Table 6.5. Summary of the trace of the simulation on problem 3. The
          * denotes productions that perform equation
          transformation and memory management.

Cycle	Production	Selected actions
1	Detect-diff-contains	No equation found relating r and t
2	Detect-diff-type	$s = 1/4 \times r$ is not a derivative
3	Retrieve-unary-operator	Differentiation formula selected and loaded
4	Remove-difference*	"Contains" difference deleted from working memory
5-6	Functional-elaboration	Functional descriptions of s and r elaborated to reflect roles played in output
7-12	Interpret-formula	Differentiation formula interpreted
13-17	Simplify-output*	Output restored to canonical form
18	States-elaboration	New derivative tagged with variables it contains
19	Application-finished*	Differentiation marked as finished
20	Detect-diff-contains	Still no equation relating r and t
21	Ret-operator-no-inputs	Chain rule loaded into working memory
22-23	Functional-elaboration	Functional descriptions of r and t elaborated to reflect roles played in inputs
24-31	Interpret-formula	Chain-rule output decomposed into inputs
32	Supply-middle-variable	Middle variable supplied
33–45	Interpret-formula	Chain-rule decomposition continued
46-47	States-elaboration	Desired inputs tagged with variables they contain
48	Application-finished*	Reverse application of chain rule finished
49	Goal-satisfied	Second input to chain rule identified as $ds/dt = 8t$
50	Detect-diff-direction	Directionality difference between ds/dr and desired first input dr/ds
51	Retrieve-unary-operator	Flip derivative selected to reduce difference
52	Flip-derivative*	Flip derivative operator applied
53-54	Simplify-output*	Output restored to canonical form
55-57	Simplify-output*	Chain rule applied to inputs and result restored to canonical form
58	Detect-diff-value	Goal set to evaluate $dr/dt = 32t$
59	Retrieve-binary-operator	Evaluate operator selected
60-61	Evaluate*	Evaluate operator applied and result simplified

initial and goal states: first, no equation in the initial state relates *r* and *t*, and second, equation 6.14 is of the wrong type. Since the differentiation operator reduces the type difference and also applies directly to equation (6.14), the differentiation formula is retrieved and loaded into working memory. On the third cycle, a goal is set to differentiate equation (6.14).

Before the formula can be applied, however, the functional descriptions of the variables in equation (6.14) need to be elaborated. In cycles 5 and 6, the simulation recognizes that the ordinate of equation (6.14) will also serve as the ordinate of the new derivative, and likewise for the abscissa. At this point, the actual form of the new derivative is generated by interpreting the formula via function-to-form analogy. A number of rounds of this analogy process take up cycles 7-12. In cycles 13 through 18, the new derivative is simplified, put into canonical form, and elaborated by P11, states-elaboration. On cycle 19, the goal of differentiating equation (6.14) is marked as satisfied.

The simulation is now ready for its next round of difference detection and, subsequently, its next operator selection. On cycle 20, the contains difference is again detected, but no operator applies directly to reduce the difference. The chain rule is identified as the operator whose preconditions are least violated, and on cycle 21 subgoals are set to find the appropriate inputs. The chain rule formula is loaded into working memory.

At this point, the analogy mechanism would apply the chain rule formula in the forward direction if it could, but it can find no inputs that satisfy the preconditions of the formula. The simulation, then, does what it can, which is to specify the inputs it needs. An important feature of the simulation is that the declarative representations of the operators, most notably the chain rule and substitution, allow for application in both the forward and backward direction. Once the chain rule formula has been loaded into working memory, the analogy mechanism can be quite opportunistic in choosing source elements from either the inputs or the output of the formula. In other words, if equations are available in working memory that match the inputs, the output is generated. Likewise, if equations are available that match the output, the inputs are generated. The direction of application depends solely upon the type of information present at loading.

In this case, the goal of the problem matches the output of the chain rule formula. However, since the goal is only partially specified (it has no right-hand side), the inputs can only be partially specified as well (with the chain rule, even if the output were completely specified, there would be some indeterminacy concerning the inputs; this is why P12, supply-middle-variable, is needed). Before even this partial specification can go through, however, the simulation has to elaborate the functional descriptions of the variables in the goal dr/dt (cycles 22 and 23). The simulation must realize (by analogy to the chain rule formula) that the variable r serves not only as the ordinate of dr/dt but also as the ordinate of the first input to the chain rule. Similarly, the variable t serves not only as the abscissa of dr/dt but also as the abscissa of the second input. Once this functional elaboration is made, the analogy mechanism successfully decomposes dr/dt into the two inputs dr/ds and ds/dt. During this process, the variable s is supplied not by the analogy mechanism but by production P12.

The simulation is now on its 49th cycle and three goals are outstanding: specification of the right-hand sides of the chain rule output (dr/dt) and the two inputs (dr/ds and ds/dt). Like the output, the inputs are represented as equations with the right-hand sides missing. At this point, production P8, goal-satisfied, examines the current set of equations and discovers that the second input to the chain rule already exists, namely equation (6.15). This goal is marked as satisfied. On cycle 50, the simulation goes into another round of difference detection, this time discovering a directionality difference between the first input to the chain rule and the derivative of equation (6.14). The flip derivative operator is identified in the means-end table as the operator that changes the directionality of derivatives. In cycles 52 through 54, the flip derivative operator is applied, and the first input to the chain rule is generated. All the preconditions for the chain rule are now satisfied.

The simulation has now done most of its serious work. On cycles 55 and 56, the chain rule is applied in the forward direction, producing $dr/dt = 32t$, and there are no more outstanding operator applications to perform. On the next round of difference detection, the simulation detects a value difference between the previous result and the goal, and the evaluate operator is selected. In cycles 60 and 61, the output of the chain rule is evaluated with $t = 4$, the result is simplified, and the problem is solved.

Production Compilation

We have now described in some detail a model of novice problem solving in calculus. The model relies heavily on the interpretation of declarative structures by general-purpose analogical processes. These declarative structures are not use-specific and support both operator application and operator selection. However, according to recent developments in the ACT* theory of skill acquisition (Anderson and Thompson, in press), one byproduct of problem solving by analogy is the creation of new use-specific productions which essentially summarize the computation performed by the analogy. These new productions are useful in that they do away with the need for analogical processing when the same situation is encountered again. It is well known that analogical processing is quite expensive. In PUPS, the process of computing analogies is formally equivalent to the search for correspondences between graph structures, which is an NP-complete problem. The production rules essentially summarize the results of this search and replace what is essentially a weak method with a strong method (Newell, 1973). The theory stipulates that production compilation should produce a marked improvement in terms of both speed and accuracy. This is due to both the reduction in search and the decreased load on working memory, since the previously-interpreted declarative structures no longer have to be maintained. Indeed, we typically observe a nearly 50 percent improvement and a marked decrease in verbalization going from the first to the second trial in many problem-solving situations. This observed improvement corresponds to the compilation of productions from analogy.

In PUPS, productions are compiled from the traces of analogical processing. The creation of the productions is guided by the semantics underlying the representation of declarative structures in PUPS. The semantics is simply that the contents of the isa and function slots of a working memory element imply the contents of the form slot. This means that lurking implicitly in every declarative structure is a production rule. Depending upon how networks of declarative structures are interpreted and for what purpose, very different sets of production rules can be compiled.

As an example of production compilation, the following two rules were derived from the application of the differentiation formula to differentiate $s = \frac{1}{4} \times p$ in the solution of problem 3 (cycles 7-12). The first rule summarizes a large portion of the generation of the left-hand side of the result:

IF   the goal is to find the form of a derivative $=$ d
THEN   create a new element $=$ rate
       whose function is to be the left-hand side of $=$ d
       and whose form is $=$ num / $=$ denom where:

1. =num is a new element which is a differential and whose function is to be the
   numerator of =rate;
2. =denom is a new element which is a differential and whose function is to be the
   denominator of =rate.

This rule, which is actually the composition of two smaller rules derived from the trace, simply states that the left-hand side of the new derivative will be composed of a fraction which is in turn composed of two differentials. This inference about the structure of the result can be made in the absence of any specific information about the equation being differentiated. It is generally true of all derivatives.

In the next rule, the right-hand side of the result is generated. Specific information about the input equation is now critically important since the right-hand side is generated from the values of coefficients, exponents, and so forth, in the input:

IF   the goal is to find the form of an expression =el
     whose function is to be the right-hand side of
     derivative =output
     and the function of this derivative =output is to be
     the output of operator application =app
     and there exists an equation =input whose func-
     tion is to be the input of operator application
     =app
     and there exists an expression =e2 whose function
     is to be the right-hand side of =input
THEN   conclude that the form of =el is
       $=\exp \times =\text{coeff} \times =\text{var}^{(=\exp - 1)}$ where:
       1. =coeff is a number whose function is to be
          the coefficient of =e2
       2. =var is a variable whose function is to be
          the abscissa of =e2
       3. =exp is a number whose function is to be
          the exponent of =e2.

This rule, also a composition, summarizes much of the content of the power rule for differentiation. Once compiled, these rules can be used in service of any differentiation goal in the future, and can be transferred within and across problems.

An interesting feature of the formula for the chain rule is that it supports operator application when interpreted in the forward direction and supports operator selection when interpreted in the backward direction. An implication of this feature is that productions compiled from forward interpretations should apply to operator application but not selection, and productions compiled from backward interpretations should apply to operator selection but not application. Thus, the declarative knowledge becomes use-specific when deposited in productions. An example of this process is the following two rules, which were both compiled from analogical interpretations of the chain rule but in opposite directions. The first rule applies to operator application, and the second to operator selection:

Application:

IF   there is a variable =x whose function is to be the
        ordinate of derivative =input1
        and the function of =input1 is to be the first input
        to the chain rule
THEN   find the derivative =output whose function is to
        be the output of the chain rule
        and elaborate the function of =x to be the ordinate
        of =output.

Selection:

IF   there is a variable =x whose function is to be the
        ordinate of derivative =output
        and the function of =output is to be the output of
        the chain rule
THEN   find the derivative =input1 whose function is to be
        the first input to the chain rule
        and elaborate the function of =x to be the ordinate
        of =input1.

These rules are in a sense mirror images of one another; the left- and right-hand sides have simply been reversed. This example highlights the fact that, whereas declarative knowledge can be put to a variety of uses, procedural knowledge is directional and use-specific. Knowledge compilation yields great savings in terms of time and accuracy. However, these savings are realized only within a limited range of tasks. In short, compilation implies a certain specialization of knowledge.

Implications

We have now gone through the details of how a PUPS production system solves a calculus problem given only a declarative representation of the problem, how it compiles productions from this experience, and how these productions serve as the basis for transfer to new problems. So we have a detailed and more or less complete instantiation of the identical productions theory of transfer. This identical productions theory predicts improvement in time due to the use of compiled productions. It predicts improvement in accuracy as a side effect of the reduction in capacity demands due to compilation.

One feature of the knowledge compilation process is that it is insensitive to the underlying correctness of the declarative knowledge that it takes as input. If the underlying declarative knowledge is wrong, practice will lead to the creation of buggy rules. Indeed, we observed a variety of fundamental misconceptions in the problem solving of our subjects. For example, some students represented the chain rule as $dx/dz = dx/dy \times dz/dy$. The knowledge compilation process would not correct this kind of error. However, if operator applications are practiced in a structured environment where knowledge of the correctness of results is supplied (which was the case in our tutoring environment), subjects will have an opportunity to detect errors in their representations and change them. In keeping with recent developments in the ACT* theory, fixes cannot be performed directly on production rules but must instead be performed on the underlying declarative representations.

Perfecting the declarative representations of the rules turns out to be a basis for transfer across various uses of the same knowledge. That is, in using the knowledge in one form, one has the opportunity to detect errors and correct the representation for use in another form. This declarative-based transfer should occur only between initial learning in the base domain and initial learning in the target domain. This is much more limited than production-based transfer which transfers the full experience in the base domain to the full course of learning in the target domain. Still it is important because it provides a basis for transfer that is not use-specific.

Conclusion

We have presented a model of novice performance on calculus related-rates problems. The model uses structural analogy to interpret declarative representations of operators and means-ends analysis to provide problem solving power. The model is somewhat of an idealization in that many of the analogical errors and notational problems experienced by subjects are removed. The model accounts for a variety of results, most notably the selection of initial and combiner moves. Most importantly, the model predicts that, contrary to the results of the experiment reported in chapter 5, operator application should transfer to operator selection during the initial stages of learning. The basis of this transfer is in the declarative representations of the operators.

Appendix: Technical Discussion of Analogy

We present our discussion with respect to the function-to-form analogy in P9, but the same algorithm works, mutatis mutandi, for function-to-function analogy in P10. The analogy mechanism is largely supported by two data structures, called the correspondence list and the expansion queue. The correspondence list is a cumulative record of all elements in the source and target domains which have been found analogous in some way and brought into correspondence. The content of the correspondence list ultimately determines whether the analogy is successful (all elements in the form slot of the source element must have corresponding elements in the target domain for the form slot to be rewritten). The expansion queue manages the search for correspondences by keeping track of the pairs of elements in the source and target domains that have not yet been examined.

The analogy process starts by putting the pair of elements identified by production P9 as analogous onto the correspondence list and also onto the expansion queue. The problem now is to find corresponding elements in the target domain for each element in the form slot of the source. The elements in the form slot of the source are here called the *writing nodes,* since the new form slot will ultimately be written using the bindings for these nodes. Each of the writing nodes is first checked to see whether it already has a correspondence on the list. If it does, the corresponding element is inserted in the position of the writing node in the form slot of the target. Initially, however, these elements almost certainly do not have correspondences, since there is only one pair on the list. Clearly, more correspondences need to be drawn. Before giving up on the current list, however, the analogy mechanism does a depth-first recursive search of the function slots of the writing nodes to see whether any elements in them already have correspondences on the list. If the function slot of any "ancestor" of a writing node can be rewritten using correspondences, a new working memory element is generated and bound to the writing node. In other words, if the functional description of a writing node can be rewritten using elements from the target domain, but no element can be found to correspond to the writing node itself, a new element is created in the target domain and is given the analogous (rewritten) functional description. This, then, is how new structure is generated by the analogy mechanism.

If this foray down the function slots of the writing nodes fails, then the system adds more pairs to the correspondence list, if it can. New correspondences are drawn by popping the pair of elements off the expansion queue and matching all elements in the function and form slots from each element (on the initial iteration, the matching of elements in the form slot is fruitless, because the target has no form elements). This matching process occurs only if (1) the slots have the same number of elements in both source and target, so that no element is left unbound, and (2) the main relational terms in both slots, which identify the type of structure in a slot, are the same. The resulting correspondences are added to both the correspondence list and the expansion queue, and once again the system tries to find (or generate) correspondences for the writing nodes. This process is repeated until either all writing nodes have correspondences (success) or the expansion queue is empty (failure). In the latter case, the two networks representing the source and target domains have been brought into maximal correspondence, but still no bindings can be found for all the writing nodes. At this point, the system abandons the attempt to use the source node as an analog. If it can find a new source node from which to gather correspondences, it will try to use this for analogy.

Rule compilation

As a byproduct of the analogy process, a new production rule is formed which summarizes the successful search for correspondences. The left-hand side of this new rule makes reference to all the pairs of correspondences on the correspondence list which were used in writing the form slot in the target network. Specifically, a variabilized node is introduced on the left-hand side for each distinct pair of correspondences. Tests are added to each variabilized node depending upon the method by which the pair was initially added to the correspondence list. For example, if a pair of correspondences was added to the list by matching values in the function slots, then the test would check for matches in the function slots. Similarly, if the pair was added by matching form slots, the test would check for matches in the form slots. The right-hand side of the rule simply generates any and all new structures that were generated by the analogy process. In the case of function-to-form analogy, this would be the new value for the form slot of the target node. Once again, references to all pairs of correspondences are replaced by variabilized nodes. Thus, the resulting production rule is guaranteed a certain range of application.

7 / Declarative Transfer

From the theoretical analysis of the early stages of skill acquisition, we have derived the following predictions:

1. There should be an initial period of positive transfer among
tasks to the degree that the tasks share a common declarative
base.

2. After the initial phase of training, continued positive transfer between tasks should depend on the degree to which they
share common productions. Thus, transfer should be use specific after this initial phase.

Our predictions about transfer up to this point have been
production-based and have rested on the identical productions
logic of prediction (2). We have not considered the initial declarative component in prediction (1), which adds another basis
for positive transfer and constitutes an important elaboration to
the identical productions model. Indeed, in our experiments,
we have often been haunted by more positive transfer than we
could readily predict. However, it has been unclear whether the
surplus positive transfer could be attributed to a common declarative base.

The Declarative-Procedural Distinction

Ultimately, our claims about the separate contributions of declarative and procedural knowledge to transfer rest on assumptions in ACT* about the fundamental distinction between
declarative and procedural memory. Although this distinction

has had a checkered past in both artificial intelligence and cognitive science (see e.g. McDermott, 1981), there is ample experimental and anecdotal evidence to support it. Generally, the distinction is based upon a number of perceived differences between the two memory systems.

Conscious access

Declarative knowledge tends to be knowledge that can be accessed and stated verbally, whereas procedural knowledge cannot. A typical instance of declarative knowledge is a fact, such as *Mary's phone number is 246-3267*. According to ACT*, as a particular skill is practiced (such as dialing Mary's phone number), conscious access to the declarative precursors may be lost as they are superseded by productions and fall into disuse. Indeed, some people report that, if they dial a phone number long enough, they lose the ability to recall the number verbally. Similar examples can be found in domains as diverse as learning to drive a car or learning the syntactic rules of a foreign language. A particularly intriguing experimental demonstration of this effect can be found in the work of Posner (1973), who asked skilled typists to label a diagram of a standard typewriter keyboard with the appropriate letters in alphabetical order. He found that, whereas the typists could type the letters in a few seconds with no errors, the diagramming task required several minutes and was highly error-prone. Subjects were often unable to recall the visual location of a letter and had to type it to determine its position. This is a dramatic demonstration of lack of conscious access to procedural knowledge.

Retention

A popular piece of psychological folklore is that, whereas factual, declarative knowledge is particularly sensitive to the ravages of time, procedural skills like riding a bicycle or swimming the backstroke are retained relatively intact over long periods. Bunch and his colleagues (Bunch, 1936; Bunch and McCraven, 1938; Bunch and Lang, 1939) performed a series of experiments with animal and human subjects which suggested that there were in fact two components to skilled performance, one that was forgotten rather quickly and one that was retained more permanently. For example, Bunch (1936) trained human subjects to solve a mazelike puzzle and then tested them after various intervals on either the same puzzle or similar puzzles.

Figure 7.1 shows that performance on the same puzzle was virtually perfect at no delay, but rapidly declined as the delay was increased (the periods of delay were two weeks and one, two, three, and four months). In contrast, performance on the similar puzzles was worse than performance on the same puzzle at first, but stayed relatively constant over the four-month period. In other words, the transfer effect was much more persistent than the specific effects of learning a particular puzzle. After a four-month delay, the performance of subjects on the same and similar puzzles was virtually identical. Whereas these results were explained at the time in terms of "narrow" and "broad" transfer factors, they may be reinterpreted now as arising from the differential role of declarative and procedural memory in transfer. The high performance of subjects on the same puzzle at no delay was due to the combined effects of declarative and procedural memory. However, as time passed, memory for specific facts about the training puzzle decayed and performance deteriorated. After a four-month delay, subjects solving the same puzzle had forgotten all of the declaratively encoded details and were performing at the same level as subjects who

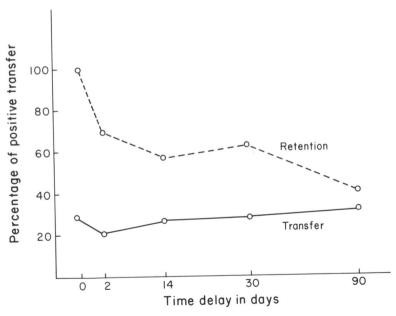

Figure 7.1. *Effect of delay between training and transfer tasks (the retention curve denotes performance on the same puzzle, and the transfer curve denotes performance on similar puzzles).*

were solving similar puzzles. Presumably, this relatively stable baseline of performance was provided by the procedural component.

Neurophysiological dissociation

Perhaps the most striking evidence to date for the declarative-procedural distinction is the long line of clinical studies initiated by Milner (1962) showing a dissociation between the two memory systems in certain stroke victims (for a review, see Schacter, 1987). Specifically, a wide variety of studies have shown that certain amnesic patients can learn complex cognitive and motor skills, retain them over time, but have no declarative memory of ever performing the skill. For example, in a study by Cohen and Corkin (1981), the subject H.M. was taught procedures for solving the five-disk tower-of-Hanoi puzzle and showed great improvement over trials. However, when asked at the beginning of each session whether he had ever seen or solved the puzzle before, he would respond with an emphatic no. In keeping with the ACT* theory, our interpretation of this situation is that H.M.'s procedural memory system was relatively unimpaired, but that the connection between short and long-term declarative memory had been severed. Thus, H.M. was able to compile productions from declarative structures in short-term memory but was unable to retrieve anything from long-term declarative memory about the problem-solving episode.

Asymmetry of access

Perhaps the most critical difference between declarative and procedural memory in terms of transfer is that knowledge is broadly accessible when stored declaratively but is narrowly accessible when stored procedurally. Specifically, unlike declarative structures, production rules imply a certain directional asymmetry in that knowledge of conditions gives rise to knowledge of actions, but not vice versa. This is simply a consequence of how production rules are matched; that is, they are matched on the basis of the contents of their conditions and not their actions. Our calculus experiment and Kessler's LISP programming experiment demonstrated the encapsulation of procedural knowledge. We now argue that transfer based on declarative knowledge is not so characterized. Thus, the experiments that follow that investigate declarative transfer may be regarded as additional evidence for the declarative-procedural distinction in human memory.

Declarative Transfer in Calculus

We performed an experiment to reexamine transfer in calculus to see if we could find some evidence for an initial declarative transfer component. A tentative conclusion from the first calculus experiment was that the operator selection and application components were largely independent. This conclusion was based on the fact that a second day of application practice had no effect on selection in terms of either time per selection or extra moves per problem. Specifically, subjects who practiced application but not selection on day 2 were no better at selection on day 3 than the selection control group on day 2. However, all subjects in the experiment started with a single day of application practice. Thus, our test involved a comparison of subjects with one versus two days of application practice. Our conclusion concerning the independence of selection and application components would have been much stronger had it been based on a transfer manipulation involving the first rather than the second day of practice. Contrary to the initial results, our prediction in this case is that a group with no operator application practice prior to problem solving would do much worse in terms of both time per operator selection and extra moves per problem than a group with a single day of application practice prior to problem solving. This prediction has its roots in our simulation model of related rates problem solving. Although selection and application components share no productions in the model, they in fact share a common base of declarative knowledge. Therefore, one might expect to see substantial transfer between the application and selection components if either is practiced separately before problem solving begins. Furthermore, all positive transfer effects should be restricted to the first day of practice on application, since it is on this first day that subjects acquire their declarative representations. According to the model, the second day of practice in the first calculus experiment had no measurable effect because subjects had already acquired their declarative representations of the operators and were then working primarily with procedural representations.

The second calculus experiment is concerned with determining the effect of a first day of practice on selection and application. Once again, subjects work in the context of our minimal calculus tutor. On the first day of this two-day experiment, subjects receive either selection practice or application practice, both, or neither. In the "selection only" condition, subjects are given differentiation problems to solve but are required only to select the operators, not apply them. Following the selections, the results of the applications are supplied automatically by the tutor. In the "application only" condition, subjects apply operators but do not select them. The operator applications are drawn from the optimal solution paths of the differentiation problems. These two conditions constitute the off-diagonals for the design. In the "both" condition, subjects solve full-scale differentiation problems, performing both the selections and the applications. Finally, in the "neither" condition, subjects practice moving the mouse and typing equations in the Student Workspace window. Subjects go through the same motions as if they were solving differentiation problems using optimal methods. However, the subjects' mouse selections and equations are prompted by the tutor and therefore require minimal cognitive involvement.

On day 2 of the experiment, all subjects transfer to the "both" condition; that is, they all solve full-scale differentiation problems. Thus, the "both" condition is the control against which the performance of the other groups is judged. By comparing the performance of the "selection only" and "application only" groups on the second day with the performance of the "both" group on the first day, it is possible to measure with greater sensitivity the magnitude of transfer between the operator selection and application components. Similarly, by comparing the performance of the "neither" group on the second day with the "both" group on the first, it is possible to factor out the perceptual-motor subcomponent from overall measures of learning and transfer.

Method

Subjects

Subjects were 32 high-school juniors and seniors from a local private girls' school. All subjects were taking either trigonometry or precalculus concurrently with the experiment and were maintaining a B average or better. As in the first calculus experiment, none of the subjects had had any direct calculus instruction.

Design

The two-day experiment used a 2 × 2 between-subjects design. The first factor was whether subjects received operator selection practice on the first day, and the second was whether subjects received application practice. On the second day of the experiment, all subjects transferred to the condition involving both operator selection and application practice.

Materials

Subjects in all conditions on both days solved differentiation problems. Rather than having subjects spend extra time translating the problem text into a set of equations, this experiment simply presented subjects with the initial states of problems. This meant that, over the course of a day, subjects could solve more problems and so have comparatively more practice on operator selection and application, which would provide for a more stringent test of the independence of these two components.

In that condition where subjects practiced both operator selection and application on the first day, the tutor behaved just as it did in the first experiment. Subjects were given a goal statement, such as "Find dx/dz when $z = 5$," and were then set free to select operators from the Operations menu. Following each selection, subjects were required to apply the operator, that is, calculate its result. They then typed the result of their calculations in the Student Workspace window.

In the condition where subjects practiced only operator selection, they made their own selections but were supplied the resulting equations. In other words, the tutor acted as a kind of sophisticated calculator that would supply the results of any operators that had been selected. Although subjects performed no calculations themselves, they were still required to read the answer presented to them in the Prompt window and type it into the Student Workspace window. Subjects were given two chances to type the equation correctly, which was eventually displayed in the Equations So Far window, as always. This meant that, although subjects had no practice on the more cognitive aspects of operator application, they did have practice typing equations.

In the condition where subjects practiced only operator application, the reverse situation prevailed; that is, the tutor supplied the selections and the subjects supplied the calculations. Subjects were told by the tutor which operators to choose from the Operations menu and then which equations to select from the Equations So Far window. These instructions were displayed in the Prompt Window. Subjects had two chances to make each selection, and in the event of two mistakes, the tutor simply continued ahead as if the right selection had been made (subjects made practically no errors with the mouse under these conditions). The operator-equation selections themselves were drawn from the optimal solution paths of the differentiation problems. However, since no information concerning problem goals was ever displayed in this condition, the underlying significance of these selections was never understood by subjects, who were told that the selections were random and that this was simply an exercise for moving and clicking the mouse (which it was). Once the operator had been selected, subjects were required to calculate the result and type it into the Student Workspace window.

In the final condition, the tutor supplied both the operator selections and the results of operator applications. Subjects were engaged in following a set of mindless instructions concerning mouse movements and equations to be typed. However, the concatenation of these simple actions constituted the same sequence of physical actions involved in the optimal solution of the problems. Indeed, a selectively informed observer might be fooled into thinking subjects were actually solving problems in this condition were it not for the breakneck speed in which they worked.

Figure 7.2 summarizes the various components practiced on day 1 in the four conditions. The perceptual-motor components of operator selection and application are practiced in all four conditions, so the experimental manipulation in fact pertains to only the cognitive components of these subskills.

		Selection	
		yes	no
Application	yes	*Cognitive* both *Perceptual-motor* both	*Cognitive* application only *Perceptual-motor* both
	no	*Cognitive* selection only *Perceptual-motor* both	*Cognitive* neither *Perceptual-motor* both

Figure 7.2. *Practiced components on day 1 of calculus experiment 2.*

Procedure

The experiment lasted two hours per day for two days. On day 1, subjects read the calculus instruction booklet from the first experiment, which took approximately 30 minutes. Subjects spent the remaining 90 minutes solving problems from one of the four conditions. The problems were presented in the same fixed order as in the first experiment. In each condition, the experimenter demonstrated use of the interface on two problems before subjects began. No explicit instruction was given on either the strategic aspects of operator selection or the computational details of operator application. On day 2 of the experiment, all subjects spent the entire two hours solving problems in the "both" condition. Once again, subjects were given a demonstration of the interface on two problems before actual problem solving began. The order of the problems was the same as day 1.

Results

As in the first calculus experiment, all summary statistics are based on performance on the first six problems.

Transfer from application to selection

In order to test the hypothesis that operator selection and application are not independent components, we first examine the transfer from application to selection. The primary question of interest is whether a day of practice at applying operators results in better performance at selecting operators. As in the first calculus experiment, the dependent measures used to measure selection performance are time per operator selection and extra moves per problem.

Figure 7.3 presents mean time per operator selection for the four conditions on both days of the experiment. On day 1, subjects spent approximately twice as much time making selections themselves as following directions from the system (31.8 vs. 14.6 seconds), which is not surprising. In addition, subjects who had to perform the calculations themselves took more time making operator selections than those who did not (27.6 vs. 18.7 seconds). A two-way between-subjects ANOVA on this data confirmed the main effects for both selection and application practice ($F(1,28) = 16.7$, $p < .001$ and $F(1,28) = 4.5$, $p < .05$, respectively). The main effect for application practice is the first

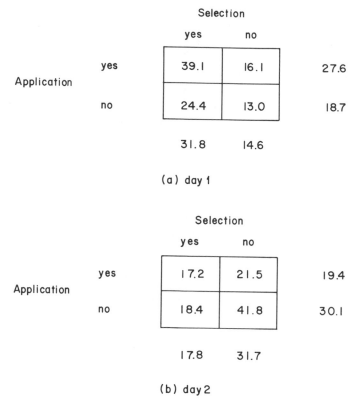

(a) day 1

(b) day 2

Figure 7.3. *Time per operator selection (sec.) on both days (the four conditions refer to type of practice on day 1; on day 2 all subjects transfer to the yes-yes condition).*

sign of some kind of interdependence between selection and application. However, this is merely a performance effect and in no way implies that selection and application share knowledge structures. One interesting possibility is that subjects who are spared the calculations become more reckless with their operator selections, since each move in the problem space is comparatively cheap. It was discovered in the first experiment (and observed again here) that operator applications on average take more than twice as long as the selections.

Looking to the results from day 2, we see that subjects who have had one day of selection practice make selections more quickly than those who have had no practice (17.8 vs. 31.7 seconds), which is certainly to be expected. Most important, however, is that those subjects who have had one day of application practice make operator selections more quickly than those who have had none (19.4 vs. 30.1 seconds). A two-way between-subjects ANOVA showed that both of these differences were statistically significant (both $F(1,28) > 10.2$, $p < .01$). Coupled with the results from the first experiment, this means that, although a second day of application practice makes no difference in terms of operator selections, a first day can be very beneficial. Indeed, if we compare the off-diagonals on day 2, we see that the group which made only applications on day 1 is performing virtually identically to the group which made only selections (21.5 vs. 18.4 seconds). This is quite interesting, given that a simple-minded procedurally based identical elements model of transfer would predict that a group which practiced selection should be substantially better on measures of selection than a group that practiced something else.

Finally, if we compare the day 2 performance of the group that did neither selection nor application on day 1 (41.8 seconds) with the day 1 performance of the group that did both (39.1 seconds), we see that there is no measurable savings in terms of time per operator selection associated with practicing the perceptual-motor component of selection. In other words, a day of practicing mouse movements and learning to locate operators in the Operations menu had a negligible effect on the time subjects took to make strategic selections for themselves on the second day.

Another measure of selection performance is extra moves per problem, which gives a somewhat more qualitative indication of the strategic abilities of subjects. Figure 7.4 presents the results for this dependent measure. On day 1, subjects wasted substantially more moves when they were making selections for themselves than when they were told which selections to make, which is no surprise. In fact, one might regard the low number of extra moves in those conditions where the tutor dictates the selections (.2) as the baseline of menu slips, which might be subtracted from the other values to give a truer indication of the actual number of cognitive-based mistakes. The other result on day 1 is that, among those subjects who made their own selections, those who were spared the calculations made more extra moves per problem (7.6 vs 4.1). This difference was significant at only the .2 level, though, and should be regarded as merely suggestive. It is consistent, however, with the view that subjects in the "selection only" condition were less deliberate in their problem solving.

On day 2, a two-way between-subjects ANOVA yielded no significant effects. We can conclude from this that the transfer from application to selection manifests itself primarily as a re-

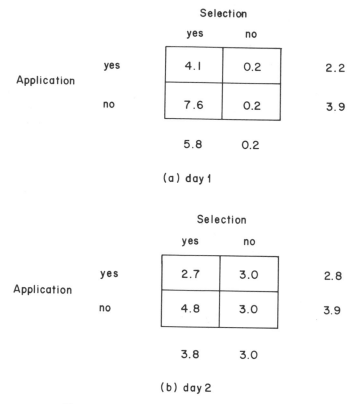

Figure 7.4. *Extra moves per problem on both days.*

duction in time and not extra moves. This agrees generally with the result from the first experiment that subjects working with the preliminary version of the tutor exhibit most of their improvement in terms of speed and not accuracy.

Transfer from selection to application

We have just seen that a day of practice on operator application improves selection in terms of time. We now explore the effect of selection practice on application. As measures of application performance, we use both time per operator application and percentage of incorrect applications.

Figure 7.5 presents results in terms of time per operator application. An ANOVA on the day 1 data yielded a main effect for the application factor ($F(1,28) = 70.3$, $p < .0001$), which means simply that it took subjects longer to calculate the result of an

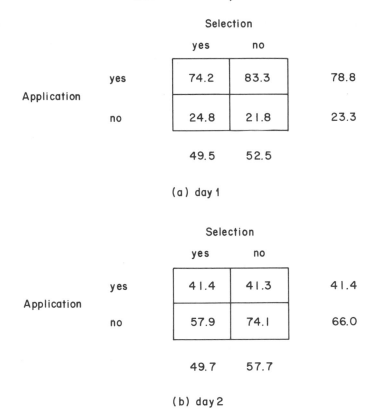

Figure 7.5. *Time per operator application (sec.) on both days.*

operator application and type it than it took them to read it and type it.

An ANOVA on the day 2 data once again yielded a main effect for the application factor ($F(1,28) = 13.5$, $p < .001$). Subjects with one day of application practice performed faster than subjects with no application practice (41.4 vs. 66 seconds). There may be a small effect of selection practice (49.7 vs. 59.7 seconds), but it is not statistically significant ($F(1,28) = 1.4$, $p = .24$). This means that, whereas application transfers to selection in terms of time, selection does not transfer much to application. If true, this is clearly a case of asymmetric transfer and contrasts with the symmetric transfer observed in the selection time results.

Our claim that such a contrast exists is less than totally convincing as it stands, because the difference in transfer is based upon the rejection of the null hypothesis in the case of selection time versus the failure to reject in the case of application time. It

would be more advantageous to have a direct comparison between the magnitudes of transfer, but standard statistical techniques do not apply because of the difficulty in calculating
transfer scores for individual subjects. This problem was resolved in the following manner: transfer scores for individual
subjects in particular conditions were calculated by comparing
them with subjects of equal rank in the relevant controls. For
example, to determine the magnitude of transfer from application to selection time, subjects in the "application only" condition were rank ordered in terms of time per selection on day 2.
These subjects were then matched with subjects of identical
rank from the "selection only" and "neither" conditions, so-
called "macrosubjects" were created. Here is the formula for
transfer from application to selection for each macrosubject:

$$(7.1) \ T_{macrosubject} = \frac{neither_i - application \ only_i}{neither_i - selection \ only_i}$$

The denominator of the formula calculates the speedup in selection time associated with one day of selection practice and
uses time from the ith subjects in the "neither" and "selection
only" conditions. The numerator calculates the speedup in selection time associated with one day of application practice and
uses time from the ith subjects in the "neither" and "application
only" conditions. Transfer, then, is expressed as a percentage of
the theoretical maximum speedup associated with practicing the
same task. These calculations yielded transfer percentages for
each of the eight macrosubjects. An analogous procedure was
performed to calculate eight scores for transfer from selection to
application. This time, however, the off-diagonal conditions
were switched in the formula, and time per application served
as the dependent measure.

The mean transfer scores calculated by this method were 85
percent from application to selection and 48 percent from selection to application. This difference was confirmed by a standard
independent-samples t-test ($t = 4.3$, $df = 14$, $p < .001$). This,
then, is statistical confirmation of the asymmetric transfer result.

We now return to our analysis of the time per application
results. Comparing the day 2 performance of the group that did
neither selection nor application on day 1 (74.1 seconds) with
the day 1 performance of the group that did both (74.2 seconds),
we see that there is no measurable savings in terms of time per
operator application associated with practicing the perceptual-
motor component of application. A day of typing equations had

a negligible effect on the time subjects took to make their calculations and type in the results. This is somewhat puzzling, because the typing of equations was an unpracticed subcomponent
of operator application, and its practice should have had some
payoff. Apparently, the cognitive aspects of this task completely
dominated patterns of learning and transfer.

Figure 7.6 presents results in terms of percentage of incorrect
applications. Looking at the day 1 data, we see the large difference between the percentage of mistakes when subjects perform
their own calculations and type the results (48 percent) and
when they just type the results (11 percent). Using this 11 percent figure as a baseline, we can conclude that nearly a quarter
of all application errors are typing slips.

A two-way between-subjects ANOVA on the day 2 percentage of incorrect applications data yielded no main effects and no
interactions. This implies both that a day's practice at perform-

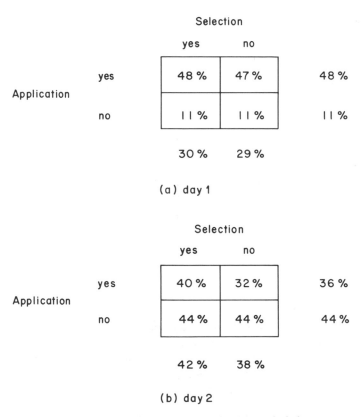

Figure 7.6. *Percentage of incorrect applications on both days.*

ing calculations led to no measurable improvement in terms of number of mistakes and that operator selection does not transfer to application in terms of number of mistakes.

Summary of Second Calculus Experiment

One interesting result from this experiment is that there is asymmetric transfer between operator selection and application. Application transfers to selection, but not vice versa. An additional qualification on this result from the first experiment is that only the first day of application practice produces a measurable effect on selection; the second day does no good. This pattern of results is completely consistent with our simulation model. The transfer from application to selection is explained as follows. On the first day of application practice, subjects first acquire declarative representations of the operators which specify in detail the critical features of the inputs and outputs. Ideally, these declarative representations are sufficient for the successful interpretation of the formulas by the PUPS analogy mechanism. These declarative representations are useful in selection on the second day in two ways. First, in the course of making an operator selection, some operators (such as the chain rule and substitute equations) are applied in reverse to determine the critical features of required inputs. This mechanism is absolutely critical to the successful execution of the backward-chaining strategy found in means-ends analysis. Second, the declarative representations have more than enough detail to allow for the derivation of the difference table required for means-ends analysis. This derivation process was not explicitly modeled in the simulation but must occur at some point for the means-ends analysis strategy to work. Presumably, detailed knowledge of the inputs and outputs of operators and the differences between them is a prerequisite to this derivation process.

Transfer is asymmetric primarily because the declarative knowledge required for selection is a proper subset of the declarative knowledge required for application. A subject who knows the formulas well enough to grind through the calculations certainly knows enough to operate in the abstracted planning space of operator selection. The planning processes draw on just a few critical features of the formulas and ignore much of the detail. For example, to select the differentiation operator properly, the planning processes need only know that the operator takes as input an equation stating x in terms of y and produces as output the derivative dx/dy. Therefore, if in some situation the goal is to obtain a particular derivative and an equation relating the ordinate and abscissa of the derivative is available, the differentiation operator can be selected. Further details of the differentiation transformation are unnecessary for this decision. However, the knowledge used in planning is not detailed enough for the subsequent application of the operator. For example, to apply the differentiation operator, one must know additionally that the exponent of the abscissa in the input is decremented in the output and that the coefficient of the input is multiplied by the exponent of the input and becomes the coefficient of the output. In no way can these details be logically derived from the minimal set of features used in making operator selections. Presumably, the declarative representations acquired by those subjects who practice only selections contain just the minimal set and are therefore insufficient for operator application. However, the representations acquired by those subjects who practice applications are completely sufficient for selection. This superset-subset relationship is at the root of the asymmetric transfer observed in the experiment.

Finally, it was observed that practicing the perceptual-motor components of application and selection in isolation prior to problem solving had virutally no effect on eventual performance. This is somewhat counterintuitive, given the unfamiliarity of the tutorial interface. In a questionnaire completed prior to the experiment, however, 88 percent of subjects reported having had prior computer experience, and 78 percent regarded themselves as fair typists. It is therefore conceivable that the perceptual-motor components were already somewhat practiced and that any speedup in them was completely overshadowed by speedup in the cognitive components (this in fact mirrors the results obtained in the text-editing experiments). The most important implication of this result is that the substantial transfer from integration to differentiation problems observed in the first calculus experiment cannot be attributed to improvement in the perceptual-motor component.

Declarative Transfer in Logic Theorem Proving

An experiment by Lewis and Anderson (in preparation) sheds further light on the role of declarative knowledge in the transfer of cognitive skill. The paradigm they used was the logic theorem-proving task, which was introduced by Moore and Anderson (1954) and studied extensively by Newell and Simon (1972). This paradigm was adapted somewhat by Lewis and

Anderson to explore the declarative-procedural distinction. Specifically, their goal was to give separate declarative and procedural practice and to observe transfer between the two memory systems within a single skill.

Table 7.1 shows the logical rules to which all subjects in the experiment were exposed. In one condition, the "rule recognition" condition, subjects were asked to treat these rules as they would any other declarative facts; that is, the task was simply to encode them and recognize them. This condition constitutes declarative practice and was modeled after the fact retrieval paradigm, which has been the subject of extensive study (Anderson, 1983).

Table 7.1.   Rules used by Lewis and Anderson (in preparation) in the logic experiment. Arrows show the direction in which recoding may take place.

1. A OR B $\rightarrow$ B OR A
2. A AND B $\rightarrow$ B AND A
   Use *only* with AND or OR. Trade places. *No* negation change.
3. A $\rightarrow$ B $\rightarrow$ $-$B $\rightarrow$ $-$A
   Use *only* with $\rightarrow$. Trade places. *Two* negation changes: *A* part and *B* part.
4. A OR A $\rightarrow$ A
5. A AND A $\rightarrow$ A
   No negation change.
6. A OR (B OR C) $\leftrightarrow$ (A OR B) OR C
7. A AND (B AND C) $\leftrightarrow$ (A AND B) AND C
   No place changes. *No* negation changes. *Only* grouping changes.
8. A OR B $\leftrightarrow$ $-$($-$A AND $-$B)
   Use *only* with OR or AND. *Three* negation changes: *A* part, *B* part, and *total* OR or AND expression.
9. A $\rightarrow$ B $\leftrightarrow$ $-$A OR B
   Use *only* with OR or $\rightarrow$. *One* negation change: *A* part.
10. A OR (B AND C) $\leftrightarrow$ (A OR B) AND (A OR C)
11. A AND (B OR C) $\leftrightarrow$ (A AND B) OR (A AND C)
    No negation changes.
12. A AND B $\rightarrow$ A
    Use *only* with *major* AND and *positive* total expression. *No* negation changes.
13. A $\rightarrow$ B, A $\rightarrow$ B
    The "$\rightarrow$" line must be *positive;* $\rightarrow$ must be the *major* connective. *No* negation changes.
14. A $\rightarrow$ B, B $\rightarrow$ C $\rightarrow$ A $\rightarrow$ C
    Both "$\rightarrow$" lines must be *positive.* $\rightarrow$'s must be the *major* connectives. *No* negation changes.

In the other condition, the rule selection condition, subjects had to derive four-step proofs along the lines of Newell and Simon (1972). Subjects were given a set of one or more premises and a statement to be proven and were asked to find a sequence of inference steps which would go from the premises to the conclusion. The proof problems were selected to provide equal practice on all the inference rules. This condition constitutes procedural practice since the rules were being applied in a problem-solving context.

The experiment was run on a computer system which provided a structured interface for proving theorems. In the rule selection condition, subjects saw a menu of all the logical rules and simply pointed with a mouse to select the next rule to apply. If it was a correct inference (an inference which kept the subject on one of the problem's four-step solution paths), the system provided the subject with the conclusion that logically followed from the premise and the rule. If it was an incorrect inference, the system so informed the subject and provided the next correct step. Figure 7.7 illustrates a completed proof. A point system was instituted to motivate the student to try to achieve high speed and accuracy. The two dependent measures of principal interest were number of errors and time for correct judgments. Time was measured from the display of the previous conclusion to the mouse click indicating the next rule selection.

The rule recognition condition was designed to bear a superficial resemblance to the rule selection condition. Subjects were shown what was purported to be one of the rules from the proof set and hard to select either a yes or a no response from a menu to indicate whether the item was in fact such a rule. Fifty percent were correct rules, and the rest were foils created by permuting, substituting, adding, or deleting one syllable. Again, Lewis and Anderson instituted a point system to keep motivation high and recorded number of errors and time for correct judgments. Subjects went through a sequence of four such lines before getting a rest. Figure 7.8 shows the screen after four such lines.

Lewis and Anderson assumed that, in the rule selection condition, subjects would compile rules specific to the problem-solving task. So a subject might acquire a procedurally encapsulated rule of the form:

> IF the goal is to prove a statement involving $=X$ and $=Y$
> and there is no premise involving $=X$ and $=Y$

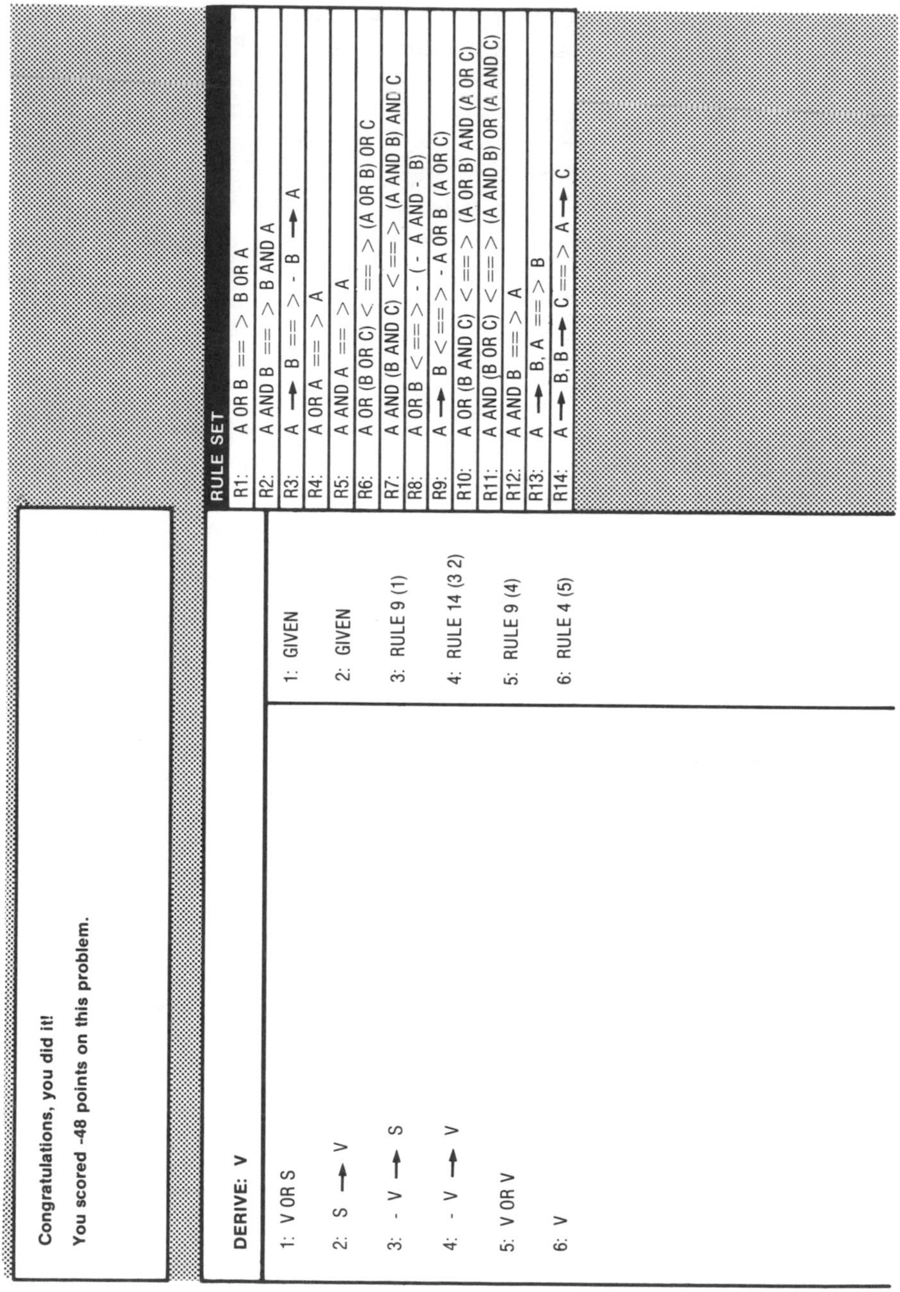

Congratulations, you did it!

You scored -48 points on this problem.

DERIVE: V

1:	V OR S	GIVEN
2:	S → V	GIVEN
3:	- V → S	RULE 9 (1)
4:	- V → V	RULE 14 (3 2)
5:	V OR V	RULE 9 (4)
6:	V	RULE 4 (5)

RULE SET

R1:	A OR B == > B OR A
R2:	A AND B == > B AND A
R3:	A → B == > - B → A
R4:	A OR A == > A
R5:	A AND A == > A
R6:	A OR (B OR C) < == > (A OR B) OR C
R7:	A AND (B AND C) < == > (A AND B) AND C
R8:	A OR B < == > - (- A AND - B)
R9:	A → B < == > - A OR B (A OR C)
R10:	A OR (B AND C) < == > (A OR B) AND (A OR C)
R11:	A AND (B OR C) < == > (A AND B) OR (A AND C)
R12:	A AND B == > A
R13:	A → B, A == > B
R14:	A → B, B → C == > A → C

Figure 7.7. *Configuration of interface in the rule selection condition (subject has just finished the proof).*

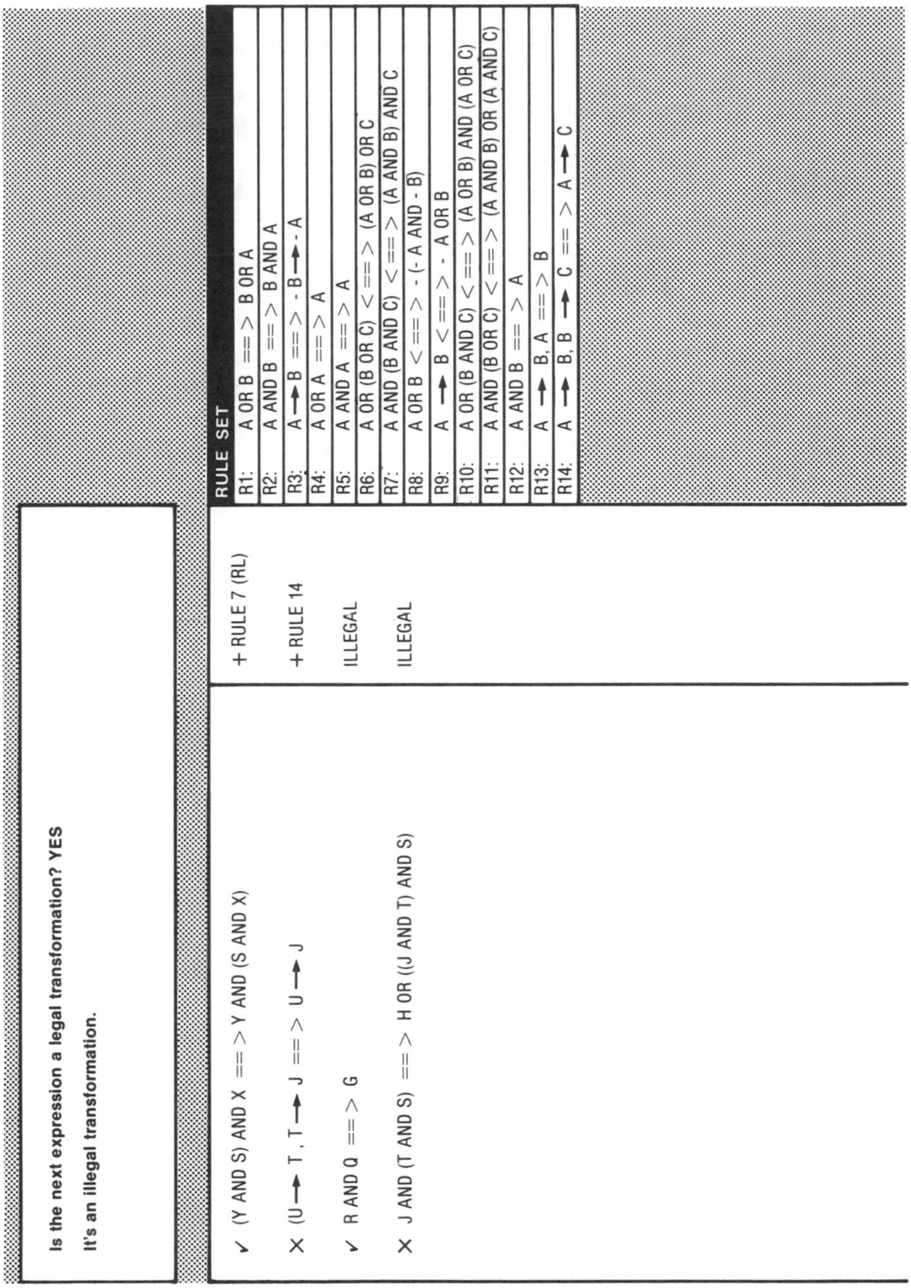

Is the next expression a legal transformation? YES

It's an illegal transformation.

✓ (Y AND S) AND X ==> Y AND (S AND X)	+ RULE 7 (RL)
✗ (U→T, T→J ==> U→J	+ RULE 14
✓ R AND Q ==> G	ILLEGAL
✗ J AND (T AND S) ==> H OR ((J AND T) AND S)	ILLEGAL

RULE SET

R1:	A OR B ==> B OR A
R2:	A AND B ==> B AND A
R3:	A→B ==> -B→-A
R4:	A OR A ==> A
R5:	A AND A ==> A
R6:	A OR (B OR C) <==> (A OR B) OR C
R7:	A AND (B AND C) <==> (A AND B) AND C
R8:	A OR B <==> -(-A AND -B)
R9:	A→B <==> -A OR B
R10:	A OR (B AND C) <==> (A OR B) AND (A OR C)
R11:	A AND (B OR C) <==> (A AND B) OR (A AND C)
R12:	A AND B ==> A
R13:	A→B, A ==> B
R14:	A→B, B→C ==> A→C

Figure 7.8. *Configuration of interface in the rule recognition condition.*

        but there is a = premise1 involving = X and = Z
        and a = premise2 involves = Y and = Z
    THEN   set as a subgoal to apply rule 14 to = premise1 and
        = premise2.

This is an encapsulation of the connection between the means-ends goal of getting terms together in a conclusion and the particular rule of logic which is relevant to that goal. In contrast, it was expected that the rule recognition subjects would continue to retrieve the declarative encodings of the rules and match them against the list probes. No domain-specific rules applicable to problem solving would be derived in this condition.

The design involved four groups of subjects working an hour per day for five days. On the last day, all subjects performed both tasks, alternating between doing proofs and recognizing rules. One group had spent the first four days doing just proofs. A second group had spent the first four days doing just rule recognition. The third group had spent the first two days doing proofs and the second two days rule recognition. The fourth group spent the first two days doing rule recognition and the second two days doing proofs.

Given such a design, Lewis and Anderson were able to measure the effect of declarative practice (rule recognition) on problem-solving performance (rule selection) and vice versa. Specifically, the experiment examined the effect of 0 versus 2 days' prior practice of each task on the performance of each task. Figure 7.9 shows the results. Part (a) shows the effect in terms of time per rule selection. We can calculate the effect of practicing rule recognition on rule selection with our standard transfer formula:

$$(7.2) \quad T_{\% learning} = \frac{Initial - Transfer}{Initial - Learning} = \frac{161 - 121}{161 - 66} = 42\%$$

This formula indicates a moderate level of positive transfer. Furthermore, the comparison between 0 versus 2 days' prior recognition practice is significant in the case of both 0 days' practice on selection (161 vs. 121 seconds) and 2 days' practice (66 vs. 49 seconds). The results are rather different in part (b), which presents results in terms of time to recognize a rule. Here the transfer score is only 27 percent and the effect of 0 versus 2 days' selection practice is not significant for either comparison.

This apparent asymmetry in transfer between declarative and procedural tasks is to be expected. On the one hand, the declar-

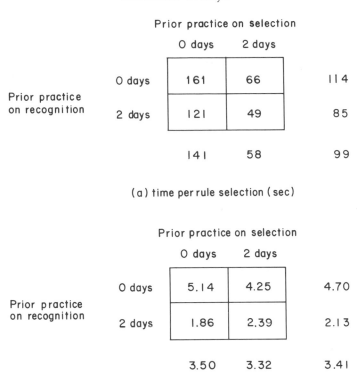

Prior practice on selection

		0 days	2 days	
Prior practice on recognition	0 days	161	66	114
	2 days	121	49	85
		141	58	99

(a) time per rule selection (sec)

Prior practice on selection

		0 days	2 days	
Prior practice on recognition	0 days	5.14	4.25	4.70
	2 days	1.86	2.39	2.13
		3.50	3.32	3.41

(b) rule recognition latencies (sec)

Figure 7.9. *Transfer results from the logic experiment.*

ative knowledge is constantly being practiced in the declarative task and is so being strengthened and debugged for its eventual use in the procedural task. On the other hand, task-specific productions arise in the procedural task, and repeated practice of these productions offers no benefit on the declarative task. This explanation is similar to the explanation for the asymmetry in transfer observed between selection and application in the calculus experiment, namely that the application task provided a better situation for practicing the declarative knowledge common to both tasks.

Our position is that declarative transfer should be short-lived and its effects should be restricted to the initial phases of skill acquisition. The Lewis and Anderson experiment offers another opportunity to test this prediction. We have already observed that there is moderate positive transfer between rule recognition and selection after two days of practice. By comparing the results of those groups that had four days of practice on either of the tasks prior to transfer (not shown in Figure 7.9) with those that had two days of practice, we can determine the marginal benefit of the two additional days of practice. To summarize the results, there is no benefit from this extra practice on either transfer task. Subjects with two days of prior recognition practice take an average of 121 seconds on their first day of selection. Subjects with four days of practice take an average of 125 seconds which, if anything, is slightly worse. Similarly, subjects with two days of prior selection practice take 4.2 seconds on their first day of recognition; subjects with four days of practice take an identical 4.2 seconds.

Thus, the total benefit is derived from initial practice, and sustained practice does not produce additional benefit. This is consistent with the idea that the basis for declarative transfer is the acquisition and subsequent debugging of the declarative knowledge, and this is done relatively early in the learning of the first task. Again, these results are consistent with the result in the calculus experiment that there was no marginal benefit associated with additional days of operator application practice on transfer to selection. In that experiment, a single day of application practice accounted for all of the positive transfer.

Conclusion

The calculus and logic experiments are generally consistent with the idea that declarative knowledge provides a basis for transfer between different uses of the same knowledge. Indeed, one could argue that the defining feature of declarative knowledge is that it serves as the basis for transfer to multiple tasks. Thus, our earlier claims concerning use specificity were somewhat overstated in that they ignored the role of the declarative component. Although its effects are short-lived and sometimes overshadowed by the effects of extended practice, initial declarative training does represent somewhat of an antidote to the encapsulation of knowledge.

While declarative knowledge is freely accessible in any problem-solving situation, however, the processes of analogical interpretation make the actual application of that knowledge somewhat problematic. The basic problem is that, since declarative knowledge is not committed to a particular use, vast amounts of it are potentially relevant in any problem-solving situation, and this leads to serious problems of search.

The search problem disappears when the source of the analogy is supplied, as it is in most "learning by example" paradigms. Indeed, the analogical transfer in our calculus experiments involved supplied sources, and this undoubtedly is largely responsible for the positive results that we obtained. However, when the source of the analogy is not supplied explicitly, the probability of retrieving and successfully applying the appropriate knowledge is often quite low. The experimental evidence is not very encouraging about the prospect of spontaneous analogical transfer. A study by Gick and Holyoak (1980), whose results are more or less typical, examined subjects' ability to solve Duncker's radiation problem after reading the solution of a military analogue. Without special prompting, few subjects were able to notice the analogy between the two problems and solve the radiation problem. Holyoak, Junn, and Billman (1984) found even poorer ability to use analogies when they studied children. However, Brown and Kane (in press) criticized these experiments on a number of grounds. They argued that the experimental situations are unnatural in that people do not normally present two stories with an analogical similarity and fail to comment on the fact. Also, the research with children has often required world knowledge that the children did not even possess, let alone apply. When Brown and Kane repaired these problems, they were able to obtain analogical transfer with children as young as three years of age. These results suggest that if the problems of search can be overcome, the processes of analogical transfer are quite robust and can serve quite well as a learning and transfer mechanism.

8 / The Theory in Review

As we start this penultimate chapter, we now have before us a more or less complete theory of transfer of cognitive skill. The theory draws heavily on the ACT* theory of skill acquisition, which states that initial representations of skill are declarative and are interpreted by general-purpose analogy mechanisms. Through this process of analogical interpretation, new domain-specific productions are compiled which are somewhat abstract but nevertheless use-specific. Although both declarative and procedural components can contribute to transfer, in many situations (especially those characterized by hours of practice), it is a useful approximation to ignore the initial declarative component and simply base transfer predictions on the procedural overlap of the skills. The procedural overlap is figured by doing simple set comparisons of the production system representations of the skills. In addition to counting the number of shared productions, it is often useful to take into consideration the relative frequency of production firings in the transfer task. In short, what we have presented is a modern version of Thorndike's theory of identical elements. We have identified the elements of cognitive skill to be production rules, which, as noted elsewhere (Anderson, 1976), are simply computationally enhanced versions of the stimulus-response bonds proposed by Thorndike.

The main points of the transfer theory can be sharpened by considering relevant research conducted in other laboratories. Of special interest is the work of David Kieras, Peter Polson, and their colleagues. For several years they have been independently pursuing a research program very similar to our own, and with notable success.

Identical Productions Theory of Transfer

In previous chapters, we have shown that the transfer of programming skill in the LISP tutor, the transfer of text-editing skill, and the transfer of calculus skill can be modeled quite well by assuming that productions are the identical elements. Our learning and transfer results were consistent with the following properties of productions as the identical elements:

1. *Independence.* Productions are learned independently and transfer independently. More specifically, the performance of a particular production in a transfer task should depend only on the level of strength accumulated in a prior training task. Aside from difficulties arising from differences in problem representation, access to particular rules should not be affected by problem context. The independence of production rules provides a kind of modularity which greatly simplifies the modeling process, since interactions between rules need not be considered as they appear in new combinations in transfer tasks.

2. *All-or-None Learning Followed by Strength Accrual.* Productions are compiled in a single trial. Following compilation, productions continue to accumulate strength with continued practice. This accounts for the effects of degree of training on transfer.

3. *Abstractness.* Productions are compiled as a byproduct of an analogy process which compares two distinct but related declarative representations (the source and the target) and extracts common features. Thus, productions are necessarily generalizations and as a result are guaranteed to have a certain range of application. The actual level of abstraction at which a production is cast depends upon the declarative encoding of the source and target and, as such, is an issue of representation.

4. *Lack of Negative Transfer.* One prediction of the identical productions theory is that, in reactive and instructive learning environments where differences between training and transfer tasks are identified and quickly repaired, negative transfer should be minimized. In fact, negative transfer should be largely restricted to a specific type of Einstellung where a particular method acquired during training turns out to be legal but nonoptimal in the transfer task. These predictions were supported in a study examining transfer between two text editors designed for maximal interference.

5. *Condition-Action Asymmetry of Productions.* One property of production rules that has strong implications for the identical productions theory is that access to knowledge is asymmetrical. In particular, the conditions of a rule imply the actions but not vice versa. This property implies the use specificity of knowledge (that is, no transfer) in certain situations where two sets of production rules are based on the same abstract knowledge but have been dedicated to different uses. This prediction was borne out in studies of calculus and LISP programming where highly related components of the skills showed little or no transfer to one another.

6. *Role of the Declarative Component.* The methodology used predominantly in our research has been to give extended practice in both training and transfer tasks. Such a methodology necessarily enhances the role of procedural knowledge while diminishing the role of declarative knowledge in transfer. According to the ACT* theory of skill acquisition, however, all productions arise initially from declarative encodings which, unlike productions, are not use-specific. It follows that a variety of different productions could be compiled from the same declarative knowledge. As demonstrated in our experiments on calculus and logic, in those situations where we are examining transfer between distinct production sets compiled from the same declarative knowledge, the declarative component cannot be overlooked. In these situations, the declarative component provides somewhat of an antidote to the encapsulation of knowledge. One prediction of the theory, supported by our experiments on calculus and logic, is that any declarative transfer effect should be quite short-lived. Specifically, all the beneficial effects of declarative transfer should be restricted to the first day of practice on the training task. Following the first day, subjects are merely strengthening their procedural representations, which provide no basis for transfer.

Productions as Identical Elements

David Kieras, Peter Polson, and their colleagues have been engaged in an extended research program which likewise has been dedicated to the identification of production rules as the elements of learning and transfer. In two representative experiments, Polson and Kieras (1985) looked at subjects learning to perform a series of text-editing commands, while Kieras and Bovair (1986) looked at subjects operating a simple device. In both cases, subjects were taught a series of overlapping procedures. For instance, in Polson and Kieras (1985) subjects learned procedures for both moving and copying a set of lines. The shared component in these two procedures is the specification of the lines to which the procedure applies.

Kieras, Polson, and Bovair brought considerable leverage to the analysis of these tasks in the form of precise production rule models for task execution. Using these models, they tried to predict task performance as a function of the number of new productions and the number of old productions required for the task. They found a contribution of both variables, but found that each new production contributed twice as much as each old production to execution time. For example, Kieras and Bovair (1986) estimated about 20 seconds for each new production and only 10 seconds for each old production. To predict subject performance accurately, they had to include a large intercept as well as these production times. The intercept presumably reflects aspects of the task that are not modeled by these productions.

One aspect of the Kieras and Bovair data might appear to be at odds with the position advanced here. They make a distinction between what they call *old* production rules and what they call *generalizations*. This turns on their production system notation which represents the rules for a particular task totally with constants (that is, no variables). Generalizations are production rules that can be derived from others by replacing certain constants by variables. They note that, in all their analyses of transfer, generalizations cost no more time than old rules and are much faster than new rules. They note that such cost-free generalizations are surprising from an ACT* point of view. However, the conclusion that subjects make such generalizations depends on their assumption that rules are originally acquired in constant-only form. If one assumes that rules are acquired in variabilized form, then no additional learning is required as the rule applies directly to the transfer task. Thus, the ACT* learning mechanisms which produce generalized productions do account for these results.

In what is perhaps their most impressive demonstration to date, Polson, Bovair, and Kieras (1987) accounted for both lateral and vertical transfer effects in the same experiment. Once again, their domain of study was text editing. They taught subjects five editing methods (insert, delete, copy, move, and transpose) for each of two full-screen editors. The two editors shared methods for positioning the cursor and inserting text, and also had identical control structures. The major difference between the editors was that, for the editing methods other than insert, one editor required specifying the command and then its argument (the verb-noun editor) and the other required the reverse (the noun-verb editor). Thus, the editors were quite similar, and large amounts of positive transfer between them was expected. Two experimental groups learned the editors in either order, spending one day on each editor. Additionally, training on the five editing methods was blocked on each day, so that measurements of transfer between commands within a particular editor were possible. Two different training orders for the five commands were included in the design, as well as a control group that practiced the same editor on both days, which yielded a total of 60 cells (3 groups × 5 commands × 2 command orders × 2 days).

Using explicit production system models, Polson et al. set out to predict training times for each of the 60 cells. Training time was defined as the time subjects took to reach a criterion of 10 consecutive error-free edits. Subjects were timed as they first read a description of the command and then practiced it interactively at the terminal. It was predicted that training time would be primarily a function of the number of new production rules subjects had to learn for each command. The number of new rules for each method was derived from the theoretical analysis and depended critically on the serial position of the method within a particular training order. Rules were considered familiar (that is, not new) either if the rule had been learned on a prior editor or if the rule had been learned on a prior command from the present editor. Thus, lateral and vertical transfer effects were accommodated within the same framework.

Training times were fit to the regression equation:

(8.1) $M_{training} = nt + c$

Here n is the number of new rules for a particular editing method, t is the time per rule, and c is a constant intercept. Using the above equation, the number of new rules in each method accounted for 77 percent of the variance in the 60 cell means. The regression analysis yielded values of 40 seconds for t and 474 seconds for c.

These impressive results provide further support for the identical productions theory of transfer. The fact that rules were observed to transfer equally well from a variety of sources both inside and outside the confines of a particular editor provides strong evidence for the claim that production rules operate independently. The Polson et al. theoretical analysis of text editing was guided largely by the rational and empirical task analysis of Card, Moran, and Newell (1983), as was ours. This suggests that transfer predictions should be informed by well-documented models of performance.

There is a substantial difference between the data Kieras and Polson are addressing and our data. Their typical measure is time to reach some criterion of mastery, while ours is time to perform a unit task. Our measurements often extend long after their mastery criteria would have been reached. With this difference in mind, it is easy to understand why their equations tend to take the form of linear functions of number of new productions plus a large intercept. The number of new productions determines when the mastery criterion is reached, and the large intercept reflects the time spent performing the parts of the task not involving the new productions. One might view the slope as reflecting the compilation time for each new production and the intercept as the cost of performing the task once the productions are compiled. In contrast, our approach is to predict total task time by adding together component times for all productions weighted by their level of practice. In most of our modeling situations, the compilation process is long past.

Effects of Lesson Sequencing

Taken to its logical conclusion, our claim that production rules are learned and transferred independently leads to a host of counterintuitive predictions concerning the sequencing of lessons in a curriculum. One such prediction is that total training time is a constant for any set of skills irrespective of training order. This is because training time depends solely on the number of new rules in a set of skills, and the total number of new rules is the same regardless of training order. Given this position, one could conceivably teach calculus to elementary-school children with no long-term negative effects. Of course, it would take these young children longer to master the subject than the average calculus student, but this is simply because there are more new rules for the young children to master. The strong prediction of the theory is that there are no second-order, interactive effects; that is, the total time to master all the rules would be identical for both groups. The only difference is that training is spaced and presented in a variety of contexts for the older group.

This of course flies in the face of theories of curriculum design like Gagné's that purpose rigid skill hierarchies which identify strict prerequisite relations among skills. In this regard, many evaluations (such as the so-called scramble studies) have failed to find any effect of principled curriculum design on the rate of learning. It may be that the importance of lesson sequence is not as critical as previously supposed. However, we ourselves believe that the extreme position that lesson sequencing has absolutely no effect on learning rate is too strong for a variety of reasons. These reasons all represent potential restrictions on the independence of production rules and argue for the use of skill hierarchies in lesson sequencing:

1. *Limits on Attention and Motivation.* ⁻Learners may not have the patience to work through complex problems involving lots of new rules. In addition, learners may benefit from more frequent positive reinforcement than that offered by complex problems.

2. *Difficulties with Credit-Blame Assignment.* Mastering the subcomponents of skills before integrating them undoubtedly simplifies credit-blame assignment in many complex problem-solving situations. For example, students faced with the prospect of debugging faulty algorithms for performing two-column subtraction can simplify their induction problem by ruling out knowledge of basic single-digit subtraction facts as a source of bugs. This can be done if students master basic subtraction facts before taking on two-column subtraction. This problem of credit-blame assignment is only an issue in those learning environments that are less than totally reactive, that is, those environments where feedback is based on the overall *product* and not the *process* of problem solving. However, recent advances in intelligent tutoring now make it possible to give feedback on every production that fires in the course of problem solving. This kind of highly reactive learning environment should greatly simplify the problem of credit-blame assignment and should lessen this credit-blame restriction on the independence of productions.

3. *Meaningful Encoding of Examples.* The content of a production rule is based upon the underlying content of the declarative knowledge from which it is compiled. If the underlying declarative knowledge reflects a shallow or even rote understanding of some procedure, then the resulting production rules will have that same character. One of the most important roles of prior knowledge is to enable students to encode declarative knowledge, or examples, meaningfully. This will cast the resulting

productions at the proper level of abstraction and ensure a broad range of application. Perhaps the greatest danger of presenting complex subject matter to students who have not been properly prepared is that those students will have a shallow encoding of the examples and eventually a production set that is in a sense too specific or rote. Indeed, this was the result observed in the Kessler and Anderson (1986) negative transfer experiment. Subjects adopted a rote learning strategy when taught recursion before iteration, presumably because the examples of recursive programs were not sufficiently meaningful.

4. *Reducing Working Memory Load.* One important negative consequence of an unstructured curriculum is that working memory is unduly burdened because complex component skills are not automated and are competing for space with higher-level skills (Shiffrin and Schneider, 1977). It is for this reason that knowledge of typing is helpful when learning a text editor and that knowledge of addition is helpful when learning multiplication. In this vein, research on reading and writing (Flower and Hayes, 1977; Lesgold and Curtis, 1981; Lesgold and Resnick, 1982) has shown that overall performance suffers when component processes (such as word recognition and spelling) are not automated. Similarly, Kotovsky, Hayes, and Simon (1985) have shown that an insightful solution to the tower-of-Hanoi problem follows after subjects have automated the procedures for making moves. However, tutoring systems which offload working memory and maintain high-level goal structures for students should somewhat lessen this restriction on curriculum design.

Productions as Abstractions

Productions differ from Thorndike's elements in that productions are mentalistic abstractions containing variables and goal structures. Given that productions have these features, it might in principle be possible to revive the doctrine of formal discipline in our framework by finding a production system cast at a high enough level of abstraction so that it applies profitably to a wide range of problems. In fact, such production sets have already been identified and go under the name of weak methods (Newell, 1969). Examples of weak problem-solving methods include means-ends analysis, hill climbing, and pure forward search. One very important weak method in our theory is the set of productions that implement the process of analogical interpretation, which was used extensively in our calculus simulation. This analogy process derives prescriptions for action from declarative knowledge and thus provides a bridge from declarative to procedural knowledge.

The one problem with reviving the doctrine of formal discipline under the banner of weak methods is that, by the time problem solvers reach adulthood, the various weak methods are already well-practiced and are a well-established part of the standard repertoire of problem-solving methods (Newell and Simon, 1972). Since the weak methods are so overlearned, they cannot serve as the basis for transfer between tasks. In order to have any impact on transfer, a shared component must be measurably strengthened in the training task. Even though the various weak methods play a large role in the initial stages of skill acquisition, they simply drop out of any calculations of transfer.

So the question still remains: are there general problem-solving methods that transfer broadly across content domains and can be taught? A long line of research (starting with the work of Thorndike and James) casts a gloomy pall on the prospect of general transfer. The identical productions theory puts the following restrictions on any proposal for general transfer:

1. The general method must be cast in the form of production rules.

2. The production rules must be shown demonstrably (that is, in a simulation) to contribute to the solution of wide-ranging problems.

3. The production rules must not already be well-practiced in subjects (this eliminates the weak methods).

To our knowledge, no theory of general transfer has yet been proposed that meets these criteria.

Although our outlook is rather pessimistic concerning the prospect of truly general transfer, this does not mean that representations of skills do not differ in terms of generality and that more general representations are not preferable. There have been several noteworthy efforts at identifying and teaching novel problem-solving methods to students in the domains of mathematical problem solving, logic, and computer programming. These methods are not truly general, in that their range of application is restricted to a particular content domain. Nevertheless, their discovery represents a significant advance in terms of the conceptualization of these domains.

Teaching mathematical heuristics

Schoenfeld has been engaged in teaching heuristics for mathematical problem-solving to college students (Schoenfeld, 1979; 1980; 1985). His basic strategy has been to take the heuristics of Polya (1957) as a starting point and to elaborate these heuristics with more specific rules and guidelines. Prior to Schoenfeld's work, many attempts had been made to teach mathematical heuristics in general form, and without exception the results were largely negative (Lucas, 1972; Smith, 1973; Goldberg, 1974; Harvey and Romberg, 1980). This led Schoenfeld (1985) to conclude that "Heuristics are complex and subtle strategies, and it is dangerous to underestimate the amount of knowledge and training required to implement them." Schoenfeld conducted an experiment in which he taught five problem-solving heuristics to a group of experimental subjects over a two-week period. Subjects spent most of their time in the experiment solving problems; the heuristics were introduced and reinforced as part of the remedial instruction following failed solution attempts (the problems used during training were very difficult, and the solution rate was quite low, so there was ample opportunity for remedial instruction). He compared the performance of this group with a control group that had no exposure to the heuristics but had attempted to solve an equivalent number of problems during the training phase. The experimental group solved significantly more problems than the control group on a post-test containing problems that could be solved with the heuristics. Actual use of the heuristics on the post-test by the experimental subjects was confirmed through protocol analysis.

One interesting aspect of Schoenfeld's results was that not all five heuristics were mastered equally well by subjects. Table 8.1 presents the five heuristics taught, and Table 8.2 presents the post-test on which mastery of the heuristics was judged. The five problems were chosen so that each heuristic would be helpful on a single problem (subjects were unaware of this fact). The entries in the two tables are ordered so that the problems and their corresponding heuristics appear in the same serial position. The only heuristics for which experimental subjects showed clear improvement were heuristics 2 and 4. These heuristics are the only ones that specify conditional tests which indicate when the heuristic might be applicable. For example, heuristic 2 states that "if there is an integer parameter" in the statement of the problem, look for an inductive argument. Similarly, heuristic 4 states that "if the problem contains a large

Table 8.1.   Schoenfeld's five mathematical problem-solving heuristics.

1. Draw a diagram if at all possible.

    Even if you finally solve the problem by algebraic or other means, a diagram can help give you a "feel" for the problem. It may suggest ideas or plausible answers. You may even solve a problem graphically.

2. If there is an integer parameter, look for an inductive argument.

    Is there an "*n*" or other parameter in the problem that takes on integer values? If you need to find a formula for $f(n)$, you might try one of these.

    a. Calculate $f(1)$, $f(2)$, $f(3)$, $f(4)$, $f(5)$; list them in order, and see if there's a pattern. If there is, you might verify it by induction.

    b. See what happens as you pass from *n* objects to $n + 1$. If you can tell how to pass from $f(n)$ to $f(n+1)$, you may build up $f(n)$ inductively.

3. Consider arguing by contradiction or contrapositive.

    Contrapositive. Instead of proving the statement "If *X* is true, then *Y* is true," you can prove the equivalent statement "If *Y* is false, then *X* must be false."

    Contradiction: Assume, for the sake of argument, that the statement you would like to prove is false. Using this assumption, go on to prove either that one of the given conditions in the problem is false, that something you know to be true is false, or that what you wish to prove is true. If you can do any of these, you have proved what you want.

    Both of these techniques are especially useful when you find it difficult to begin a direct argument because you have little to work with. If negating a statement gives you something solid to manipulate, this may be the technique to use.

4. Consider a similar problem with fewer variables.

    If the problem has a large number of variables and is too confusing to deal with comfortably, construct and solve a similar problem with fewer variables. You may then be able to (a) adapt the method of solution to the more complex problem, or (b) take the result of the simpler problem and build up from there.

5. Try to establish subgoals.

    Can you obtain part of the answer, and perhaps go on from there? Can you decompose the problem so that a number of easier results can be combined to give the total result you want?

Source: A. H. Schoenfeld, *Mathematical problem solving* (New York: Academic Press, 1985).

number of variables," construct and solve a similar problem with fewer variables. In contrast, the other heuristics specify actions but no conditions. For example, heuristic 1 simply states to draw a diagram, and heuristic 5 to establish subgoals. Given that previous attempts at teaching heuristic strategies have been criticized for failing to deal with issues of control, it may be that

Table 8.2.   The post-test used by Schoenfeld to measure transfer of
the five heuristics. Each problem is solved using the
heuristic of the same number in Table 8.1.

1. For what values of a does the system of equations
   $$x^2 - y^2 = 0, \qquad (x + a)^2 + y^2 = 1$$
   have (a) no solutions?
       (b) 1 solution?
       (c) 2 solutions?
       (d) 3 solutions?
       (e) 4 solutions?

2. Let S be a set which contains n elements. How many different subsets of S are there, including the null set?

3. Let A and B be two given whole numbers. The *greatest common divisor of A and* B is defined to be the largest whole number C that is a factor of both A and B. For example, the GCD of 12 and 39 is 3, and the GCD of 30 and 42 is 6. Prove that the greatest common divisor of A and B is unique.

4. Suppose p, q, r, and s are positive real numbers. Prove the inequality
$$\frac{(p^2 + 1)(q^2 + 1)(r^2 + 1)(s^2 + 1)}{pqrs} \geq 16.$$

5. Prove that the product of any three consecutive whole numbers is divisible by 6.

Source: A. H. Schoenfeld, *Mathematical problem solving* (New York: Academic Press, 1985).

heuristics 2 and 4 are superior to the rest because they contain information that provides some basis for their selection.

One could argue that the conditions for transfer were ideal in Schoenfeld's experiment. Thorny problems of control (that is, heuristic selection and evaluation) which have plagued other training efforts were mitigated by having a relatively small number of heuristics from which to choose. Also, Schoenfeld included no foils in the post-test. In other words, there were no problems that could *not* be solved by one of the heuristic strategies, and this further simplified control decisions. Additionally, the experimental procedure encouraged the use of the heuristics. During the post-test, experimental subjects were prompted every five minutes to examine a sheet containing the five heuristics and consider their use. This encouraged subjects to consider different options and once again mitigated problems of control.

In summary, Schoenfeld's experiment represents a modestly successful attempt at teaching moderately general yet domain-specific heuristics under more or less ideal experimental conditions. Considering the prior lack of success in this area, however, Schoenfeld's work is a substantial achievement and in a sense represents a beachhead from which further attempts at heuristic training can be launched.

Teaching deductive and statistical reasoning

A controversial issue in modern cognitive psychology is whether people either naturally use or can be taught to use formal, abstract rules to solve everyday problems in deductive logic and statistics. Of course, the early logicians subscribed to the doctrine of formal discipline and believed that abstract, formal rules of deductive logic provided the basis for human reasoning in all domains. However, much recent research, exemplified by Wason and Johnson-Laird (1972) in logic and Tversky and Kahnemann (1974) in statistics, has shown that people are generally quite poor at applying general logical and statistical principles. What is more, people seem particularly resistent to formal instruction in these domains.

The classic demonstration of fallacious reasoning in deductive logic is the card selection task of Wason (1966). Subjects are shown four cards that have letters on one side and numbers on the other. Subjects are asked to evaluate the correctness of rules that describe the cards, such as "If a card has a vowel on one side, then it has an even number on the other." On a particular trial, subjects might be shown cards that have the symbols A, E, 4, and 7 printed on them. Subjects are asked which cards they would need to turn over in order to either confirm or reject the rule, which in this case would be cards A and 7. The operative rule of logic in this task is the conditional, which states "if *p*, then *q*" (*modus ponens*) and equivalently, "if not *q*, then not *p*" (*modus tollens*). Subjects must turn over card A to evaluate the former case of the rule (if there is a vowel on one side, then there is an even number on the other) and card 7 to evaluate the latter (if there is not an even number on one side, then there is not a vowel on the other). Typically, subjects choose the A card, but turn over the 4 rather than the 7, mistakenly thinking that the rule implies a vowel on the other side of the 4. This fallacy is known as *affirming the consequent*. It has been shown in a wide variety of situations that people perform quite poorly in these formal situations involving arbitrary relations and little semantic content. For example, the solution rate on Wason's selection task is typically between 10 percent and 20 percent. Even more discouraging is the fact that formal instruction in deductive logic has little impact on performance. In a study by Cheng, Holyoak, Nisbett, and Oliver (1986), college students who had just taken a semester course in logic did only 3 percent better than those who had no formal logic training on the card selection task.

Although people do quite poorly on the card selection task, research has shown that the probability of solution increases dramatically if the problems are presented in realistic, thematic contexts. For example, Johnson-Laird, Legrenzi, and Legrenzi (1972) studied performance on a problem that was formally equivalent to the card selection task but involved a rule relating sealed letters and postage. This rule, which was well known in Britain at the time of the study and at one time actually described British postal system practice, stated that "if a letter is sealed, then it has a 5-pence stamp on it." In an experiment involving British subjects, performance on the "postal" version of the selection task was 81 percent correct, compared with 15 percent on the standard version. Interestingly, subsequent studies showed that people not familiar with the rule, such as Britons raised after the rule was revoked or people from other countries, showed no improvement. This led some researchers (e.g. D'Andrade, 1982; Griggs and Cox, 1982) to propose that people relied on extremely specific domain knowledge involving particular instances and counterexamples to solve such problems. This represents a radical specificity position that denies the potential generality of knowledge encoded as production rules and is almost as extreme as the position originally advanced by Thorndike.

Recently, Nisbett, Holyoak, and their colleagues have undertaken research aimed at disconfirming the radical specificity position and salvaging some of the generality lost in the demise of the formal discipline view. Their claim is that, although people do not seem to use the completely general and abstract system of deductive logic championed by the logicians, they do use a family of rule systems that are still somewhat general and domain-independent. These rule systems, which are acquired naturally through the solution of recurrent everyday problems, are called *pragmatic reasoning schemas.* Examples of such pragmatic schemas include the "causal" schema (Kelley, 1973), which provides an abstract framework for reasoning about necessary and sufficient conditions, and the "contractual" or "permission" schema, which provides rules for checking whether contracts or other social obligations have been violated. In the latter case, these checking procedures can be put into perfect correspondence with the logic of the conditional, which underlies performance on Wason's selection task. The basic "logic" of the permission schema, which people come to understand through everyday experience, is that one may not do action p unless first securing permission q. In order to check whether a permission such as this has been violated, one would first check cases where the action was taken to make sure the permission was granted, and then cases where the permission was not granted to make sure that the action was not taken. This corresponds perfectly to the forms of *modus ponens* and *modus tollens*.

Cheng and Holyoak (1985) have shown that, if Wason's card selection task is represented in such a way that it makes contact with the permission schema, performance is greatly enhanced. In one experiment, one group of subjects was asked to evaluate the following senseless rule against a set of instances: "If the form says 'entering' on one side, then the other side includes cholera among the list of diseases." Another group was given the same rule but also the rationale behind it which made explicit contact with the idea of permission. The rationale was that, in order to satisfy immigration officials upon entering a particular country, one must have been vaccinated for cholera. The performance of the group given the rationale was significantly better than that of the group given just the senseless rule.

Perhaps the most striking demonstration of the power of the permission schema was another experiment by Cheng and Holyoak (1985) where the problem was cast in terms of the schema but at the highest possible level of abstraction: "If one is to take action A, then one must first satisfy precondition P." Subjects performed three times better on this task than on the standard card task (60 percent vs. 20 percent). This is a clear demonstration that subjects are not using specific information about the situation to make their judgments but really are being guided by the abstract concept of permission.

Follow-up studies by Cheng, Holyoak, Nisbett, and Oliver (1986) showed that, whereas abstract training in the logic of the conditional by itself did not improve performance on the card selection task, abstract training in the permission schema did. Furthermore, abstract schema training was helpful on both arbitrary (that is, those not placed in a real-world context) and meaningful (that is, those more naturally thought of in terms of permissions and obligations) problems. One explanation offered for the observed facilitation was that, rather than learning anything substantive about the permission schema itself, subjects were learning more general rules for encoding situations in terms of the permission schema.

This encoding explanation is consistent with recent findings in the realm of statistical reasoning which suggest that the failure to apply certain statistical principles (such as the law of large numbers) is due in part to a failure to encode ambiguous situations in a way that allows for application of the principle. A study by Kunda and Nisbett (1986) found that subjects were much more likely to apply the law of large numbers and simple versions of the regression principle to situations that could be objectively coded (such as academic or athletic performance) than more ambiguous and subjective social situations (such as another person's friendliness toward new acquaintances). This is consistent with what Ross (1977) termed the "fundamental attribution error," which is the tendency of people to overestimate the role of dispositional at the expense of situational factors in social interactions. Presumably, if people could be prompted to code social situations more objectively, they would be more inclined to see elements of chance at work and subsequently more likely to apply statistical principles.

The importance of encoding was further demonstrated in a study by Fong, Krantz, and Nisbett (1986). In this experiment, subjects with widely varying levels of statistical training were told a story about a person who had had an outstanding meal at a restaurant on the first visit but on subsequent visits had been disappointed. Subjects were asked to generate possible explanations for the inconsistent quality of the food, and these explanations were rated by the experimenters for their statistical content. For example, an explanation with high statistical content might be that only the very best restaurants turn out excellent meals consistently for every customer and that the first meal received by the character in the story was probably a fluke. Alternatively, a nonstatistical explanation might be that the restaurant had changed chefs between the first and subsequent meals. In addition to measuring the likelihood of statistical explanation at the various skill levels (subjects ranged from undergraduates with minimal statistical training to statistically sophisticated Ph.D.–level scientists), the experimenters introduced an experimental manipulation in the form of a "randomness cue" which they predicted would encourage subjects to adopt a statistical point of view. Specifically, half of the subjects read stories where the unhappy diner selected his meals by randomly dropping his pencil on the menu. It was found that, at least for those subjects with low and middling levels of training, the presence of the cue led to a greater percentage of statistical explanations. This reinforces the basic point that, in many problem-solving situations, novices may have the necessary rules but fail to encode situations in a way that makes contact with those rules. In these situations, training in encoding may have a much greater impact on performance than further training on the rules themselves.

To summarize, moderately general methods have been discovered and successfully taught in the areas of mathematical problem-solving, deductive logic, and statistical reasoning. Transfer across problems in these domains takes place through identical elements, but at a much higher level of abstraction than Thorndike proposed. Within a domain, certain ideas may have broader application than others, and it may be possible to package these ideas and present them to students. Pedagogical success is largely dependent on the ingenuity and patience of the teacher. However, there are limits to generality, as there are certain costs associated with representing disparate phenomena similarly so that a particular generalized procedure will apply. Specifically, a general procedure may involve more rules and take longer to learn than a specific procedure (see Katona, 1940).

Teaching general methods in computer programming

The identical productions theory of transfer is quite capable of explaining transfer at an abstract level. Unfortunately, in many transfer studies there is no attempt either before or after the collection of data to simulate with production rules or any other computational formalism the abstract reasoning required of subjects. Many attempts at teaching abstract reasoning would benefit from a preliminary task analysis to determine whether the methods being taught can in fact be formalized. The exercise of writing a computer simulation would most probably reveal a great deal of complexity that had been overlooked. Additionally, once completed, these task analyses can be used as a guide to instruction.

The research of Klahr and Carver (1988) on the acquisition and transfer of LOGO programming skills in children has amply demonstrated the utility of this approach. Like Schoenfeld, Klahr and Carver set out to demonstrate transfer in a domain that was strewn with negative results. Although some have held out great hope that computer programming would emerge as the mental discipline that would revolutionize children's thinking, most empirical studies have shown little benefit of learning to program on general problem-solving skills (Gorman and Bourne, 1983; Pea, 1983; Dalbey and Linn, 1984; Garlick, 1984; McGilly, Poulin-DuBois, and Shultz, 1984). Undaunted by these results, Klahr and Carver set as their goal to teach high-level debugging skills to elementary-school children and measure transfer of those skills to nonprogramming contexts. The leverage they brought to the task was an in-depth task analysis and production system model of debugging which they used to guide instruction. Most important to their model and subsequent instruction was a reification of the high-level goal structure of debugging, which included the four subgoals of describing the discrepancy between the actual and desired program output, representing the structure of the program as a necessary preliminary step for locating the bug, finding the bug using the information gathered in steps 1 and 2, and correcting the bug by writing new code. They found, first, that instruction based on the simulation model improved children's debugging skills over the span of a two-semester course and, second, that the children were able to transfer their debugging skills to nonprogramming contexts. The transfer tests involved the debugging of sets of written instructions for such tasks as arranging furniture, ordering food, or running errands. Transfer was facilitated by the fact that the directions for these tasks were given a procedure-subprocedure structure similar to the LOGO programs children had learned to debug. Specifically, children who had received training in LOGO debugging were much more likely to do a selective search of the directions and localize the bug to a particular subprocedure than a control group. These positive results suggest that simulation models may contribute much to the teaching of high-level thinking skills by providing a precise definition of exactly what is being taught. This philosophy lies behind much of our work on intelligent tutoring systems, such as the LISP tutor.

Limited Effects of Negative Transfer

The identical productions theory claims that negative transfer should be quite limited in scope in transfer environments that are highly reactive and instructive. In our second text-editing experiment, we found little evidence of negative transfer between a pair of screen editors designed for maximal interference. However, there has been a dearth of research on interference between complex cognitive skills, and we must regard our conclusions as tentative. Fortunately, a study by Polson, Muncher, and Kieras (in preparation) provides further support for our position.

The Polson et al. study is very similar to our own in that the domain of study was text editing. Subjects spent three days learning one of four screen editors and then all transferred for two days to a common editor. Subjects learned methods for performing fifteen kinds of edits defined by crossing the editing operations delete, copy, and transpose by the editing objects character, word, phrase, line, and sentence. There were four groups of approximately 25 subjects. One of these groups spent all five days learning the common editor and acted as a control group.

The four editors used in the experiment shared identical methods for positioning the cursor (LL) and had common high-level control structures, so there was an ample basis for positive transfer. However, the methods for performing the edits (MT) differed in ways that, at least according to the classical literature on verbal learning, would tend to promote interference. Two of the editors were called *single-character* editors (one was called SK1 and the other SK2), because each of the fifteen edits was associated with a single control character. These two editors differed from one another in that the same keys were used but rebound to different commands (thus, the relationship between them was equivalent to the relationship between the two editors used in our second text-editing study). In these single-character editors, subjects first positioned the cursor at the beginning of the range of the edit and simply pressed the appropriate control key to perform the edit. The bindings for the fifteen commands were equally nonmnemonic in both editors. One of the single-character editors, SK1, was designated as the common editor which served as the transfer condition for all groups. One of the experimental groups transferred from SK2 to SK1.

The two remaining experimental groups transferred from the other two training editors to SK1. One of these training editors, called the *cross-product* editor (CP), had fifteen two-character commands that were generated by combining the first letter of the editing operation (d, c, or t) with the first letter of the editing object (c, w, p, l, or s). Thus, to delete a phrase, one would type dp. The fourth and final training editor, called the *block mode* editor (BM), had three generic commands: delete, copy, and transpose, which were bound to labeled function keys. After selecting a particular editing operation, subjects were required to specify the range of the edit by highlighting a range of text with either the cursor keys or a single-character find function. Once both the operation and range were defined, the edit was terminated by pressing the enter key.

Subjects spent the first and fourth days of the experiment going through a structured training program which consisted of three phases: reading an instruction booklet, practicing a blocked set of exercises for each of the three command operations until reaching a criterion of ten correct edits, and then editing a short manuscript containing a mixed selection of thirty edits. In the last two phases, immediate feedback was given on each edit by a simple CAI program, and subjects were required to redo incorrect edits. On the second, third, and fifth days of the experiment, subjects had extended practice on their assigned editor on larger manuscripts. Again, immediate feedback was given and mistakes were corrected.

Given the results of our text-editing experiment, it should come as no surprise that massive positive transfer was observed between all training editors and the transfer editor in this experiment on both day 4 and day 5. Positive transfer was observed in terms of both time to reach criterion on day 4 and total editing time on day 5. There was no evidence of negative transfer or interference of any kind.

The value of this experiment is that it provides an interesting comparison between the amount of transfer between "rebound" editors (which is the replication of our experiment) and the amount between editors that likewise share many common elements but intuitively have a less interfering relationship. This provides a sensitive test for the presence of interference of any kind. For example, the cross-product training editor and the single-character transfer editor (called SK1) share nearly as many elements as the two single-character editors (SK1 and SK2), yet one would intuitively expect there to be little or no interference between the cross-product editor (CP) and SK1, since the command structures are rather dissimilar. Since these two transfer conditions are based on nearly the same number of common elements, one would expect the level of transfer to be about the same in both, if only common elements were in play and there were no interference effects. However, if transfer between SK2 and SK1 was substantially less than that between CP and SK1 (though still positive), this would be strong evidence that some kind of interference was reducing the level of positive transfer between SK2 and SK1.

Figure 8.1 presents the mean time to reach criterion during the training phases on both day 1 and day 4. The data from day

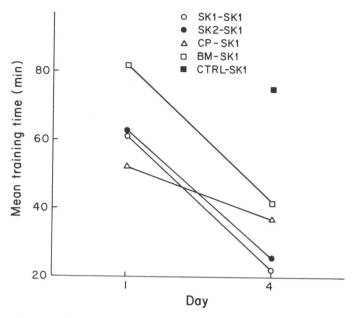

Figure 8.1. *Transfer results from the Polson, Muncher, and Kieras text-editing experiment. Reprinted by permission of the authors.*

1 are not important here; more interesting are the transfer results from day 4. The SK2-SK1 condition exhibits nearly total positive transfer and, surprisingly, even *more* than that shown by CP-SK1. Statistical analysis confirmed that the performance of SK2-SK1 was superior to that of CP-SK1 on day 4; interestingly, the SK2-SK1 condition was not found significantly different from the SK1-SK1 control. Thus, it appears that the SK2-SK1 group is exhibiting full positive transfer and is able to show the positive effects of all of its common elements. There is no evidence for interference of any kind.

A repair analysis

In the interpretation of these results, Polson et al. rightly point out that their experimental training procedure greatly eased the transition between editors, and that in such a situation the effects of interference are likely to be minimized. Subjects were told explicitly about the structure of the transfer editor, and practice was accompanied by immediate feedback. To explain the beneficial effects of explicit instruction and feedback, they propose that transfer between overlapping complex skills is largely a repair process where the representation of a training skill is "edited" in order to reflect the new demands of the transfer task. This repair process is composed of three steps: determining which elements of the old skill need to be repaired, namely which elements are no longer valid in the transfer task; determining what the new, replacement elements should be; and making the repair. Polson et al. point out that, in transfer environments that offer both instruction and feedback, the first two steps in the repair process are greatly simplified. However, in situations where the transition between tasks is poorly defined and must be discerned by the subjects themselves, the effects of interference may be much stronger. Indeed, the classic Einstellung phenomenon (Luchins, 1942) can be described as a transfer situation where the changing demands of the transfer task have not been pointed out explicitly to subjects.

A dramatic demonstration of this effect in a somewhat different setting is the classic part-whole negative transfer effect in verbal learning (Tulving, 1966; Tulving and Osler, 1967; Sternberg and Bower, 1974). The basic phenomenon is that subjects exhibit negative transfer in the learning of a second list of words after learning an initial list that is either a subset (part-whole transfer) or superset (whole-part transfer) of the transfer list. However, if subjects are explicitly informed that the transfer list either contains or is a part of the training list, the negative transfer turns to strong positive transfer, which is what one would have originally expected given an identical elements theory. Anderson and Bower (1973) offered an explanation of these results which claimed that, without an explicit mention of the relationship between the lists, subjects were having trouble determining which items went with which list. In present terminology, subjects were having trouble with the first step of the repair process, namely identifying which elements needed to be changed. Apparently, subjects were entertaining the possibility that something more complex than a part-whole or whole-part relationship held between the two lists. Once subjects are informed of the relationship, they can quickly incorporate the representation of the first list into the representation of the second.

Karat, Boyes, Weisgerber, and Schafer (1986) report preliminary results from yet another text-editing experiment which supports this notion that, as repairs become more difficult to characterize, the likelihood of negative transfer increases. They took subjects who were already skilled users of a word-processing system and transferred them to a new version of the system that differed somewhat in low-level editing functions. The critical difference between their experimental procedure and that of Polson et al. is that they provided no explicit instruction or feedback to ease the transition between systems, but simply handed subjects a set of reference manuals and asked them to go to work. This may be somewhat more representative of what happens in the standard office environment. Although the results were somewhat preliminary and the appropriate controls were missing, the experiment did seem to suggest that subjects were showing less transfer than would be expected given a formal analysis of similarity between the editors.

While the repair analysis can be used to accommodate these results, it is not clear that it is necessary. Our analysis handled results similar to those of Polson, Muncher, and Kieras without assuming such a process. Indeed, it is contrary to the ACT* theory to suppose that subjects have conscious access to productions in order to execute repairs. Also, we do not think that evidence of poor transfer in uninformed conditions requires such an explanation. If subjects cannot characterize what a new text editor requires, it is of little surprise that knowledge does not transfer. For example, if they do not know they are supposed to move a cursor to the position of an edit, they will not set the goal to do so, and productions relevant to that goal will not apply. The problem seems to be simply knowing what knowledge is applicable, not repairing that knowledge.

Use Specificity of Knowledge

Finally, recent research has a bearing on the issue of use specificity of knowledge. Much work in the areas of naive mental models (Clement, 1983; McCloskey, 1983) and situated reasoning (Lave, Murtaugh, and de La Rocha, 1984; Scribner, 1984) has shown that the use specificity of knowledge is not the exception but rather the rule in many content domains. For example, McCloskey (1983) has shown that trained physics students regress to "phenomenological" explanations when asked to interpret physical events outside of the classroom context. Most of these mistaken explanations conform to what McCloskey calls the naive "impetus" theory of motion, which conforms to a pre-Newtonian view of physics popular during the fourteenth through the sixteenth centuries. The impetus theory states that a proximal force is required to move an object, and without a proximal force an object will quickly stop, or at least stop moving in the direction of the force. Figure 8.2 shows some exam-

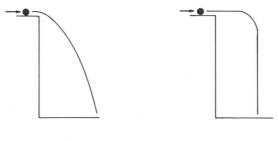

(a) rolling off a table top

(b) shot out of a circular tube

Figure 8.2. *Erroneous predictions of ball trajectories from the experiments on naïve theories of motion. The diagrams on the left show the correct Newtonian motion. M. McCloskey, Naïve theories of motion, in D. Gentner and A. L. Stevens, eds.,* Mental models *(Hillsdale, N.J.: Erlbaum Associates, 1983).*

ples of this misconception at work. In the task depicted in Figure 8.2(a), subjects are asked to predict the trajectory of a ball rolling off a cliff, assuming no friction or air resistance. Instead of predicting the correct curvilinear path shown in the first panel, subjects often predict a path that is initially completely horizontal, followed by a short curvilinear segment, followed by a segment that is completely vertical, which is shown in the second panel. Clearly, formal knowledge of physics is not being applied in this task. Similarly, in Figure 8-2(b), subjects are asked to predict the trajectory of a ball as it shoots out one end of a circular tube. Instead of predicting the correct straight-line path tangent to the circle at the point of departure (shown in the first panel), subjects often predict that the ball will continue for a while in its circular motion, but will eventually straighten out (as shown in the second panel). As shown in these two examples, subjects appear to have different sets of rules for reasoning about physics in the classroom and physics in the real world, and these rules make little contact with one another. McCloskey claims that the naive view actually dominates the formal view, to the extent that information presented in the classroom is often misinterpreted or distorted to fit the naive view.

Similarly, work in situated reasoning has shown that certain people develop specialized, pragmatic mathematical procedures for reasoning about everyday situations that make little contact with formal mathematics instruction. Ethnographic studies (Lave, Murtaugh, and de La Rocha, 1984; Scribner 1984) have shown that educated adults may show a particular competence at performing mathematics in everyday situations such as shopping, managing money, and loading dairy trucks, but are incapable of performing the same tasks stated in the form of abstract mathematical problems in the laboratory.

Most interesting is a study by Carraher, Carraher, and Schliemann (1985), which investigated the mathematical strategies used by Brazilian school children who also worked as street vendors. They found that, on the job, these children used quite sophisticated strategies for calculating the total cost of orders involving different numbers of different objects (such as the total cost of four coconuts and twelve lemons) and, what is more, could perform such calculations reliably in their heads. Carraher et al, actually went to the trouble of going to the streets and posing as customers for these children, making various purchases and recording the percentage of correct calculations. The experimenters then asked the children to come with them to the laboratory, where they were given written mathematics tests that involved the same numbers and mathematical operations that had been handled successfully in the streets. For example, if a child had correctly calculated the total cost of five lemons at 35 cruzeiros each on the street, the child was given the written problem: $5 \times 35 = ?$

The results showed that, whereas children solved 98 percent of the problems presented in the situated context, they solved only 37 percent of the problems presented in the laboratory context. Once again, these problems involved the exact same numbers and mathematical operations. Interestingly, if the problems were stated in the form of word problems in the laboratory, performance improved to 74 percent. This runs counter to the usual finding, which is that word problems are more difficult than equivalent number problems (Carpenter and Moser, 1982). Apparently, the additional context provided by the word problem allowed students to make contact with their pragmatic strategies. Protocol analyses of the children's solution processes revealed that, whereas in the laboratory children were using formal mathematical algorithms, in the streets they were using an informal grouping strategy which took advantage of commonly recurring sums and products. For example, if the task was to compute the cost of four coconuts, and the cost of three coconuts was well known, the child would restate the problem as an addition of the cost of three and the cost of one.

Conclusion

Recent research thus provides a rather contented perspective on the identical productions theory and the ACT* theory on which it is based. It offers a great deal of support for the theory and gives it very little difficulty. However, this optimistic assessment ignores some deep representational problems associated with application of the identical productions theory. The focus of the last chapter is to expose these problems in some detail.

9 / Representation and Transfer

The essence of this book is that Thorndike's identical elements theory is alive and well in a new body. We have resurrected Thorndike's theory by redefining his identical elements as the units of declarative and procedural knowledge in the ACT* theory. In short, we propose that initial transfer can be explained in terms of overlap in the declarative component and sustained transfer in terms of overlap in the procedural component. The key difference between his proposal and ours is that, whereas Thorndike's elements referred only to external behaviors, ours include purely cognitive operations that reference abstract mental objects. In the process of resurrecting Thorndike, we have given support to the ACT* theory of knowledge representation.

There is a serious problem, however, lurking in this otherwise rosy picture. The problem is that all of our transfer predictions turn critically on assumptions about the representation of the skill. We are in danger of having a vacuous theory because we may be able to accommodate any potentially embarrassing result by suitable assumptions about knowledge representation. This was not a problem for Thorndike because he did not propose a mental representation.

A series of experiments by Elio (1986) illustrate how potentially conflicting transfer results can be resolved by making appropriate assumptions about representation. She had subjects learn procedures that involved calculating a hypothetical pollution rating for a sample of water. Table 9.1 shows the four procedures, which consisted of three component steps (where

Table 9.1. Examples of procedures from the four conditions of the Elio experiment. The component steps are particulate rating, mineral rating, and marine hazard. The integrative steps are index 1, index 2, and overall quality.

Quantity calculated	Formula
Initially learned procedure	
1. Particulate rating	Solid $\times$ $(\text{lime}_4 - \text{lime}_2)$
2. Mineral rating	Greater of (algae/2) and (solid/3)
3. Index 1	Particulate + mineral
4. Marine hazard	$(\text{Toxin}_{max} + \text{toxin}_{min})/2$
5. Index 2	Index 1/marine
6. Overall quality	Index 2 $-$ mineral
Old component, new integrative condition	
1. Particulate rating	$(\text{Toxin}_{max} + \text{toxin}_{min})/2$
2. Mineral rating	Solid $\times$ $(\text{lime}_4 - \text{lime}_2)$
3. Marine hazard	Greater of (algae/2) and (solid/3)
4. Index 1	Mineral/marine
5. Index 2	Particulate $\times$ index 1
6. Overall quality	Index 2 + index 1
Old integrative, new component condition	
1. Particulate rating	$(\text{Lime}_{min} \times 3)$ + algae
2. Mineral rating	Lesser of $(\text{solid} + \text{lime}_1)$ and $(\text{algae} + \text{toxin}_3)$
3. Index 1	Particulate + mineral
4. Marine hazard	$\text{Solid}/\text{lime}_1$
5. Index 2	Index 1/marine
6. Overall quality	Index 2 $-$ mineral
Both new condition	
1. Particulate rating	$(\text{Lime}_{min} \times 3)$ + algae
2. Mineral rating	Lesser of $(\text{solid} + \text{lime}_1)$ and $(\text{algae} + \text{toxin}_3)$
3. Marine hazard	$\text{Solid}/\text{lime}_1$
4. Index 1	Mineral/marine
5. Index 2	Particulate $\times$ index 1
6. Overall quality	Index 2 + index 1

Source: R. Elio, Representation of similar well-learned cognitive procedures, *Cognitive Science*, 10, 41–74 (1986).

raw data presented to subjects were used to calculate intermediate quantities) and three integrative steps (where the intermediate quantities were combined into an overall score). Subjects
had to commit these procedures to memory and perform the
calculations at a computer terminal, as shown in Figure 9.1.

Elio reported a series of five experiments, but for our purposes, transfer results from only two are relevant. In both of
these experiments, subjects learned a couple of pollution procedures and then transferred to one of four new procedures that
involved either: (1) old component steps and new integrative
steps, (2) old integrative steps and new component steps, (3) all
old steps, or (4) all new steps. The critical difference between the
two experiments was that in one experiment, when component
steps were familiar in the transfer task (case 1 above), they
appeared in the same serial positions as in training, and in the
other experiment they appeared in different serial positions.
Before these experiments were run, there was no reason to
expect that serial position would have any effect on accessing
and executing familiar steps. Indeed, one property of production rules that we have proposed is that they fire independently
of context. However, Elio observed that transfer was nearly total
when the steps appeared in the same serial positions, but much
less when the serial positions were scrambled. To explain these
results, she proposed that the rules for the component steps test
for the serial position of the step on the left-hand side.

Thus, Elio was able to accommodate potentially conflicting
results by suitable assumptions about knowledge representa-

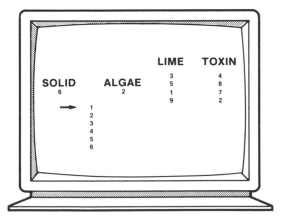

Figure 9.1. *Screen configuration in the pollution index experiments (subjects are given
this raw data to make a series of calculations). R. Elio, Representation of similar well-
learned cognitive procedures,* Cognitive Science, 10 (1986), 41–74.

tion. Her goal was not to salvage the identical elements model, as far as we can tell. Nonetheless, her work illustrates how certain representational assumptions can blunt the disconfirmation of the identical elements model.

As we face up to the problem of representation and its implications for theories of transfer, our discussion is dominated by two issues. First, to what degree can tests be made of our identical elements model that do not depend on detailed assumptions about representation? Second, what can we do to constrain a representation on independent grounds so that we can make real tests of the identical elements hypothesis?

Mathematical Analysis of Transfer

What predictions can the identical elements model make about transfer without a strong commitment to a particular knowledge representation? Without any representational assumptions, no predictions are possible. To get started, it is helpful to assume minimally that the transfer task has the same organization before and after a subject's exposure to the training task. This is not always the case. Specifically, most instances of negative transfer are due to the fact that training on task A causes subjects to choose a nonoptimal procedure for task B.

Overlooking this complication for the moment, suppose we can assume that learning task A does not affect the structure of task B or vice versa. In many situations this is a good first approximation. Then what can we predict? We can decompose the tasks into the elements that are shared and those that are unique. Let i index the components (such as productions) that occur in either task. Let A_i give the frequency of component i in task A and B_i its frequency in task B. For components unique to task A, $B_i = 0$. For components unique to task B, $A_i = 0$. A common component has both A_i and B_i greater than zero. This framework allows for the very real possibility that common elements may occur with very different frequencies in the two tasks.

Now let us turn to calculation of our transfer formula:

$$(9.1) \quad T_{\%learning} = \frac{I - T}{I - L} \times 100$$

where I is some measure of initial performance, T is a measure of performance following training on a related task (the transfer condition), and L is a measure of performance following an equal amount of training on the same task (the learning control condition).

The initial performance I is typically some aggregate measure over a series of trials, as is T and L. For the sake of simplicity in our calculations, let us assume that I, T, and L are based on performance on the median (not the mean) trial of the aggregate. We define m as the index of the median trial that goes into calculating I, and n the index that goes into calculating T and L (for example, if I is based on performance on the first ten trials, $m = 5.5$). In the case of calculating T, we can break n into two parts; j, which is the total number of trials on the training task, and k, which is the median trial on the transfer task. In calculating T, $n = j + k$.

Now we are in a position to calculate the I, T, and L terms in the transfer equation. In our calculations, we sum over all components to determine total task time. $I(A)$ denotes initial performance on task A, $I(B)$ initial performance on task B, $L(A)$ learning performance on task A, $L(B)$ learning performance on task B, $T(AB)$ transfer performance on task B having studied task A, and $T(BA)$ transfer performance task on A having studied task B.

Assuming power-law speedup, the total times are:

$$(9.2)\ I(A) = \sum_{i \in A} t_i(A_i m)^{-d}$$

$$(9.3)\ I(B) = \sum_{i \in B} t_i(B_i m)^{-d}$$

$$(9.4)\ L(A) = \sum_{i \in A} t_i(A_i n)^{-d}$$

$$(9.5)\ L(B) = \sum_{i \in B} t_i(B_i n)^{-d}$$

$$(9.6)\ T(AB) = \sum_{i \in B} t_i(A_i j + B_i k)^{-d}$$

$$(9.7)\ T(BA) = \sum_{i \in A} t_i(B_i j + A_i k)^{-d}$$

Here t_i is the time to execute the ith component on the first trial. Again, we are assuming that all of the components are speeding up as a power function of practice with exponent d.

What we cannot do without representational assumptions is specify the t_i, A_i, and B_i in the preceding equations. We now want to explore what can be predicted without full specification of these components. Two equations give the percentage savings in going from A to B versus going from B to A:

$$(9.8) \ T_{\% learning} \ (AB) \quad = \quad \frac{I(B) \ - \ T(AB)}{I(B) - L(B)}$$

$$= \quad \frac{\displaystyle\sum_{i \in B} t_i(B_i m)^{-d} - \sum_{i \in B} t_i(A_i j + B_i k)^{-d}}{\displaystyle\sum_{i \in B} t_i(B_i m)^{-d} - \sum_{i \in B} t_i(B_i n)^{-d}}$$

$$(9.9) \ T_{\% learning} \ (BA) \quad = \quad \frac{I(A) \ - \ T(BA)}{I(A) - L(A)}$$

$$= \quad \frac{\displaystyle\sum_{i \in A} t_i(A_i m)^{-d} - \sum_{i \in A} t_i(B_i j + A_i k)^{-d}}{\displaystyle\sum_{i \in A} t_i(A_i m)^{-d} - \sum_{i \in A} t_i(A_i n)^{-d}}$$

A reasonable experimental assumption is that we aggregate over the same number of trials in calculating both I and T. Thus, $m = k$. Then we can rewrite these equations:

$$(9.10) \ T_{\% learning} \ (AB) = \frac{\displaystyle\sum_{i \in A \cap B} t_i B_i [m^{-d} - ((A_i / B_i)j + m)^{-d}]}{\displaystyle\sum_{i \in B} t_i B_i [m^{-d} - (j + m)^{-d}]}$$

$$(9.11) \ T_{\% learning} \ (BA) = \frac{\displaystyle\sum_{i \in A \cap B} t_i A_i [m^{-d} - ((B_i / A_i)j + m)^{-d}]}{\displaystyle\sum_{i \in B} t_i A_i [m^{-d} - (j + m)^{-d}]}$$

Here the numerator now represents the intersection of elements in A and B (in equation (9.10) some of the A_i might be zero, and in equation (9.11) some of the B_i might be zero). With the equations stated in this form, it is clear that transfer is always positive in that the numerators are always greater than 0. For example, in equation (9.10), since $(A_i / B_i)j > 0$, then $((A_i / B_i)j + m)^{-d} < m^{-d}$. It follows simply that the numerator is always greater than 0.

In addition, equations (9.10) and (9.11) reveal the remote possibility of transfer greater than 1. $T_{\%learning}(AB)$ can be greater than 1 if the ratios A_i / B_i are very large, indicating that the common components get much more practice on a trial in task A than in task B. This would happen only in perverse experimental situations, for example, when training trials involve solving two problems and transfer trials only one.

A reasonable simplifying assumption at this point is that the ratios A_i / B_i and B_i / A_i are close enough to 1 that we can get rid of them in equations (9.10) and (9.11). As a result, the complex terms involving m, j, and d can be brought outside the summation signs and canceled, yielding the equations:

$$(9.12) \quad T_{\%learning}(AB) = \frac{\displaystyle\sum_{i \in A \cap B} t_i B_i}{\displaystyle\sum_{i \in B} t_i B_i}$$

$$(9.13) \quad T_{\%learning}(BA) = \frac{\displaystyle\sum_{i \in A \cap B} t_i A_i}{\displaystyle\sum_{i \in A} t_i A_i}$$

Here we see a remarkable result. Our measure of transfer is independent of j, the number of initial learning trials, or m, which reflects the number of transfer trials ($m = k$). Interestingly, this prediction seemed true of the various experiments we analyzed. The equations also predict transfer less than or equal to 1, since $A \cap B$ is a subset of A and also of B.

A further simplification at this point would be to assume that all components (such as productions) take the same time to execute on the first trial; that is, t_i is a constant. The t_i terms in the preceding equations could then be canceled, yielding transfer formulas which involved simple summations of component frequencies. This in fact is the form we used to make our theoretical predictions of transfer in text editing.

As a final simplification, we might assume that, for the common elements, $A_i = B_i$. In other words, the common elements co-occur with equal frequency in the two tasks. This leads to the prediction that absolute amount of transfer would be equal in both directions. This prediction tended not to be confirmed in our data.

To summarize, with increasingly strong assumptions, the following predictions can be made concerning identical elements models of transfer:

1. The transfer ratio will be greater than 0.
2. The transfer ratio will be less than 1 and will be independent of the number of learning trials and transfer trials.
3. The transfer ratio will depend solely on the number and frequency of shared components versus total components.
4. Transfer in terms of absolute savings (not ratio savings) will be symmetric.

The first three predictions seem to be confirmed in our data, but the last is not. Any stronger predictions about transfer will be based on more detailed assumptions about skill representation.

Determining Representations of Cognitive Skill

The preceding mathematical analysis has shown that certain interesting qualitative properties of transfer can be determined in the absence of specific representational assumptions. However, quantitative predictions of transfer can be made only in the context of explicit cognitive models, which necessarily embody a host of representational assumptions. This problem has troubled cognitive psychologists for years: how do we determine the representations used by subjects? There are numerous examples (such as the early work of the gestalters and the Elio experiments) where subtle differences in representation can sometimes have a major impact on transfer outcomes. It follows that the accuracy of transfer predictions ultimately rests on the fidelity of the cognitive models upon which they are based. In turn, the fidelity of the models depends upon the strength of the tools available for model building and the skill with which they are deployed.

Model building in cognitive science is a complex task, and we can provide no effective algorithm for success. Given the current state of the art, we can only list some of the methods used, cite some of their problems, and present what we feel are examples worth emulating. We should first point out the obvious: every model is an approximation, and no model is perfect. A model of performance may account for more or less behavior and incorporate more or less of the complexity of the task. One common simplification is to model only error-free performance (e.g. Card, Moran, and Newell, 1983). This is despite the fact that error recovery may contribute to the performance of the skill and may serve as a basis for substantial transfer. Generally, one would expect that the more detailed and extensive the task analysis, the more accurate the prediction (but cf. Abruzzi, 1956). Never theless, our text-editing results and the results of Kieras and Polson (1985) suggest that approximate production system models may often do quite well at predicting transfer. Our calculus experiments, however, show that in some cases this production system approximation is inadequate and must be supplanted by a more detailed analysis which involves the consideration of declarative precursors in calculations of transfer. This adds a whole new dimension of complexity to the models.

Although individual task analyses may be more or less detailed, the history of task analysis in psychology shows a general trend toward the assimilation of greater and greater levels of complexity. This is made possible by theoretical advances in the understanding of complex behavior. Complex task analysis began with Thorndike, who reduced skilled performance to a set of stimulus-response bonds. This position was developed by Skinner (1957) and his colleagues, who applied task analysis techniques to the design of programmed instruction. This line of research culminated in Gagné's work on complex skill hierarchies (Gagné and Paradise, 1961). However, the task analyses of Thorndike, Skinner, and Gagné were purely behavioral and made no reference to cognitive constructs like goals, plans, and strategies. This omission was remedied with the advent of cognitive psychology in the late 1950s. Initially, researchers like Newell and Simon (1972) explored the role of goals and plans in knowledge-impoverished domains like logic and cryptarithmetic. As cognitive psychology matured, the emphasis shifted to the study of knowledge-intensive domains like physics problem solving (Larkin, McDermott, Simon, and Simon, 1980), medical diagnosis (Shortliffe, 1976), and writing (Flower and Hayes, 1977). This period was marked by numerous detailed comparisons of problem solving in experts and novices and led to the enumeration of many differences in knowledge and strategy (Chi, Feltovich, and Glaser, 1981). Most recently, researchers like Johnson-Laird (1983), Young (1983), and Kieras and Bovair (1984) have documented the role of complex mental models in skilled behavior. Thus, cognitive psychology has witnessed a steady growth in the taxonomy of "elements" that comprise skilled performance.

As cognitive theories become more sophisticated, so do task analyses, which are simply embodiments of those theories. Realizing that theories of the future will undoubtedly capture more complexity and provide even more kinds of "identical elements" upon which to base calculations, we adopt a relativist outlook: current representations of cognitive skill, though admittedly deficient, are useful to the extent that they both make accurate transfer predictions and highlight mistakes or omissions and therefore suggest better representations. With this kind of disclaimer, we hope to avoid arguments concerning the exact nature of the representations. Model building is necessarily an inductive prcoess, fraught with indeterminacy and approximation. A proposed model is often just one of many equally good models satisfying a set of empirical constraints (Anderson, 1976). In the absence of discriminating features, the well-traveled and oft-maligned principle of parsimony may be applied to choose among competitors. Ultimately, however, it is predictive power that validates all modeling decisions.

Dimensions of representation

Representations may vary along a number of dimensions. Model building involves working in a three-dimensional space defined by the dimensions of organization, specificity, and grain size.

Organization. The dimension of organization refers to the basic decomposition of the task, and it is revealed by a subject's goals and plans. Although the task itself may place severe constraints on skill decomposition, it is often the case that more than one organization is possible. Most notable are the "rote" and "meaningful" organizations studied by the gestalters. Another interesting instance is the classic work of Simon (1975) on the functional equivalence of problem-solving strategies for solving the tower-of-Hanoi puzzle. Through a formal analysis, Simon identified four strategies for solving the puzzle that radically differed in terms of memory demands, concepts used, and perceptual tests performed. Surprisingly, all predicted the same move sequences and could only be discriminated (if at all) through protocol analysis.

Not surprisingly, the basic organization of a skill has broad implications for transfer. Indeed, Wertheimer discriminated between rote and meaningful organizations on the basis of a transfer test. Similarly, Simon (1975) pointed out that, whereas a complex, goal-recursive strategy for the tower-of-Hanoi puzzle will transfer to puzzles with any number of disks, a simpler perceptual strategy may not.

Working within a production system formalism, movement

along the organization dimension is associated with the casting and recasting of productions that define goal structures. A rote strategy may be defined as the absence of a hierarchical goal structure, and as such, it represents an endpoint of sorts along the organization dimension. A rote strategy for any task can be modeled by a single goal and a set of operators which fire in some predetermined sequence in service of that goal. Control is supplied by working memory tests which make explicit reference to previous steps in the procedure. For example, here are several rules which might appear in some rote procedure for baking a cake:

> IF   the goal is to bake a cake
> and the batter has just been mixed
> THEN light the oven.

> IF   the goal is to bake a cake
> and the oven has just been lit
> THEN grease the pan.

> IF   the goal is to bake a cake
> and the pan has just been greased
> THEN dump the batter into the pan.

Alternatively, the task of baking a cake could be organized by some hierarchical control structure. In this case, certain rules would exist which simply test for the current goal and set appropriate subgoals rather than operate directly on the environment. Here is an example of one such rule, perhaps the first rule to fire in a meaningful cake-baking procedure:

> IF   the goal is to bake a cake
> THEN set as subgoals to:
>   1. read the recipe
>   2. assemble the ingredients
>   3. prepare the batter
>   4. bake in the oven.

Each of these four subgoals might be decomposed further into additional subgoals. Finally, when operators fire, they do so in the context of some hierarchical goal structure. It is interesting to note that the rote procedure is more efficient than the meaningful procedure in terms of number of rule firings; each rule that sets subgoals is additional overhead in terms of both learning and performance. A classic result from Katona (1940) is that rote procedures are in fact often easier to learn and perform than meaningful procedures. The advantage of meaningful procedures is in their wider applicability and potential for transfer.

Specificity. Given a particular organization, a representation may vary in terms of specificity (or conversely, in terms of generality). In production systems, specificity is often achieved by replacing variables in the tests with constants or by adding conditional clauses to individual rules. These processes were called *proceduralization* and *discrimination*, respectively, in Anderson (1982) and were regarded as two of the primary learning mechanisms. As examples of variability along the dimension of specificity, here are some possible variants of a rule from our text-editing simulation:

> IF   the goal is to specify a command symbol
> and the command is = command
> and the symbol for = command is = symbol
> THEN   set as a subgoal to type = symbol.

This rule retrieves the alphanumeric symbolic for a command and sets the goal to type that symbol. Given the variabilization, this rule is quite general and will work for any command in our text editors, assuming that the association between command and symbol is stored in working memory. However, one could replace the variables with constants and have a rule specialized to a particular command:

> IF   the goal is to specify a command symbol
> and the command is replace line
> and the symbol for replace line is r
> THEN   set as a subgoal to type r.

This rule has eliminated the need for memory retrieval and variable instantiation but, as a consequence, has sacrificed much of its generality. In the language of Anderson (1982), this rule has been *proceduralized*. Issues of proceduralization arise frequently when building production system models of transfer. The issue is essentially whether to store task-specific knowledge declaratively in working memory and have that knowledge interpreted by general-purpose productions or to embed the knowledge directly in the productions themselves. If one is making predictions of transfer solely on the basis of production set overlap, it seems wise to use fully proceduralized rules, since otherwise the task-specific component of the skill will be grossly underestimated. In fact, we used proceduralized rules in our text-editing simulations.

Aside from proceduralization, our text-editing rule can be

made even more specific by adding a discriminating contextual test on the left-hand side:

IF   the goal is to specify a command symbol
     and the command is replace line
     and the symbol for replace line is r
     and the editor is EDT
THEN   set as a subgoal to type r.

This rule now only fires when the editor is EDT. In general, it is quite a thorny problem to decide how many contextual tests to include on the left-hand sides of rules. Perhaps a defensible position is to include enough context so that the rule fires correctly in the training task(s) but no more. So, for example, if training involved learning two editors, ED and EDT, and the replace command differed in the two editors, then the preceding contextual test would be required for the rule to fire properly.

Although movement along the specificity dimension is associated largely with decisions concerning discrimination and proceduralization, sometimes subtler situations arise which may require local reorganizations of small sets of rules. Specifically, certain abstractions involve the creation of entirely new rules rather than the modification of existing rules. For example, in our text-editing simulations, we were faced with the situation that in the line editors, all commands are terminated with carriage return. Do we include this carriage return as part of each command, or do we write a separate rule to supply the carriage return? This has implications for transfer, because a rule that stood independently and supplied a terminating carriage return would transfer between the line editors. To illustrate this situation further, we present two production rule representations for the print command in ED. First, we have a rule that includes carriage return as part of the method for printing lines:

IF   the goal is to execute a command
     and the command is print
     and the target line is = line
     and the editor is ED
THEN   set as subgoals to:
        1. type = line
        2. type p
        3. type carriage return.

Next, here are two rules which simulate the same behavior. The difference is that a piece of goal structure has been added which captures the regularity of carriage return as a terminator for all commands in ED:

    IF   the goal is to enter a command
THEN   set as subgoals to:
        1. enter the command
        2. type carriage return.

    IF   the goal is to enter a command
        and the command is print
        and the target line is = line
        and the editor is ED
THEN   set as subgoals to:
        1. type = line
        2. type p.

We chose the latter representation for our simulation. This decision was based upon a small informal experiment conducted with several expert users of ED. First, we asked subjects to describe the various methods for printing, substituting, and appending text in ED. None made reference to carriage return in any of their descriptions. This suggests that carriage return is not stored as a part of each method. Second, we gave subjects hypothetical new commands, such as a command to change lines of text from upper to lower case. Although none of our descriptions made reference to carriage return, all subjects were able to supply the missing carriage return when using the commands. Thus, we have reason to believe that the carriage return is represented as an independent rule.

In sum, we used a miniature transfer experiment to discriminate between possible representations of particular rules. Ultimately, many such microdecisions contributed to an overall model of the skill which was used to make a series of transfer predictions in another, totally independent context: transfer between the line editors. Small pilot tests such as these can serve a useful bootstrapping function in many modeling situations.

Grain Size. Finally, within a particular organization and level of specificity, representations may vary in terms of grain size. Grain size simply refers to the size of operators, that is, the number and scope of actions on the right-hand sides of productions. Movement along the grain size dimension is accomplished through what in Anderson (1982) is called *composition*. Composition takes two rules and combines them into one. For example, the first two rules of our rote cake-baking procedure could be combined into the rule:

> IF   the goal is to bake a cake
>   and the batter has just been mixed
> THEN 1. light the oven
>   2. grease the pan.

This rule has two actions on the right-hand side rather than one. Composition does not change the performance of a model in terms of the sequence of actions taken. However, composition does have a large effect in terms of speed. Generally, the composition process predicts an exponential speedup in terms of execution time on a single task, since the total number of rules is being cut by some constant proportion from trial to trial. However, Rosenbloom and Newell (1986) showed that the composition process in fact predicts learning rates that more closely approximate a power function if one looks at performance across trials that involve slight variations of the same task, which is the case in most learning situations. This slower learning rate is due to the fact that only certain compositions apply from trial to trial. Many of the larger compositions are based on the idiosyncrasies of particular problems and are often useless on similar problems.

This learning effect nicely illustrates the effect of composition on transfer. Generally, as rules get larger, that is, have more tests and actions per rule, they become less applicable. For this reason, in our production system models of transfer, we have avoided composed rules.

Factors influencing representation

A number of factors influence the representation that subjects use. Newell and Simon (1972) pointed out that severe constraints are placed on representation by the task environment itself. This position is derived from the principle of limited rationality (Simon, 1947), which states that, within the processing limits set by the human information-processing system, individuals act more or less rationally to attain their goals. This means that, often when we examine expert behavior on routine tasks, we are learning more about the structure of the task than the psychology of the subject. The expert has adapted completely to the demands of the task and is doing precisely what is required. However, there may still be a certain amount of variance in the kinds of representations that subjects adopt. This variance can be attributed to three major sources: task instructions, previous experience on similar tasks, and practice.

Task Instructions. Although it is often thought that subjects arrive at their representations through some mysterious means, it is often the case that the task instructions provided by the experimenter go a long way toward defining the representation. Typically, instructions provide descriptions of objects to be manipulated, operators for manipulating them, initial and goal states of the problem, and perhaps even some subgoal structure. For example, in our text-editing experiments, we told subjects in our instructions that to perform an edit, they first had to locate the line containing the edit and then modify the text on that line. This rule, derived from the GOMS model of text editing of Card et al. (1983), was encoded directly as a rule in the simulation.

With the use of intelligent tutoring systems as data collection tools, the experimenter's conceptualization of the problem space normally provided only in the task instructions is enforced to a much greater degree throughout the course of problem solving. The interface of the tutor completely determines the operators and the objects to be manipulated, as well as the form of external memory. For this reason, intelligent tutoring systems are very promising as test-beds for identical elements theories of transfer. They reduce variability in representation between subjects by enforcing the designer's conceptualization of the problem space.

Hayes and Simon (1974) and Simon and Hayes (1976) performed a set of experiments comparing isomorphs of the tower of Hanoi which nicely illustrates the strong linkage between task instructions and representation. In conjunction with this empirical work, they developed a model of comprehension called UNDERSTAND whose purpose was to take the written problem instructions and develop a representation that could be used to solve the problem. Specifically, the model derived information about goals, problem states, and operators from the task instructions and presented that information to a general-purpose problem-solving program called GPS. The UNDERSTAND model made explicit predictions concerning the kinds of representations subjects would adopt when given a particular set of problem instructions.

Hayes and Simon studied two basic isomorphs of the tower of Hanoi. The first, called the *move* isomorph, involves the physical movement of disks from peg to peg. This is the standard configuration of the problem, where moves are constrained by two principles: if a peg has more than one disk, only the smallest disk can be moved; and a larger disk may not be placed on a peg where there is already a smaller disk. The second isomorph, called the *change* isomorph, involves changing the sizes of disks on pegs of differing sizes. A single, stationary disk is associated with each peg, and the rules state that it is illegal to make a disk larger if there is already a disk of greater or equal size on a larger peg. These problems are actually equivalent in terms of the space of moves. The change representation differs from the move representation in that the referents for disks and pegs have simply been switched. A peg in the change representation represents a disk in the move representation, and changing sizes maps perfectly onto changing locations. In the change representation, each peg always has a single disk, since in the move representation, disks have only a single location.

The UNDERSTAND model predicted that problem states and moves would be represented differently for these two isomorphs and that the representation adopted would be determined completely by the instructions provided. In the move problems, a move would be represented as removing a disk from one of the pegs and placing it on another peg. In the change problems, a move would be represented as changing the name of the peg with which some disk is associated. Thus, the same move is represented by a different rule, depending upon the isomorph from which it is drawn.

Simon and Hayes (1976) gathered verbal protocols from subjects solving both kinds of problems to support their claim that the representations differed. They presented the isomorphs within the context of a particular cover story involving monsters and globes rather than pegs and disks. Table 9.2 shows the problem instructions for both isomorphs. Two kinds of statement were analyzed from the protocols: those concerning descriptions of moves and those concerning descriptions of problem states. In both cases, the analysis was quite straightforward, and the evidence was overwhelming that subjects adopted the representation given by the experimenter. For example, this protocol excerpt reveals a move representation: "So the small globe goes over to the guy with the medium-sized globe"; whereas this excerpt reveals a change representation: "The medium-sized monster changes his into a small globe."

Protocols were scored by two coders who agreed in all cases on the representation adopted. Furthermore, in all cases but one, the representation was consistent with the problem instructions. This leads to two important conclusions: task instructions strongly influence the representation a subject adopts, and

Table 9.2. Isomorphic versions of the tower-of-Hanoi monster problems.

(a) Move isomorph

Three five-handed extraterrestrial monsters were holding three crystal globes. Because of the quantum-mechanical peculiarities of their neighborhood, both monsters and globes come in exactly three sizes with no others permitted: small, medium, and large. The medium-sized monster was holding the small globe, the small monster was holding the large globe, and the large monster was holding the medium-sized globe. Since this situation offended their keenly developed sense of symmetry, they proceeded to transfer globes from one monster to another so that each monster would have a globe proportionate to his own size. Monster etiquette complicated the solution of the problem since it requires:

1. that only one globe may be transferred at a time;
2. that if a monster is holding two globes, only the larger of the two may be transferred; and
3. that a globe may not be transferred to a monster who is holding a larger globe.

By what sequence of transfers could the monsters have solved this probem?

(b) Change isomorph

Three five-handed monsters were holding three crystal globes. Because of the quantum-mechanical peculiarities of their neighborhood, both monsters and globes come in exactly three sizes with no other permitted: small, medium, and large. The medium-sized monster was holding the small globe, the small monster was holding the large globe, and the large monster was holding the medium-sized globe. Since this situation offended their keenly developed sense of symmetry, they proceeded to shrink and expand the globes so that each monster would have a globe proportionate to his own size. Monster etiquette complicated the solution of the problem since it requires:

1. that only one globe may be shrunk or expanded at a time;
2. if two globes are of the same size, only the globe held by the larger monster can be changed; and
3. a globe may not be changed to a size that is held by a larger monster.

By what sequence of transfers could the monsters have solved this problem?

Source: J. R. Hayes and H. A. Simon, Psychological differences among problem isomorphs, in J. Castellan, D. B. Pisoni, and G. Potts, eds., *Cognitive theory,* volume two (Hillsdale, N.J.: Erlbaum Associates, 1977).

it is possible to use verbal protocol data to discriminate between possible representations.

Neves (1977) performed a similar kind of experiment investigating the link between instruction and representation. He taught subjects different strategies for solving the tower of Hanoi and subsequently sought evidence for use of a particular strategy from subjects' verbal protocols. Two of the strategies he used were called the *goal-recursive* strategy and the *perceptual* strategy by Simon (1975). These two are quite similar, and it was something of a challenge for Neves to be able to discriminate between them. The goal recursive strategy involves decomposing the goal of moving the largest pyramid into a series of goals involving smaller pyramids. Thus, given the situation in Figure 9.2, a subject taught the goal-recursive strategy gave the following protocol: "Go to peg 2 and try to move the next to largest, which is the 3."

In the perceptual strategy, one does not worry about pyramids but simply tries to move the largest disk to the goal peg. If it is blocked, one must detect the largest disk blocking the move. From a subject taught this strategy, Neves collected the following protocol: "The 4 has to go in to the 3 but the 3 is in the way."

Neves developed production systems for these strategies and was able to put the protocol statements he collected into close correspondence with the firing of individual rules.

The Neves study demonstrates once again that instruction exerts a major influence on representation, and that representations can be determined through protocol analysis. In the case illustrated here, the discrimination made was quite fine, and in a sense it demonstrates the power and precision of protocol analysis in the limit. In many cases, choice of representation is revealed by an almost cursory inspection of a protocol. For example, Neves (1977) stated that discrimination of yet another strategy, the radically different move-pattern strategy, from the two strategies described here was quite trivial, given a smattering of protocol data.

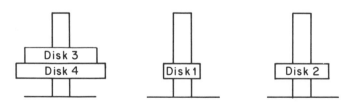

Figure 9.2. *Tower-of-Hanoi configuration corresponding to the Neves (1977) protocol excerpts.*

Previous Experience on Similar Tasks. In the typical transfer experiment, subjects learn task A and transfer to task B. The experimenter's concern is to identify the knowledge that is acquired in task A that applies to task B. This fixation on the transition between tasks A and B is an experimental convenience, because in fact every learning situation is a transfer situation. A much less well-defined yet equally interesting transfer situation is the one between pre-experimental knowledge and initial performance on task A. To take a trivial example, most preschool children or non-English-speaking adults would do very poorly on most psychological experiments administered to college sophomores in the United States. In this country, psychologists rely on a body of shared culture (minimally, knowledge of English) that makes compliance to experimental demands possible.

Since a subject's pre-experimental history exerts an influence on his representation of task A, and since transfer predictions require models of both task A and task B, studies of transfer must give at least some consideration to a subject's pre-experimental history. This is done implicitly in most experiments by drawing subjects from a certain, restricted population. For example, in our calculus experiments, we were sure to get students who had completed high-school trigonometry. Thus, we could assume a certain level of basic mathematical competence, no more and no less, in our subjects (transfer is well-behaved within a very narrow band of competence; if subjects come into the experiment knowing too little, they cannot learn and cannot transfer; the same is true if they know too much). These assumptions are often ill-founded, and violations are responsible for much of the within-subjects variance we observed in our learning experiments. Indeed, Gagné and Paradise (1961) claimed that most individual differences in learning rates arise not from differences in native ability but rather from differences in prerequisite knowledge.

Taken to its logical conclusion, this point concerning prior knowledge puts cognitive psychologists in the quixotic position of not being able to say anything about current behavior without knowing the entire past intellectual history of subjects. Indeed, concern over this point led to the initial emphasis on the study of tasks with low semantic content, such as tower of Hanoi. In these tasks, the subject's prior knowledge had little or no effect. However, even in more complex, semantically rich tasks, there is reason to believe that the influences on representation are quite proximal and the picture is not so gloomy. Most encouraging is the work of several researchers on early skill acquisition, which shows that subjects rely heavily on task instructions and prefer analogies drawn from within the domain (Ross, 1982; VanLehn, 1983; Anderson, Farrell, and Sauers, 1984). This suggests that some of the more insidious and nonspecific influences of prior knowledge may be washed out by task instructions in many experimental situations.

Practice. A third influence on representation is practice on the task. It is a well-documented fact that, as subjects acquire expertise, their representations change, in terms of both grain size (Chase and Simon, 1973) and basic strategy (Larkin, McDermott, Simon, and Simon, 1980). Production systems typically model the effects of practice by either adding rules or modifying existing rules (Klahr, Langley, and Neches, 1987). Some of the mechanisms for change are composition, proceduralization, and discrimination.

The fact that representations are not static but rather are changing throughout the course of skill acquisition presents a subtle problem to those interested in modeling transfer. Exactly what level of expertise serves as the basis for the models? The exact nature of this problem can be illustrated by an example drawn from the text-editing models. These models were somewhat misleading in that they suggested that expertise could be captured by a finite number of rules. In fact, expertise is quite open-ended in that any number of special-case methods and decision rules can be acquired. For example, here is a sophisticated rule for choosing the substitution method over the line replacement method in the line editors:

> IF   the goal is to replace = text1 with = text2 in = line
>   and the length of the resulting line is greater than
>   the sum of the lengths of = text1 and = text2
> THEN   choose the substitution method.

Generally, in text editing, one method is to be preferred to another when the number of keystrokes required is fewer. In the present instance, substitution is more efficient than line replacement in those cases where relatively small portions of a particular line are to be replaced. This is because, in substitution, both the text to be deleted and the text to be inserted have to be typed as arguments, whereas in line replacement the line is deleted automatically and only the text to be inserted has to be typed. The preceding rule states that the break-even point for these two methods is roughly when the sum of the lengths of the two arguments to the substitution command equals the length of the entire line.

This rule did not appear in our simulations of the line editors. If it had, it would have led us to predict a slightly higher level of transfer between them, since this is a method that applies to both. We excluded the rule because there was no evidence in the keystroke protocols that the length of the arguments had any effect on choice of method. The point is that determining the level of expertise acquired by subjects after a certain amount of practice may be a subtle undertaking. As the level of expertise increases, the number of rules required to represent that expertise grows, and the predictions of transfer become more complex (this is a violation of one of the principles derived earlier from the transfer equation, that transfer is independent of the amount of practice on the training task).

There are two encouraging aspects to the relationship between practice and representation. First, in most laboratory studies of learning and transfer, the amount of time devoted to both training and transfer tasks (such as several hours) is quite small relatively speaking, and many of the more subtle effects of practice may be profitably ignored in most modeling situations. Second, practice curves are negatively accelerated, which means that after a certain point, additional practice has very little effect on overall performance. This effect may be due in part to the fact that many of the additional rules acquired through extended practice are limited in scope and apply only in special situations. The fact that these additional rules have little impact on performance implies that, in many practical situations, they will have little impact on transfer as well.

Methods for determining representation

Given the current state of the art, there is no substitute for careful experimentation and empirical analysis of representation questions. We are currently years away from making the kinds of back-of-the-envelope calculations of transfer advocated by Newell and Card (1985). In most cases, there are just too many subtle effects to make reasonably accurate transfer predictions in the absence of data. Currently, it is best to first sample behavior in the training and transfer tasks and develop models for both, bringing to bear as many empirical constraints as possible. Only then can we expect transfer predictions to be reasonably accurate.

What tools, then, are available to cognitive psychologists for the construction of models? This is a complicated question, and we can offer only a cursory answer here. Often the kinds of evidence brought to bear on model construction are limited only by the ingenuity of the model builder. This is especially true in a young science such as cognitive psychology, where new methodologies (such as eyetracking) are continually being developed.

Rational and Empirical Task Analysis. Typically, model building involves a combination of rational and empirical task analysis conducted within the context of some theoretical framework. The sophistication of the underlying theoretical framework tends to determine the kinds of elements identified as components of the skill. Furthermore, the computational formalism within which a process model is stated carries with it a host of processing assumptions. Thus, any model stands upon a long and convoluted chain of inference.

The goal of rational task analysis is to determine what kinds of knowledge are necessary for optimal performance on a task. Such analyses are guided by the *principle of rationality*, which states that an adaptive agent's behavior is completely determined by the agent's goals and the task environment. Through rational task analysis, it is possible to develop a model of optimal behavior which serves as a useful comparison point with actual human behavior. If the task is simple and if extended practice is given, subjects may in fact reach the optimal level defined by this analysis, and in these situations, the "rational" model may be quite good. However, in most cases, rational task analysis is only the first step in model building and must be quickly supported by empirical task analysis, which measures actual human behavior on the task. Empirical analyses are necessary because human beings often fall short of the ideal of total rationality. This fact is captured by the *principle of limited rationality* (Simon, 1947), which states that total rationality is often thwarted by the processing limits imposed by the human information-processing system.

Empirical task analysis is often an iterative process that starts with a model defined through rational task analysis. Successive refinements are made to the model in accordance with experimental evidence. Typically, the model tries to account for the sequence of behaviors and perhaps also the latencies between behaviors. Less often, error data is accounted for (but see Brown and Burton, 1982; VanLehn, 1983). The crowning achievement of the analysis is to use the model to predict some new set of data.

A good example of the use of rational and empirical task analysis is the development of the GOMS model of text editing (Card, Moran, and Newell, 1983), which served as the basis of some of our transfer predictions. We felt we were on fairly solid ground making our predictions because the GOMS model had been validated through an exhaustive modeling process. Card, Moran, and Newell proposed that complex text-editing behavior could be modeled by a simple sequence of elementary information processes consisting of the setting of goals, the execution of operators, and the selection among methods. They supported their model through extensive keystroke analyses of experts. The GOMS model did quite well at accounting for the sequence of keys struck, interkeystroke latencies, and aggregate times. The model was used to make predictions on a new set of expert data, and again it did quite well.

Verbal Protocols. In most empirical task analyses, many of the more superficial elements of the skill (those elements representing operators) can be determined by simply observing a subject's manipulation of objects in the task environment. For example, in text editing, the stream of keystrokes can be examined to determine the operators a subject is using and further to determine common combinations of those operators (such as methods). Similarly, in the LISP and calculus tutoring systems, operators were defined as discrete operations on objects defined by the interface. In these cases, much of the skill can be defined behaviorally, that is, by examining an overt sequence of behaviors. However, what is missing in these observations and what is perhaps most difficult to determine using standard task analysis techniques is the purely cognitive component of a skill, namely the component that represents goal structures and plans. To get a fix on this component, the most powerful tool available is verbal protocol analysis.

The technique of verbal protocol analysis and its role in the development of process models is well documented in Newell and Simon (1972) and Ericsson and Simon (1984). To take a verbal protocol, one simply instructs a subject to think aloud while solving a problem or performing a skill. The simple model of verbalization presented in Ericsson and Simon states that subjects are capable of verbalizing the running contents of working memory. Working within the production system framework, the contents of working memory would include elements matched by the left-hand sides of productions as well as elements deposited by the right-hand sides. Since goal structures are often included in the tests and actions of productions, it

follows that subjects have conscious access to them. Goal structures and plans are therefore candidates for verbalization (Nisbett and Wilson, 1977). In fact, "protocols almost always contain
information that reveals the subjects' control and evaluative
processes and goals" (Ericsson and Simon, 1984, p. 264).

A good illustration of the use of protocol analysis to determine
goal structures is the work of Ericsson (1975). Ericsson told his
subjects to think aloud as they solved a simple problem called
the Eight puzzle. Figure 9.3 shows this puzzle, consisting of a 3
× 3 matrix of numbered tiles, with one missing. Typically, the
subject is presented with an initial, unordered configuration of
the tiles and is asked to put the tiles in order. Attainment of this
goal involves the repeated shuffling of tiles in and out of the
single space to change the overall arrangement.

Individual statements within the protocols were classified as
relating goal information on the basis of a very superficial analysis. If the statement contained verbs of a type such as shall,
will, want, must, or need, the statement was categorized as a
goal statement. Included in the analysis were 274 goal statements gathered from 10 subjects. Although Ericsson observed a
variety of goal statements, the clear majority or 59 percent,
involved the placement of a single tile. Moreover, most of these
single-tile statements expressed the intention of getting the tile
into its final resting position rather than next to a contiguously
numbered tile. Of the remaining statements that referred to
more than one tile, only one made reference to tiles that were
not contiguously numbered, and only one referred to tiles that
were on different rows in the final configuration. Given the
combinations of tiles that are logically possible in goal statements, this restricted pattern is quite remarkable, and it reveals

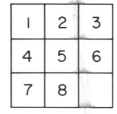

(a) initial state   (b) goal state

Figure 9.3. *Classic eight puzzle.*

much about the overall plan for the solution of this problem.

Although protocol analysis is a useful tool for revealing cognitive structures, it is in fact a rather blunt instrument and is not without its problems. One of these problems is incompleteness of reports. Although in theory subjects have conscious access to all elements in working memory, it is unreasonable to expect that they will verbalize all contents at all times. The incompleteness of verbal protocols becomes evident when comparing the verbalizations of a single subject on different trials of the same task, or when comparing concurrent verbalizations with retrospective reports.

Another problem of protocol analysis is lack of coverage. Ericsson and Simon (1984) pointed out that protocol analysis does not work well with all kinds of tasks. Particularly troublesome are tasks that involve heavy doses of text comprehension, perceptual, or recognition processes. Another way of stating this is that protocol analysis does not reveal much about the underlying cognitive structure of tasks that have been highly automated. This does not pose much of a problem in analyses of transfer, since automated processes like text comprehension show little learning and can therefore be excluded from calculations of transfer. However, in certain cases, goal structures may be learned and automated over the course of the experiment. For this reason, it may be best to take protocols from subjects at middling levels of performance.

Protocol analysis has other problems of induction. Aside from problems stemming from incompleteness, it is often difficult to derive the exact nature of a rule from a protocol statement. For one thing, it is difficult to establish the generality of a rule, since subjects rarely if ever state the rule in variabilized form. For example, Newell and Simon (1972) gathered this protocol statement from a subject solving a cryptarithmetic problem: "Since D + D = G, G must be even." It seems obvious in this case that the exact letters stated in this relation are completely irrelevant and that they should therefore be variabilized in the representation of the rule in the simulation:

> IF   the sum of = number and = number is = result
> THEN   = result is an even number.

Although this case is fairly clear, consider this fictional protocol statement: "Since G is an even number, G + 1 is an odd number." In this case, is 1 a special constant, or is it simply an instance of an odd number? In other words, is the rule even plus

1 yields odd, or even plus odd yields odd? In the absence of other data, it is impossible to make this discrimination.

Another problem arises from the danger of taking protocol statements too literally. For example, Ericsson and Simon (1984) presented this segment from a subject performing mental multiplication: "First, I will put the largest number on top . . ." Ericsson and Simon warned against the strict logical interpretation of the word "largest," proposing that the subject will not heed the relative magnitudes of the two multiplicands unless they differ greatly, as they did in this case. In other words, missing from this protocol is an implicit test of the relative magnitudes of the two numbers which supplies the necessary context for this rule to fire.

In sum, protocol analysis gives us a window on the contents of working memory, but not the rules that are generating these contents. Although it is often difficult to determine the precise nature of individual rules, when used in conjunction with other modeling tools, protocol analysis provides strong additional constraints on representation. It is important to point out that protocol analysis is just one more tool in the model builder's kit.

Conclusion

The reader should not leave this chapter with the conclusion that representational issues pose a particular problem for the study of transfer. They are problems for the study of all cognitive phenomena, and for the same reason: there is the danger that the theorist can salvage a mistaken theory by suitable choice of representation. If anything, transfer is less imperiled by representational indeterminism than are most phenomena because so many constraints can be applied to the representation before making behavioral predictions.

The problem of indeterminacy of representation has been discussed at length by Anderson, (1976; 1983). The general conclusion is that, for any representation-process pair, there are many other pairs of different representations and processes that make the same behavioral predictions. In the current situation, we have proposed a process (the identical elements model of transfer) and are worried about whether it can be insulated from empirical disconfirmation by an appropriate choice of representation (the cognitive elements). None of the results on representation-process indeterminacy imply that it is impossible to test our process assumption given a sufficient set of converging constraints.

The "process" in the identical elements model of transfer is an interesting one from a formal standpoint. It is an identity operator and, as such, is really no process at all. This means that, if the identical elements model were correct, the transfer paradigm would become a very potent one for placing constraints on knowledge representation. If we see that component i of task A transfers completely to component j of task B (as we saw in some of our experiments), we are in position to assert that the rules underlying the components are the same. This in turn places strong constraints on the form of the rules. For instance, we saw in our calculus experiments that the rules for translating economics cover stories transferred perfectly to geometry cover stories. Given our assumption of a null transfer process, this result meant that the rules had to be sufficiently general to handle both types of cover stories.

Finally, we feel that, in most cases where relatively high levels of performance are achieved, rational constraints provide a substantial guide to knowledge representation. Indeed, the rules we have developed in our models have largely been the obvious ones given the demands of the task. The second author is in the process of developing a new theory of cognition called "rational analysis" which can be seen as an extension of Simon's limited-rationality hypothesis. It claims that human behavior can be predicted from a rational analysis of the task if one takes into account the basic information-processing limitations under which the person operates. Applied to the current problem of rule representation, the theory predicts that a subject will adopt a rule set which:

1. Minimizes the number of rules that have to be learned.
2. Minimizes working memory load.
3. Minimizes the amount of overt behavior (for example, this principle would favor a text editing procedure that involved fewer keystrokes).

These principles of course might conflict, in which case some joint minimum would be sought.

The results of the Elio experiment concerning representation could have been predicted by the principles of rational analysis. She proposed that subjects represented the serial position of component steps in their rules since there was no transfer when the positions did not match. It turns out that in her experimental situation there is substantial benefit in representing the rules in this way. Most importantly, working memory load is reduced because internal control elements or goals need not be maintained, and the serial position of a step can be read right off the terminal screen (see Figure 9.1). Additionally, specializing the rules in terms of serial position costs nothing in terms of number of rules to be learned. Since the step always occurred in the same position during training, there was no loss in applicability across problems. This implies that, if the rules had been practiced in different orders during training, serial position would not have been included in the rules, and transfer would have been successful. Indeed, in a follow-up experiment involving integrative rather than component steps, Elio found that subjects learned and transferred general rules only if those rules appeared in more than one context during training. In this case, subjects learned more general rules because that minimized the total number of new rules to be learned. This result is consistent with classic work (e.g. Duncan, 1958) as well as with more recent research (e.g. Gick and Holyoak, 1980) showing that subjects adopt more general representations when given variable training.

The rational analysis theory obviously needs to be developed more fully before it can be used to provide rule representations generally. We view it as a promise for the future.

References

Abruzzi, A. 1956. *Work, workers, and work measurement.* New York: Columbia University Press.

Allport, G. W. 1937. *Personality.* New York: Henry Holt.

Anderson, J. R. 1976. *Language, memory, and thought.* Hillsdale, N.J.: Erlbaum Associates.

―――― 1982. Acquisition of cognitive skill. *Psychological Review, 89,* 369–406.

―――― 1983. *The architecture of cognition.* Cambridge, Mass.: Harvard University Press.

―――― 1986. Knowledge compilation: the general learning mechanism. In R. Michalski, J. Carbonell, and T. Mitchell, eds., *Machine learning,* vol. 2, pp. 289–310. Los Altos, Calif.: Morgan Kaufmann.

―――― 1987. Production systems, learning, and tutoring. In D. Klahr, P. Langley, and R. Neches, eds., *Production system models of learning and development,* pp. 437–458. Cambridge, Mass.: MIT Press.

―――― In press. Analysis of student performance with the LISP tutor. In N. Frederiksen, R. Glaser, A. Lesgold, and M. Shaffo, eds., *Diagnostic monitoring of skill and knowledge acquisition.* Hillsdale, N.J.: Erlbaum Associates.

Anderson, J. R., and Bower, G. H. 1973. *Human associative memory.* Washington, D.C.: Winston.

Anderson, J. R., and Reiser, B. J. 1985. The LISP tutor. *Byte, 10,* 159–175.

Anderson, J. R., and Thompson, R. Forthcoming. Use of analogy in a production system architecture. In A. Ortony et al., eds., *Similarity and analogy.* Cambridge: Cambridge University Press.

Anderson, J. R., Farrell, R., and Sauers, R. 1984. Learning to program in LISP. *Cognitive Science, 8,* 87–129.

Anderson, J. R., Corbett, A. T., and Conrad, F. Forthcoming. Skill acquisition and the LISP tutor.

Anderson, J. R., Corbett, A. T., and Reiser, B. J. 1987. *Essential LISP.* Reading, Mass.: Addison-Wesley.

Anderson, J. R., Boyle, C. F., Corbett, A, and Lewis, M. W. In press. Cognitive modelling and intelligent tutoring. *Artificial Intelligence.*

Angell, J. R. 1908. The doctrine of formal discipline in the light of the principles of general psychology. *Educational Review, 36,* 1–14.

Anzai, Y., and Uesato, Y. 1982. Learning recursive procedures by middle school children. In *Proceedings of the Fourth Annual Conference of the Cognitive Science Society,* Ann Arbor, Mich.

Atwood, M. E., and Polson, P. G. 1976. A process model for water jug problems. *Cognitive Psychology, 8,* 191–216.

Ausubel, D. P. 1968. *Educational psychology: a cognitive view.* New York: Holt, Rinehart, and Winston.

Bilodeau, E. A., and Bilodeau, I. McD. 1961. Motor-skills learning. *Annual Review of Psychology, 12,* 243–280.

Bobrow, D. G. 1964. A question-answering system for high school algebra word problems. *AFIPS Conference Proceedings, 26,* 577–589.

Boring, E. G. 1950. *History of experimental psychology.* New York: Appleton-Century-Crofts.

Bower, G. H., and Hilgard, E. R. 1981. *Theories of learning.* Englewood Cliffs, N.J.: Prentice-Hall.

Bower, G. H., Black, J. B., and Turner, T. J. 1979. Scripts in memory for text. *Cognitive Psychology, 11,* 177–220.

Brain, L. 1965. *Speech disorders: aphasia, apraxia, and agnosia.* London: Butterworth.

Brown, A. L. 1981. Metacognition and reading and writing: the development and facilitation of selective attention strategies for learning from text. In M. L. Kamil, ed., *Directions in reading: research and instruction.* Washington, D.C.: National Reading Conference.

——— 1982. Learning to learn how to read. In J. Langer and T. Smith-Burke, eds., *Reader meets author, bridging the gap: a psycholinguistic and social linguistic perspective.* Newark, N.J.: Dell.

Brown, A. L., Bransford, J. D., Ferrara, R. A., and Campione, J. C. 1983. Learning, remembering, and understanding. In J. H. Flavell and E. M. Markman, eds., *Handbook of child psychology,* vol. 4, *Cognitive development.* New York: Wiley.

Brown, A. L., and Kane, M. J. In press. Preschool children can learn to transfer: learning to learn and learning from example. *Cognitive Psychology.*

Brown, J. S., and Burton, R. B. 1982. Diagnostic models for procedural bugs in basic mathematical skills. *Cognitive Science, 2,* 155–192.

Brown, J. S., and VanLehn, K. 1980. Repair theory: a generative theory of bugs in procedural skills. *Cognitive Science, 4,* 379–426.

Brownston, L., Farrell, R., Kant, E., and Martin, N. 1985. *Programming expert systems in OPS5: an introduction to rule-based programming.* Reading, Mass.: Addison-Wesley.

Bruner, J. S. 1966. *Toward a theory of instruction.* New York: W. W. Norton.

Buckland, P. R. 1968. The ordering of frames in a linear program. *Programmed Learning and Educational Technology, 5,* 197–205.

Bunch, M. E. 1936. The amount of transfer in rational learning as a function of time. *Journal of Comparative Psychology, 22,* 325–337.

Bunch, M. E., and Lang, E. S. 1939. The amount of transfer of training from partial learning after varying intervals of time. *Journal of Comparative Psychology, 27,* 449–459.

Bunch, M. E., and McCraven, V. 1938. Temporal course of transfer in the learning of memory material. *Journal of Comparative Psychology, 25,* 481–496.

Carbonell, J. G. 1983. Learning by analogy: formulating and generalizing plans from past experience. In R. S. Michalski, J. G. Carbonell, and T. M. Mitchell, eds., *Machine learning,* pp. 137–162. Palo Alto, Calif.: Tioga Press.

Card, S. K., Moran, T. P., and Newell, A. 1976. *The manuscript editing task: a routine cognitive skill.* Tech. Rep. SSL-76-8, Xerox Palo Alto (Calif.) Research Center.

Card, S. K., Moran, T. P., and Newell, A. 1980. Computer text-editing: an information processing analysis of a routine cognitive skill. *Cognitive Psychology, 12,* 32–74.

Card, S. K., Moran, T. P., and Newell, A. 1983. *The psychology of human-computer interaction.* Hillsdale, N.J.: Erlbaum Associates.

Carpenter, T. P., and Moser, J. M. 1982. The development of addition and substraction problem-solving skills. In T. P. Carpenter, J. M. Moser, and T. Romberg, eds., *Addition and subtraction: a cognitive perspective.* Hillsdale, N.J.: Erlbaum Associates.

Carraher, T. N., Carraher, D. W., and Schliemann, A. D. 1985. Mathematics in the streets and in schools. *British Journal of Developmental Psychology, 3,* 21–29.

Carroll, J. B. 1940. Knowledge of English roots and affixes as related to vocabulary and Latin study. *Journal of Educational Research, 34,* 256–261.

Chase, W. G., and Ericsson, K. A. 1982. Skill and working memory. In G. H. Bower, ed., *The psychology of learning and motivation.* New York: Academic Press.

Chase, W. G., and Simon, H. A. 1973. The mind's eye in chess. In W. G. Chase, ed., *Visual information processing.* New York: Academic Press.

Cheng, P. W., and Holyoak, K. J. 1985. Pragmatic reasoning schemas. *Cognitive Psychology, 17,* 391–416.

Cheng, P. W., Holyoak, K. J., Nisbett, R. E., and Oliver, L. M. 1986. Pragmatic versus syntactic approaches to training deductive reasoning. *Cognitive Psychology, 18,* 293–328.

Chi, M. T. H., Feltovich, P., and Glaser, R. 1981. Categorization and representation of physics problems by experts and novices. *Cognitive Science, 5,* 121–152.

Chi, M. T. H., Glaser, R., and Rees, E. 1982. Expertise in problem solving. In R. J. Sternberg, ed., *Advances in the psychology of human intelligence.* Hillsdale, N.J.: Erlbaum Associates.

Chomsky, N. 1957. *Syntactic structures.* The Hague: Mouton.

—— 1965. *Aspects of the theory of syntax.* Cambridge, Mass.: MIT Press.

Clark, E., and Hecht, B. 1983. Comprehension, production, and language acquisition. *Annual Review of Psychology, 34,* 325–349.

Clement, J. 1983. A conceptual model discussed by Galileo and used intuitively by physics students. In D. Gentner and A. L. Stevens, eds., *Mental models.* Hillsdale, N.J.: Erlbaum Associates.

Cohen, N., and Corkin, S. 1981. The amnesiac patient H.M.: learning and retention of a cognitive skill. In *Proceedings of the Eleventh Annual Meeting, Society for Neuroscience,* Los Angeles.

Cohen, J., Dunbar, K., and McClelland, J. Forthcoming. On the control of automatic processes: a parallel distributed model of the Stroop effect.

Conrad, F., and Anderson, J. R. 1988. The process of learning LISP. In *Proceedings of the Tenth Annual Conference of the Cognitive Science Society,* Montreal.

Coxe, W. W. 1925. The influence of Latin on the spelling of English words. *Journal of Educational Research Monographs, 7.*

Dalbey, J., and Linn, M. 1984. Spider world: a robot language for learning to program. In *Proceedings of the American Educational Research Association Conference,* New Orleans.

D'Andrade, R. 1982. Reason versus logic. Paper presented at the Symposium on the Ecology of Cognition, Greensboro, N.C.

Damasio, A. 1981. The nature of aphasia: signs and syndromes. In M. Sarno, ed., *Acquired aphasia.* New York: Academic Press.

Day, J. D. 1980. Training summarization skills: a comparison of teaching methods. Doctoral diss., University of Illinois.

Digital Equipment Corporation. 1982. Introduction to the EDT editor. Marlborough, Mass.

Dorsey, M. N., and Hopkins, L. T. 1930. The influence of attitude upon transfer. *Journal of Educational Psychology, 21,* 410–417.

Duncan, C. P. 1958. Transfer after training with single versus multiple tasks. *Journal of Experimental Psychology, 55,* 63–72.

Duncker, K. 1945 (1935). On problem-solving, trans. L. S. Lees. *Psychological Monographs, 58* (270).

Ekstrom, R. B., French, J. W., and Harman, H. H. 1976. Manual for kit of factor-referenced cognitive tests. Princeton, N.J.: Educational Testing Service.

Elio, R. 1986. Representation of similar well-learned cognitive procedures. *Cognitive Science, 10,* 41–74.

Ellis, H. C. 1965. *The transfer of learning.* New York: Macmillan.

Ericsson, K. A. 1975. *Instruction to verbalize as a means to study problem solving processes with the Eight Puzzle.* Report 458 from the Department of Psychology, University of Stockholm.

Ericsson, K. A., and Simon, H. A. 1984. *Protocol analysis: verbal reports as data.* Cambridge, Mass.: MIT Press.

Ernst, G. W., and Newell, A. 1969. *GPS: A case study in generality and problem solving.* New York: Academic Press.

Fawcett, H. P. 1935. Teaching for transfer. *Mathematics Teacher, 28,* 465–472.

Fitts, P. M., and Posner, M. I. 1967. *Human performance.* Belmont, Calif.: Brooks Cole.

Flavell, J. H. 1978. Reply to Brainerd: the stage question in cognitive-developmental theory. *Behavioral and Brain Sciences, 2,* 187.

Flexman, R. E., Matheny, W. G., and Brown, E. L. 1950. *Evaluation of the Link and special methods of instruction.* Aeronautics Bulletin 8, University of Illinois.

Flower, L. S., and Hayes, J. R. 1977. Problem-solving strategies and the writing process. *College English, 39,* 449–461.

Fodor, J. A., Bever, T. G., and Garrett, M. F. 1974. *The psychology of language.* New York: McGraw-Hill.

Fong, G. T., Krantz, D. H., and Nisbett, R. E. 1986. The effects of statistical training on thinking about everyday problems. *Cognitive Psychology, 18,* 253–292.

Forgy, C. 1979. *On the efficient implementation of production systems.* Doctoral diss., Carnegie-Mellon University.

Gagne, R. M. 1966. *The conditions of learning.* New York: Holt, Rinehart, and Winston.

Gagne, R, M., and Bassler, O. C. 1963. Study of retention of some topics of elementary non-metric geometry. *Journal of Educational Psychology, 54,* 123–131.

Gagne, R. M., and Paradise, N. E. 1961. Abilities and learning sets in knowledge acquisition. *Psychological Monographs, 75* (14).

Gagne, R. M., and Staff of University of Maryland Math Project. 1965. Some factors in learning nonmetric geometry. *Monographs of Social Research in Child Development, 30,* 42–49.

Gagne, R. M., Baker, K. E., and Foster, H. 1950. On the relation between similarity and transfer of training in the learning of discriminative motor units. *Psychological Review, 57,* 67–79.

Gagne, R. M., Forster, H., and Crowley, M. E. 1948. The measurement of transfer of training. *Psychological Bulletin, 45,* 97–130.

Gardner, M. 1978. *Aha! insight.* New York: W. H. Freeman.

Garlick, S. 1984. Computer programming and cognitive outcomes: a classroom evaluation of LOGO. Master's thesis, Flinders University of South Australia.

Gavurin, E. I., and Donahue, V. M. 1961. Logical sequence and random sequence. *Automated Teaching Bulletin, 1,* 3–9.

Geschwind, N. 1972. Language and the brain. *Scientific American, 226,* 76–83.

Gick, M. L., and Holyoak, K. J. 1980. Analogical problem solving. *Cognitive Psychology, 12,* 306–355.

——— 1983. Schema induction and analogical transfer. *Cognitive Psychology, 15,* 1–38.

Goldberg, D. J. 1974. The effects of training in heuristics methods on the ability to write proofs in number theory. Doctoral diss., Columbia University.

Goldin-Meadow, S., Seligman, M., and Gelman, R. 1976. Language in the two-year-old. *Cognition, 4,* 189–202.

Gomez, L. M., Egan, D. E., Wheeler, E., Sharma, D., and Gruchacz, A. 1983. How interface design determines who has difficulty learning to use a text editor. In *Proceedings of CHI '83 Human Factors in Computing Systems Conference.* New York: Association for Computing Machinery.

Gomez, L. M., Egan, D. E., and Bowers, C. 1986. Learning to use a text editor: some learner characteristics that predict success. *Human-Computer Interaction, 2,* 1–23.

Gorman, H., and Bourne, L. E. 1983. Learning to think by learning LOGO: rule learning in third grade computer programmers. *Bulletin of the Psychonomic Society, 21,* 165–167.

Gosling, J. 1981. *Unix EMACS user manual.* Technical Report, Computer Science Department, Carnegie-Mellon University.

Griggs, R. A., and Cox, J. R. 1982. The elusive thematic-materials effect in Wason's selection task. *British Journal of Psychology, 73,* 407–420.

Halasz, F., and Moran, T. P. 1982. Analogy considered harmful. In Proceeding of the Human Factors in Computer Systems Conference, Gaithersburg, MD.

Hammerton, M. 1967. Visual factors affecting transfer of training from a simulated to a real control situation. *Journal of Applied Psychology, 51,* 46–49.

———— 1981. Tracking. In D. Holding, ed., *Human skills.* New York: Wiley.

Harlow, H. F. 1949. The formation of learning sets. *Psychological Review, 56,* 51–65.

Hartung, M. L. 1942. Teaching of mathematics in senior high school and junior college. *Review of Educational Research, 12,* 425–434.

Harvey, J., and Romberg, T. 1980. *Problem-solving studies in mathematics.* Madison: Wisconsin R&D Center.

Hayes, J. R. 1980. Teaching problem-solving mechanisms. In D. T. Tuma and F. Reif, eds., *Problem solving and education,* Hillsdale, N.J.: Erlbaum Associates.

Hayes, J. R., and Simon, H. A. 1974. Understanding written problem instructions. In L. Gregg, ed., *Knowledge and cognition.* Hillsdale, N.J.: Erlbaum Associates.

———— 1977. Psychological differences among problem isomorphs. In J. Castellan, D. B. Pisoni, and G. Potts, eds., *Cognitive theory,* vol. 2. Hillsdale, N.J.: Erlbaum Associates.

Higginson, G. 1931. *Fields of psychology: a study of man and his environment.* New York: Holt.

Hilgard, E. R., Irvine, R. P., and Whipple, J. E. 1953. Rote memorization, understanding, and transfer: an extension of Katona's card trick experiments. *Journal of Experimental Psychology, 46,* 288–292.

Holding, D. 1981. Skills research. In D. Holding, ed., *Human skills.* New York: Wiley.

Holyoak, K. J. 1985. The pragmatics of analogical transfer. In G. H.

Bower, ed., *The psychology of learning and motivation*, vol. 19. New York: Academic Press.

Holyoak, K. J., Junn, E., and Billman, D. 1984. Development of analogical problem solving skills. *Child Development, 55*, 2042–55.

Huttenlocher, J. 1974. The origins of language comprehension. In R. Solso, ed., *Theories in cognitive psychology*. Potomac, Md.: Erlbaum Associates.

Inhelder, B., and Piaget, J. 1964. *The early growth of logic in the child: classification and seriation*. New York: Norton.

Jeffries, R. 1978. The acquisition of expertise on missionaries-cannibals and waterjug problems. Doctoral diss., University of Colorado.

Jeffries, R., Polson, P. G., Razran, L., and Atwood, M. E. 1977. A process model for missionaries-cannibals and other river-crossing problems. *Cognitive Psychology, 9*, 412–440.

Johnson-Laird, P. N. 1983. *Mental models*. Cambridge, Mass.: Harvard University Press.

Johnson-Laird, P. N., Legrenzi, P., and Legrenzi. M. 1972. Reasoning and a sense of reality. *British Journal of Psychology, 63*, 395–400.

Judd, C. H. 1908. The relation of special training and general intelligence. *Educational Review, 36*, 28–42.

Karat, J., Boyes, L., Weisgerber, S., and Schafer, C. 1986. Transfer between word processing systems. In M. Mantei and P. Orbeton, eds., *Proceedings of CHI '86 Human Factors in Computing Systems*. New York: Association for Computing Machinery.

Karmiloff-Smith, A. 1977. More about the same: children's understanding of post-articles. *Journal of Child Language, 4*, 377–394.

Katona, G. 1940. *Organizing and memorizing*. New York: Columbia University Press.

Katz, H., and Beilin, H. 1976. A test of Bryant's claims concerning the young child's understanding of quantitative invariance. *Child Development, 47*, 877–880.

Kay, D. S., and Black, J. B. 1985. The evolution of knowledge representations with increasing expertise in using systems. In *Proceedings of the Seventh Annual Conference of the Cognitive Science Society*, Boston.

Kelley, H. H. 1973. The process of causal attribution. *American Psychologist, 28*, 107–128.

Kernighan, B. W. 1980. *A tutorial introduction to the UNIX text editor*. Technical memorandum, Bell Telephone Laboratories, Murray Hill, N.J.

Kessler, C. 1988. Transfer of programming skills in novice LISP learners. Doctoral diss., Carnegie-Mellon University.

Kessler, C., and Anderson, J. R. 1986. Learning flow of control: recursive and iterative procedures. *Human-Computer Interaction, 2*, 135–166.

Kieras, D., and Bovair, S. 1984. The role of a mental model in learning to operate a device. *Cognitive Science, 8*, 255–273.

——— 1986. The acquisition of procedures from text: a production-system analysis of transfer of training. *Journal of Memory and Language, 25*, 507–524.

Kieras, D., and Polson, P. 1985. An approach to the formal analysis of user complexity. *International Journal of Man-Machine Studies, 22,* 365–394.

Kinsbourne, M. 1978. Reply to Brainerd: the stage question in cognitive-developmental theory. *Behavioral and Brain Sciences, 2,* 191.

Klahr, D., and Carver, S. 1988. Cognitive objectives in a LOGO debugging curriculum: instruction, learning, and transfer. *Cognitive Psychology, 20,* 362–404.

Klahr, D., Langley, P., and Neches, R. 1987. *Production system models of learning and development.* Cambridge, Mass.: MIT Press.

Kling, R. E. 1971. A paradigm for reasoning by analogy. *Artificial Intelligence, 2,* 147–178.

Kotovsky, K., Hayes, J. R., and Simon, H. A. 1985. Why are some problems hard? Evidence from tower of Hanoi. *Cognitive Psychology, 17,* 248–294.

Kunda, Z., and Nisbett, R. E. 1986. The psychometrics of everyday life. *Cognitive Psychology, 18,* 195–224.

Kurland, D. M., and Pea, R. D. 1983. Children's mental models of recursuve LOGO programs. In *Proceedings of the Fifth Annual Conference of the Cognitive Science Society,* Rochester, N.Y.

Laird, J. E., Rosenbloom, P. S., and Newell, A. (1984). Towards chunking as a general learning mechanism. In *Proceedings of the American Association of Artificial Intelligence Conference,* Austin, Texas.

Larkin, J., and Simon, H. A. 1987. Why a diagram is (sometimes) worth ten thousand words. *Cognitive Science, 11,* 65–100.

Larkin, J., McDermott, J., Simon, D. P., and Simon, H. A. 1980. Expert and novice performance in solving physics problems. *Science, 208,* 1335–42.

Lave, J., Murtaugh, M., and de La Rocha, O. 1984. The dialectical construction of arithmetic practice. In B. Rogoff and J. Lave, eds., *Everyday cognition: its development in social context.* Cambridge, Mass.: Harvard University Press.

Lesgold, A. M. 1984. Acquiring expertise. In J. R. Anderson and S. M. Kosslyn, eds., *Tutorials in learning and memory,* pp. 31–60. San Francisco: W. H. Freeman.

Lesgold, A. M., and Curtis, M. E. 1981. Learning to read words efficiently. In A. M. Lesgold and C. A. Perfetti, eds., *Interactive processes in reading.* Hillsdale, N.J.: Erlbaum Associates.

Lesgold, A. M., and Resnick, L. B. 1982. How reading difficulties develop: perspectives from a longitudinal study. In J. P. Das, R. F. Mulcahy, and A. E. Wall, eds., *Theory and research in reading disabilities.* New York: Plenum.

Levin, G. R., and Baker, B. L. 1963. Item scrambling in a self-instructional program. *Journal of Educational Psychology, 54,* 138–143.

Lewis, D. 1959. Latest news and views regarding individual susceptibility to interference in the performance of perceptual-motor tasks. Paper presented at the annual meeting of the Midwestern Psychological Association, Chicago.

Lewis, M. W., and Anderson, J. R. 1985. Discrimination of operator schemata in problem solving: learning from examples. *Cognitive Psychology, 17,* 26–65.

——— Forthcoming. Declarative and procedural transfer in logic.

Linn, M. C., and Fisher, C. W. 1983. The gap between promise and reality in computer education: planning a response. In *Making our schools more effective: a conference for California educators.* San Francisco: ACCCEL.

Lucas, J. F. 1972. An exploratory study on the diagnostic teaching of heuristic problem-solving strategies in calculus. Doctoral diss., University of Wisconsin.

Luchins, A. S. 1942. Mechanization in problem solving. *Psychological Monographs, 54* (248).

Mack, R., Lewis, C. H., and Carroll, J. 1983. Learning to use word processors: problems and prospects. *ACM Transactions on Office Information Systems, 3,* 254–271.

Martin, E. 1965. Transfer of verbal paired associates. *Psychological Review, 72,* 327–343.

Marx, M. H. 1944. The effects of cumulative training upon retroactive inhibition and transfer. *Comparative Psychology Monographs, 94.*

McClelland, J., and Rumelhart, D. 1981. An interactive model of context effects in letter perception: Part I, an account of basic findings. *Psychological Review, 88,* 375–407.

McCloskey, M. 1983. Naive theories of motion. In D. Gentner and A. L. Stevens, eds., *Mental models.* Hillsdale, N.J.: Erlbaum Associates.

McDermott, D. 1981. Artificial intelligence meets natural stupidity. In J. Haugeland, ed., *Mind design.* Cambridge, Mass.: MIT Press.

McGilly, K., Poulin-DuBois, D., and Schultz, T. R. 1984. The effect of learning LOGO on children's problem solving skills. Technical Report., Department of Psychology, McGill University.

McKendree, J. E., and Anderson, J. R. 1987. Frequency and practice effects on the composition of knowledge in LISP evaluation. In J. M. Carroll, ed., *Cognitive aspects of human-computer interaction.* Cambridge, Mass.: MIT Press.

Meiklejohn, A. 1908. Is mental training a myth? *Educational Review, 37,* 126–141.

Meredith, G. P. 1927. Consciousness of method as a means of transfer of training. *Forum of Education, 5,* 37–45.

Miller, S. A. 1976. Nonverbal assessment of conservation of number. *Child Development, 47,* 722–728.

Milner, B. 1962. Les troubles de la memoire accompagnant des lesions hippocampique bilaterale. In *Physiologie de l'hippocampe.* Paris: Centre National de la Recherche Scientifique.

Moore, O. K., and Anderson, S. B. 1954. Modern logic and tasks for experiments on problem solving behavior. *Journal of Psychology, 38,* 151–160.

Moran, T. 1983. Getting into a system: external-internal task-mapping analysis. In *Proceedings of CHI '83 Human Factors in Computing Systems Conference.* New York: Association for Computing Machinery.

Murdock, B. B. 1957. Transfer designs and formulas. *Psychological Bulletin, 54,* 313–326.

Nakatani, L. H. 1983. Soft machines: a philosophy of user-computer interface design. In *Proceedings of CHI '83 Human Factors in Computing Systems Conference.* New York: Association for Computing Machinery.

Neves, D. M. 1977. An experimental analysis of strategies of the tower of Hanoi puzzle. C.I.P. Working Paper 362, Department of Psychology, Carnegie-Mellon University.

———— 1981. Learning procedures from examples. Doctoral diss., Carnegie-Mellon University.

Neves, D. M., and Anderson, J. R. 1981. Knowledge compilation: mechanisms for the automatization of cognitive skills. In J. R. Anderson, ed., *Cognitive skills and their acquisition,* pp. 52–84. Hillsdale, N.J.: Erlbaum Associates.

Newell, A. 1969. Heuristic programming: ill-structured problems. In J. Aronofsky, ed., *Progress in operations research,* New York: Wiley.

———— 1973. Production systems: models of control structures. In W. G. Chase, ed., *Visual information processing,* pp. 463–526. New York: Academic Press.

Newell, K. 1981. Skill learning. In D. Holding, ed., *Human skills,* New York: Wiley.

Newell, A., and Card, S. K. 1985. The prospects for psychological science in human-computer interaction. *Human-Computer Interaction, 1,* 209–242.

Newell, A., and Simon, H. 1972. *Human problem solving.* Englewood Cliffs, N.J.: Prentice-Hall.

Niedermeyer, F. C. 1968. The relevance of frame sequence in programmed instruction: an addition to the dialogue. *Teaching Machines and Programmed Instruction, 16,* 301–317.

Nisbett, R. E., and Wilson, T. D. 1977. Telling more than we know: verbal reports on mental processes. *Psychological Review, 84,* 231–259.

Norman, D. A. 1973. Memory, knowledge, and the answering of questions. In R. L. Solso, ed., *Contemporary issues in psychology.* Washington, D.C.: Winston.

Orata, P. T. 1928. *The theory of identical elements.* Columbus: Ohio State University Press.

Osgood, C. E. 1949. The similarity paradox in human learning: a resolution. *Psychological Review, 56,* 132–143.

Paige, J., and Simon, H.A. 1966. Cognitive processes in solving algebra word problems. In B. Kleinmuntz, ed., *Problem solving.* New York: Wiley.

Papert, S. 1980. *Mindstorms: children, computers, and powerful ideas.* New York: Basic Books.

Payne, D. A., Krathwohl, D. R., and Gordon, J. 1967. The effect of sequence on programmed instruction. *American Educational Research Journal, 4,* 125–132.

Pea, R. D. 1983. LOGO programming and problem solving. In *Proceed-*

ings of the American Educational Research Association Conference, Montreal.

Perfetto, G. A., Bransford, J. D., and Franks, J. J. 1983. Constraints on access in a problem solving context. *Memory and Cognition, 11*, 24–31.

Pillsbury, W. B. 1908. The effects of training on memory. *Educational Review, 36*, 15–27.

Pirolli, P. L., and Anderson, J. R. 1985. The role of learning from examples in the acquisition of recursive programming skill. *Canadian Journal of Psychology, 39*, 240–272.

Polson, P. G., and Kieras, D. E. 1985. A quantitative model of learning and performance of text editing knowledge. In L. Bormann and B. Curtis, eds., *Proceedings of CHI '85 Human Factors in Computing Systems Conference*. New York: Association for Computing Machinery.

Polson, P., Bovair, S., and Kieras, D. 1987. Transfer between text editors. In J. M. Carroll and P. Tanner, eds., *Proceedings of CHI '87 Human Factors in Computing Systems and Graphics Interface Conference*. New York: Association for Computing Machinery.

Polson, P., Muncher, E., and Kieras, D. In preparation. Transfer of skills between inconsistent editors.

Polya, G. 1957. *How to solve it*. Garden City, N.Y.: Doubleday/Anchor.

Porter, L. W., and Duncan, C. P. 1953. Negative transfer in verbal learning. *Journal of Experimental Psychology, 46*, 61–64.

Posner, M. I. 1973. *Cognition: an introduction*. Glenview, Ill.: Scott, Foresman.

Post, T. R., and Brennan, M. L. 1976. An experimental study of the effectiveness of a formal vs. an informal presentation of a general heuristic process on problem solving in tenth grade geometry. *Journal for Research in Mathematics Education, 7*, 59–64.

Postman, L. 1971. Transfer, interference, and forgetting. In L. W. Kling and L. A. Riggs, eds., *Experimental psychology*, pp. 1019–32. New York: Holt, Rinehart, and Winston.

Pyatte, J. A. 1969. Some effects of unit structure on achievement and transfer. *American Educational Research Journal, 6*, 241–261.

Rapp, A. 1945. The experimental background of the problems of learning. *Classical Journal, 40*, 467–480.

Reder, L. M., and Ross, B. H. 1983. Integrated knowledge in different tasks: positive and negative fan effects. *Journal of Experimental Psychology: Human Learning, Memory, and Cognition, 9*, 55–72.

Reed, S. K., Ernst, G. W., and Banerji, R. 1974. The role of analogy in transfer between similar problem states. *Cognitive Psychology, 6*, 436–450.

Reigeluth, C. M., and Stein, F. S. 1983. The elaboration theory of instruction. In C. M. Reigeluth, ed., *Instructional design theories and models*. Hillsdale, N.J.: Erlbaum Associates.

Rescorla, L. 1980. Overextension in early language development. *Journal of Child Language, 7*, 321–335.

Resnick, L. B. 1976. Task analysis in instructional design: some cases from mathematics. In D. Klahr, ed., *Cognition and instruction*. Hillsdale, N.J.: Erlbaum Associates.

Roberts, T. L. 1979. *Evaluation of computer text editors.* Technical Report SSL-79-9, Xerox Palo Alto (Calif.) Research Center.

Robertson, S. P. 1984. Goal, plan, and outcome tracking in computer text-editing performance. Doctoral diss., Yale University.

Roe, K. V., Case, H. W., and Roe, A. 1962. Scrambled vs. ordered sequence in autoinstructional programs. *Journal of Educational Psychology, 53*, 101–104.

Rogoff, B., and Lave, J., eds. 1984. *Everyday cognition: its development in social context*. Cambridge, Mass.: Harvard University Press.

Rosenbloom, P. S., and Newell, A. 1986. The chunking of goal hierarchies: a generalized model of practice. In R. S. Michalski, J. G. Carbonell, and T. M. Mitchell, eds., *Machine learning*, vol. 2, pp. 247–288. Los Altos, Calif.: Morgan Kaufmann.

Ross, B. H. 1982. *Remindings and their effects in learning a cognitive skill*. Technical Report CIS-19, Xerox Palo Alto (Calif.) Research Center.

Ross, L. 1977. The intuitive psychologist and his shortcomings. In L. Berkowitz, ed., *Advances in experimental social psychology*. New York: Academic Press.

Rubens, A. B. 1979. Agnosia. In K. Heilman and E. Valenstein, eds., *Clinical neuropsychology*. Oxford: Oxford University Press.

Rubinstein, M. F. 1975. *Patterns of problem solving*. Englewood Cliffs, N.J.: Prentice-Hall.

––––––– 1980. An interdisciplinary problem-solving course. In D. T. Tuma and F. Reif, eds., *Problem solving and education*. Hillsdale, N.J.: Erlbaum Associates.

Ruger, H. A. 1910. The psychology of efficiency. *Archives of Psychology, 15*.

Sauers, R., and Farrell, R. 1982. *GRAPES User's Manual*. Technical Report, Department of Psychology, Carnegie-Mellon University.

Schacter, D. L. 1987. Implicit memory: history and current status. *Journal of Experimental Psychology: Learning, Memory, and Cognition, 13*, 501–518.

Schank, R. C., and Abelson, R. P. 1977. *Scripts, plans, goals, and understanding*. Hillsdale, N.J.: Erlbaum Associates.

Schoenfeld, A. H. 1979. Measures of problem-solving performance and of problem-solving instruction. *Journal for Research in Mathematics Education, 10*, 173–187.

––––––– 1980. Teaching problem solving skills. *American Mathematical Monthly, 87*, 794–805.

––––––– 1983. Beyond the purely cognitive: belief systems, social cognitions, and metacognitions as driving forces in intellectual performance. *Cognitive Science, 7*, 329–363.

––––––– 1985. *Mathematical problem solving*. New York: Academic Press.

Schustack, M. 1979. Task-dependency in children's use of linguistic rules. Paper presented at the annual meeting of the Psychonomics Society, Phoenix.

Scribner, S. 1984. Studying working intelligence. In B. Rogoff and J. Lave, eds., *Everyday cognition: its development in social context.* Cambridge, Mass.: Harvard University Press.

Shiffrin, R. M., and Schneider, W. 1977. Controlled and automatic human information processing. II. Perceptual learning, automatic attending, and a general theory. *Psychological Review, 84,* 127–190.

Shortliffe, E. H. 1976. *Computer-based medical consultations: MYCIN.* New York: American Elsevier.

Shrager, J., and Pirolli, P. 1983. *SIMPLE: a simple language for research in programmer psychology.* Computer program, Department of Psychology, Carnegie-Mellon University.

Siegler, R. S. 1986. *Children's thinking.* Englewood Cliffs, N.J.: Prentice-Hall.

Silver, E. A. 1979. Student perceptions of relatedness among mathematical verbal problems. *Journal for Research in Mathematics Education, 10,* 195–210.

Simon, H. A. 1947. *Administrative behavior.* New York: Macmillan.

―――― 1969. *The sciences of the artificial.* Cambridge, Massachusetts: MIT Press.

―――― 1975. The functional equivalence of problem solving skills. *Cognitive Psychology, 7,* 268–288.

―――― 1980. Problem solving and education. In D. T. Tuma and F. Reif, eds., *Problem solving and education: issues in teaching and research.* Hillsdale, N.J.: Erlbaum Associates.

Simon, H. A., and Hayes, J. R., 1976. The understanding process: problem isomorphs. *Cognitive Psychology, 8,* 165–190.

Simon, H. A., and Reed, S. K. 1976. Modelling strategy shifts in a problem solving task. *Cognitive Psychology, 8,* 86–97.

Singley, M. K., and Anderson, J. R. 1985. The transfer of text-editing skill. *Journal of Man-Machine Studies, 22,* 403–423.

―――― 1988. A keystroke analysis of learning and transfer in text editing. *Human-Computer Interaction, 3,* 223–274.

Skinner, B. F. 1954. The science of learning and the art of teaching. *Harvard Educational Review, 24,* 86–97.

―――― 1957. *Verbal behavior.* New York: Appleton-Century-Crofts.

Smith, J. P. 1973. The effect of general versus specific heuristics in mathematical problem-solving tasks. Doctoral diss., Columbia University.

Smith, S. 1986. An analysis of transfer between tower of Hanoi isomorphs. Doctoral diss., Carnegie-Mellon University.

Soloway, E., Ehrlich, K., and Gold, E. 1983. Reading a program is like reading a story (well, almost). In *Proceedings of the Fifth Annual Conference of the Cognitive Science Society,* Rochester, N.Y.

Sternberg, R., and Bower, G. H. 1974. Transfer in part-whole and whole-part free recall: a comparative evaluation of theories. *Journal of Verbal Learning and Verbal Behavior, 13,* 1–26.

Stratton, G. M. 1922. *Developing mental power.* New York: Houghton Mifflin.

Strom, I. M. 1960. Research in grammar and usage and its implication for teaching and writing. *Bulletin of School of Education, Indiana University, 36* (5).

Stroop, J. R., 1935. Studies of interference in serial verbal reactions. *Journal of Experimental Psychology, 18,* 643–662.

Thibadeau, R., Just, M. A., and Carpenter, P. A. 1982. A model of the time course and content of reading. *Cognitive Science, 6,* 157–203.

Thomas, J. C. 1974. An analysis of behavior in the hobbits-orcs problem. *Cognitive Psychology, 6,* 257–269.

Thompson, R. 1986. *PUPS user manual.* Technical Report, Department of Psychology, Carnegie-Mellon University.

Thomson, J. R., and Chapman, R. S. 1977. Who is 'Daddy' revisited: the status of two-year-olds' overextended words in use and comprehension. *Journal of Child Language, 4,* 359–375.

Thorndike, E. L. 1903. *Educational psychology.* New York: Lemke & Buechner.

——— 1906. *Principles of teaching.* New York: A. G. Seiler.

——— 1922. The effect of changed data upon reasoning. *Journal of Experimental Psychology, 5,* 33–38.

——— 1924. Mental discipline in high school studies. *Journal of Educational Psychology, 15,* 1–22.

Thorndike, E. L., and Woodworth, R. S. 1901. The influence of improvement in one mental function upon the efficiency of other functions. *Psychological Review, 8,* 247–261.

Thorndike, E. L., Aikens, H. A., and Hubbell, E. 1902. Correlations among perceptive and associative processes. *Psychological Review, 9,* 374–382.

Thune, L. E. 1950. The effect of different types of preliminary activities on subsequent learning of paired-associate material. *Journal of Experimental Psychology, 40,* 423–438.

Tulving, E. 1966. Subjective organization and effects of repetition in multi-trial free-recall learning. *Journal of Verbal Learning and Verbal Behavior, 5,* 193–197.

Tulving, E., and Osler, S. 1967. Transfer effects in whole/part free-recall learning. *Canadian Journal of Psychology, 21,* 253–262.

Tversky, A., and Kahnemann, D. 1974. Judgments under uncertainty: heuristics and biases. *Science, 185,* 1124–31.

Underwood, B. J. 1957. *Psychological research.* New York: Appleton-Century-Crofts.

VanLehn, K. 1983. Felicity conditions for human skill acquisition: validating an AI-based theory. Doctoral diss., Massachusetts Institute of Technology.

VanPatten, J., Chao, C., and Reigeluth, C. M. 1986. A review of strategies for sequencing and synthesizing instruction. *Review of Educational Research, 56,* 437–471.

Voss, J. F., Vesonder, G. T., and Spilich, G. J. 1980. Generation and recall by high-knowledge and low-knowledge individuals. *Journal of Verbal Learning and Verbal Behavior, 19,* 651–667.

Wallin, J. F. W. 1910. The doctrine of formal discipline. *Journal of Educational Psychology, 1,* 168–171.

Ward, L. B. 1937. Reminiscence and rote learning. *Psychological Monographs, 49* (220).

Wason, P. C. 1966. Reasoning. In B. M. Foss, ed., *New horizons in psychology.* Harmondsworth: Penguin.

Wason, P. C., and Johnson-Laird, P. N. 1972. *Psychology of reasoning: structure and content.* Cambridge, Mass.: Harvard University Press.

Waterman, D. A., and Hayes-Roth, F., eds. 1978. *Pattern-directed inference systems.* New York: Academic Press.

Weisberg, R., DiCamillo, M., and Phillips, D. 1978. Transferring old associations to new situations: a non-automatic process. *Journal of Verbal Learning and Verbal Behavior, 17,* 219–228.

Wertheimer, M. 1945. *Productive thinking.* New York: Harper & Row.

Wesman, A. G. 1945. A study of transfer of training from high school subjects to intelligence. *Journal of Educational Research, 39,* 254–264.

Winer, G. A. 1980. Class-inclusion reasoning in children: a review of the empirical literature. *Child Development, 51,* 309–328.

Winston, P. H. 1977. *Artificial intelligence.* Reading, Mass.: Addison-Wesley.

——— 1979. Learning and reasoning by analogy. *Communications of the Association for Computing Machinery, 23,* 689–703.

Winston, P. H., and Horn, B. K. P. 1981. *LISP.* Reading, Mass.: Addison-Wesley.

Woodrow, H. 1927. The effect of the type of training upon transference. *Journal of Educational Psychology, 18,* 159–172.

Woodworth, R. S., and Schlosberg, H. 1954. *Experimental psychology.* New York: Holt, Rinehart, and Winston.

Young, R. M. 1983. Surrogates and mappings: two kinds of conceptual models for interactive devices. In D. Gentner and A. L. Stevens, eds., *Mental models.* Hillsdale, N.J.: Erlbaum Associates.

Author Index

Subject Index